RAISE BACKYARD BEES

1503 S.W. 42nd St.
Topeka, KS 66609, USA.
Telephone (785) 274-4300
Fax (785) 274-4305
www.ogdenpubs.com

First Edition. Copyright © 2018 by Ogden Publishing
All rights reserved.

No part of this work may be reproduced or transmitted in any form or by any means,
electrical or mechanical, including photocopying, or by any information storage
or retrieval system, without written permission of the copyright owners.

Printed in the U.S.A.

Contents

8 Fresh Honey, Wild Bees
Remembering the experiences of tasting honey and capturing a swarm.

Chapter 1 ■ Beekeeping Basics ■ Page 10

12 Beekeeping Basics
If you're interested in raising honeybees but aren't sure you can commit, here's a rundown of equipment you'll need and the schedule you can expect to follow.

17 How to Become a Beekeeper
A certified beekeeper offers a checklist for beginners.

20 What's All the Buzz?
Bees have played an important role in pollination, nutrition, and culture throughout the ages.

22 To Bee or Not to Bee
Ten compelling reasons to encourage your inner beekeeper.

27 Remembering a Honeybee Hive
One trip for honey turns into a lifelong fascination with the buzzing makers of the sweet treat.

Chapter 2 ■ Buying Bees ■ Page 30

32 Setting Up a Beehive
Maintaining a beehive is not nearly as complicated or scary as some people believe.

38 Find Your Favorite Honeybee
A guide to the top backyard producers and pollinators.

41 The Reverend Langstroth's Beehive
Nineteenth-century invention is still on the job.

44 The Key is Location, Location, Location
Take a look around your property and decide where to place your new beehives.

46 Hive Pros and Cons
Breaking down the top-bar design with an experienced apiarist.

50 The Difference Between Beehives
Beekeeper details the pros and cons of the three top designs: Top-Bar, Warre, and Langstroth.

54 Building a Beehive
Create your own bee condo and save money in the process.

56 Beginning With Honeybees
Questions and answers help beginning beekeepers learn more about their hives.

Chapter 3 ▪ What to Do the First Year ▪ Page 60

62 Buzz-Worthy Plants
Attract native bees by transforming your backyard into a sanctuary filled with nectar-rich flowers, insect hotels, and more.

66 A Bounty to Buzz About
The art of attracting nature's pollinators to your garden.

73 Let Your Bees Do the Gardening
Work in tandem with native bees for a bountiful, beautiful garden.

80 Wise Pairings
Plant a profusion of fragrant flowers among your edible plants to help control pests, boost pollination, and provide eye-pleasing pops of color.

86 Go Native With Wild Bees
The humble little orchard mason bee is the best-kept (pollinator) secret.

90 Balm for Bees
Herbs have the power to help pollinators. Discover these plant medicines for our busy buddies.

97 Trees for Bees
Landscape with flowering trees and shrubs.

98 13 Drought-Tolerant Plants
Try these low-maintenance perennials to attract bees and other pollinators to your garden.

100 Harness a Swarm
Honeybees don't have to come at an expensive price. This spring and summer, consider the free alternative.

105 Build a Nuc Vac
A DIY project to help you gather up and remove swarms.

110 Beekeepers in the City
Pittsburgh residents swarm together to keep bees.

Chapter 4 ▪ Harvest Honey ▪ Page 116

118 Nectars in Nature
What's your favorite type of honey? Learn what all plays into honing the best-tasting honey.

124 Measure Moisture Before Honey Harvest
Using a refractometer can increase your honey production; learn how it works and how to use one.

126 Harvesting Honey
One of the most fun parts of beekeeping is harvesting honey.

131 How to Produce Comb Honey
An experienced apiarist explains why comb honey is such a valuable product of the hive.

134 Build Your Own Honey Extractor
You can make an inexpensive honey extractor from simple materials available in your local hardware store.

138 A Top-Bar Hive Honey Harvest
Honey collection differs as to the type of hive.

140 The Importance of Nectar Flow
Understanding the nectar flow in your area helps maximize colony health and honey production.

143 Honey Business Yields Sweet Rewards
What began as a hobby for her young son turned into a lucrative honey production business for one of our bloggers.

144 Watch for Robber Bees
The dearth of summer often brings out robbing behavior in honeybees. An experienced beekeeper discusses what causes it, and what to do about it.

146 From Pesky Weed to Wonderful Treat
Tall goldenrod is a fall favorite of the honeybee.

Chapter 5 ▪ Healthy Bees ▪ Page 148

150 The Latest Buzz
Honeybees have seen better days, but efforts to boost their populations haven't gone unnoticed.

153 Russians to the Rescue
America's beleaguered honeybees are getting some help from a distant relative.

158 Saving the Honeybee
Businesses educate future beekeepers.

162 A Primer for Rearing Queen Honeybees
The art of queen breeding is a valuable skill in any apiarist's arsenal.

170 Winterizing Your Bee Hives Naturally
There may be snow on the ground and ice on the trees, but your bees are a balmy 96 degrees inside their hive.

173 Feeding Honeybees
Many commercial beekeepers feed sugar syrup to their charges. Two beekeepers offer reasons to discontinue the practice.

Chapter 6 ▪ Cooking With Honey ▪ Page 176

178 How to Make Mead
Create this delicious and refreshing wine with yeast, water, and honey.

180 A Homemade Wine Recipe
Use fruits or honey to create a wine from home without fancy equipment.

181 Add Honey to Recipes
A variety of dishes lend themselves to substituting healthful honey for other sweeteners.

186 Beehive Baking
Put down the sugar bowl and switch to honey with these wholesome recipes.

192 A Guide to Cooking With Honey
Learn tips for substituting honey for sugar, and discover recipes for syrup, jams, jellies, breads, puddings, and muffins.

Chapter 7 ▪ Health and Bee-uty ▪ Page 200

202 Natural Treatments for Stings
To get fast relief, try one of these treatment options; you likely have what you need in the kitchen cupboard!

204 Health Benefits of Honey
Raw honey isn't just delicious—read on to learn some of the medicinal uses for the golden treat.

206 Bee Byproducts
Honey is but one of the items created by ever-industrious honeybees.

211 How to Render Beeswax
To make your own candles and more, utilize the wax cappings from your hives' frames.

212 15 Household Uses for Honey
Help your family thrive with honey; the all-natural nectar is a healing powerhouse.

214 Bee-Friendly Beauty Tips
Nurture and nourish skin with bee-produced ingredients straight from the hive.

219 Notes

222 Acknowledgments

223 Photo Credits

Fresh Honey, Wild Bees

Remembering the experiences of tasting honey and capturing a swarm.

Hank's friend and fellow beekeeper, Nate Lindsay, cuts into a massive ash tree to remove a wild honeybee colony and repopulate the top-bar hive at Prairie Turnip Farm.

I can still remember the first time I experienced the taste of honey—it was even more memorable than that first bitter bite from saccharin-sweetened Kool-Aid. I can't remember the reason my mother had honey in the pantry, but it was my dislike of peanut butter that earned me that first amber teaspoonful—to make a youngster's lunch go down without the usual fussing. Wow, I was amazed by the way it smelled, tasted, and made peanut butter so much more palatable. I might clarify here that I often enjoyed Miracle Whip (why that glop was in our pantry I'll never understand) sandwiches and cherry preserves with cheddar cheese sandwiches—so my childhood taste in lunch foods might not be considered normal.

Honey most definitely was not used as a regular sweetener at our place in those days. I suspect it was because my father could not cope with sticky containers of any kind. However, I looked for every opportunity to sneak honey and even suggested that eating my oatmeal, toast, and cornbread would be a lot easier if I could just have a bit of honey. In time, I realized that honey comes in many different forms and an infinite range of colors and flavors. As I made my way into fourth grade, I anticipated the science unit on social insects—ants were cool, but the honeybees illustrated on the textbook's cover captivated me completely. Since there were no beekeepers in my family, and no way for a boy to make it happen, I took to stalking honeybees to see if I could discover their hive and catch a glimpse of all the bits and pieces I'd studied so earnestly in school.

Lucky for me perhaps, I never found that wild bee nest (images of Pooh Bear in my head). I trapped many honeybees (and other kinds of insects) in jars with holes poked in the lids. I watched them, and I even got stung a few times, but the allure was always there. When I was a little older, I nearly always had a bit of cash in my pockets from performing various odd jobs for neighbors (allowances weren't part of growing up in my family—chores were expected), and when I was lucky enough to visit a favored roadside farm stand, I would plunk down my hard-earned cash for honey comb, clover honey, alfalfa honey, and even beeswax candles. Then, as now, soothing feelings passed through me whenever I was in the presence of honey and beeswax.

A couple years back, a friend built me a beehive and vowed to help me through the process of keeping some bees myself. So far, the experience has included getting chased by the bees, some fascinating observation, and the most amazing apricot and cherry yields our trees have ever delivered. We've even tasted a bit of the liquid gold. And then, in the spring shortly after the fruit trees were all set, the colony literally collapsed in the course of a week. There was plenty of honey in the comb, a viable queen, and then poof! Nothing left but a pile of dead bees.

WILD BEES, WILD TIMES

A little deeper investigation revealed that the problem may have been a combination of the colony being low on food and an unexpected cold spell. I've taken the experience into consideration each year since, when it's time to stop feeding. It was already past the optimal bee ordering date, and I just figured that we'd be bee-less until procuring a new group of bees the following spring.

A few weeks later, I took the day off to spend some quality time at the farm. I was at the pond closest to the house—and in the midst of landing my second or third largemouth bass of the morning—when my cell phone buzzed. Arghh. Why didn't I just leave that thing at home?

Then I noticed that the missed call was from my friend and expert beekeeper, Nate Lindsay. I'd been meaning to talk to him about my hive's sudden demise anyway, so I rang him back. To make a long story short, Nate had been called upon by the municipal arborists in nearby Osage City, Kansas, to help "deal" with a huge "bee tree" that had to be cut down. Part of the reason the huge old ash needed to come down was that it was largely hollowed out on the inside—which was also the reason it was so favored by several colonies of wild honeybees. Nate was looking for a home for one of the colonies and wondered if I had any room.

Within an hour, Nate had trailered a 20-foot length of hollowed-out ash trunk to my place. Wow, it was huge—and there was window screen stapled over all the openings. To say the log was abuzz is an understatement. After rolling the log over with the loader tractor, we donned bee suits, fired up the chainsaw and cut into the largest cavities—whoa, we're talking about honeycomb that approached 4 feet long by 2 feet wide—and yes, it was messy. My chainsaw was sticky for a long time.

After a little smoke, observation, and Nate "scenting" the queen, we went to work gathering brood, bees, and comb, transferring it all into my empty top-bar hive. Within about 20 minutes, the bees began to congregate at the back end of their new home. Nate looked at me and grinned. "Looks like we got her," he said.

Now, the new hive is alive and well, and the bees are much gentler than the domesticated ones I had before. In the years since, I've been committed to keeping the feeders full for a few weeks longer.

Whether you live in town or on 1,000 acres, there's plenty of room in your yard or on your urban rooftop for a hive or three. In the pages that follow, we'll help you get to know bees and embark on adventures in cooking with honey, creating queen bees, and becoming a skilled beekeeper. We'll also help you save a little money by demonstrating how to build a couple of different hives and a honey extractor. We'll even show you how to attract wild native bees to pollinate your gardens and orchards.

Keep on buzzin',

Oscar H. "Hank" Will III
Editor in Chief
MOTHER EARTH NEWS

Finding a swarm is one way to populate your hives.

BEEKEEPING BASICS

"Given the right environment, bees will work hard to add to your bottom line with increased yields — and if you treat them right, they'll pay you rent in the form of sweet, delicious, healthful honey and wax, which you can easily convert to cold cash."

— Linda Rountree Grove, "To Bee or Not to Bee," Page 22

Beekeeping Basics

If you're interested in raising honeybees but aren't sure you can commit, here's a rundown of the equipment you'll need and the schedule you can expect to follow.

By Hannah Kincaid

No wonder more and more folks are making a beeline for beekeeping a single hive of these tiny, social pollinators can provide 40 to 60 pounds of golden honey per year, as well as a few pounds of ever-useful beeswax. Plus, many crops need honeybees (*Apis mellifera*) to achieve good fruit set and high yields. This pollination benefit is becoming increasingly important because of industrial agriculture's dependency on toxic pesticides, which poison bees' food supplies and result in lower pollinator populations. For the willing homesteader or backyard gardening enthusiast, dedicating a small amount of time every couple of weeks to maintaining a beehive will render sweet returns indeed.

Like any livestock, bees need care and attention, though the time commitment can be far less than for dairy goats or even chickens. To help you decide whether beekeeping would be a good fit, we asked Kim Flottum, longtime editor of *Bee Culture* magazine, to help us outline the beekeeping essentials, including what to expect in terms of initial start-up needs and costs, along with a basic apiary to-do calendar.

TOOLS OF THE TRADE

Start with a new hive body and frames. Looking for a bargain on used beekeeping equipment may be tempting, but bees are susceptible to several diseases that can persist in old equipment. Also, you may come across suggestions to foster a wild swarm that someone has captured. The concern here is that a wild swarm (particularly one found in the western or southern United States) may

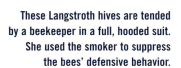

These Langstroth hives are tended by a beekeeper in a full, hooded suit. She used the smoker to suppress the bees' defensive behavior.

As the weather warms, visits to the beehive will be mainly to look at the amount of honey in storage and to make sure there's a thriving population of active, healthy bees. Begin preparations for colder weather by installing a windbreak and a mouse guard at the entrance.

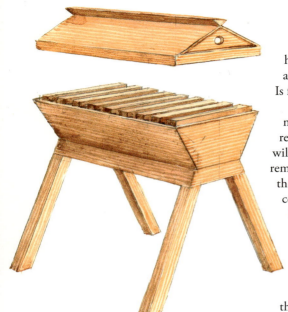

Top-bar hives allow bees to build their own U-shaped combs that will hang from the wooden bars laid across the hive's interior.

A basic Langstroth hive will include a lid, cover, two supers and one hive body — each filled with removable frames — a bottom board, and a concrete or wooden stand to elevate the hive off the ground.

have crossbred with aggressive Africanized honeybees. Buy either a package or a nucleus colony (called a "nuc") of gentle bees with a queen (see "Which Bee Is for Me?" below).

You'll choose one of two hive designs. The more common Langstroth hive, named after its inventor, consists of stacked, rectangular boxes that contain removable wooden frames with pre-formed foundations upon which the bees will build their wax comb (see illustration at the bottom of this page). The removable frames in the Langstroth system make monitoring the health of the hive easy, and its popularity means tracking down replacement parts is convenient. Expect to pay about $250 for an unassembled cedar Langstroth hive that includes one hive body and two additional boxes called "supers" for honey storage, as well as 30 frames (10 frames per box) and a lid, cover, bottom board, and screws.

The simpler top-bar hive design consists of a trough-shaped, lidded box with wooden bars laid across the top of the interior (see illustration at left). The bees establish their own U-shaped combs suspended from the bars. Expect to pay more than $200 for an unassembled top-bar kit with plans, or $50 in materials to build your own. Top-bar hives will typically produce about 20 percent less honey than a Langstroth, but the beeswax is easier to harvest. Despite yielding less honey, proponents say the top-bar design results in a gentler, happier hive that's a viable option for beekeepers more concerned with conservation and plant pollination than with maximum honey production.

To dig deeper into both types of hives, turn to Page 41 for Langstroth hives and to Page 46 for top-bar hives.

In addition to one or two initial hives, you'll need a few specialized beekeeping tools. A smoker ($20) is used to suppress defensive behavior in bees. A hive tool ($10) looks similar to a crowbar and is used to remove frames from the hive. A feeder ($15) should be filled with sugar water and placed inside your hive to provide food when you first introduce the bees to their new home and during periods when nectar is scarce. Most beekeepers start with a hooded beekeeping suit ($70), which should include gloves. You may opt to later shed some pieces as you become more comfortable around the bees. All in all, you'll probably spend between $200 and $500 for your first hive and the basic beekeeping equipment (not including bees).

WHICH BEE IS FOR ME?

A typical bee package costs about $130, plus shipping, and holds 3 pounds of loose adult bees and an individually packaged queen. Alternatively, a nuc is made up of Langstroth-fitting frames already populated with bees, including a queen, and you simply slide the frames into your hive.

Nucs are slightly more expensive than packages because they contain working frames — expect to pay approximately $150 for a nuc, which must be picked up rather than mailed.

Just as different breeds of cows or chickens are better suited to certain homesteads and purposes, some specific types of honeybees are best for home beekeepers. Flottum says every bee supplier strives to produce the calmest bees possible, but that Carniolan bees tend to be more subdued than the more readily available Italian bees. Some types of bees also have more resistance to pests and diseases. For example, Minnesota Hygienic Italians and bees with Varroa Sensitive Hygiene (VSH) traits have a high degree of resistance to varroa mites, American foulbrood, and chalkbrood.

THE APICULTURAL CALENDAR

Before your bees arrive, do some homework and consider shadowing an experienced beekeeper so you're able to recognize normal hive behavior and honeycomb structure, as well as what potential invaders, such as mites, look like. According to the Backyard Beekeepers Association, you can plan on spending about 30 hours a year maintaining your hives. Your time commitment will parallel the pollen and nectar flows—when it's peak gardening season, it's also peak beekeeping season.

Place your package or nuc order in winter for pickup in warmer weather. Make sure your hive is assembled and ready to immediately house its new residents by the time they arrive. Carefully read directions about how to best install the bees into your hive.

Wait one week after you've installed your bees to do your initial inspection. Your goal will be to make sure the queen is laying eggs. Return at least once every week or two to check the hive's overall health and monitor its growth.

As the weather warms, visits to the beehive will be mainly to look at the amount of honey in storage and to make sure there's a thriving population of

A novice beekeeper would be wise to purchase a full suit and other equipment.

BEEKEEPING SUPPLIES

Beekeeping does involve some initial expense. Here's a list of what you will need to start two hives. The cost can be divided into one-time startup expenses for hive components (about $550) and other equipment (about $250). If you get everything new, the cost comes to about $950 for two hives, plus bees and shipping. You can cut costs by starting with swarms instead of purchasing bees. You can also buy some equipment secondhand, although you should not buy used hive and frame components because of the threat of spreading mites and disease. Before you order any equipment, you will need to decide whether you want liquid or comb honey (see "The Sweetest Reward," Page 16).

HIVES, FRAMES & FOUNDATIONS

Two hives, commercial-grade. This is a one-time expense of about $400. It includes these parts of the boxes: four hive bodies (boxes), six 6⅝-inch honey supers (boxes), two reversible bottom boards, two telescoping covers with inner covers, two queen excluders, two top feeders, two screened bottom boards, and two entrance reducers.

Frames and foundations. These will need to be gradually replaced every three years or so, and cost about $150. That estimated cost includes commercial frames and foundation sheets. Be sure to get correctly sized frames for your supers. Also, if you decide to make liquid honey, you'll need to order crimp-wired foundation sheets. For comb honey, order thin, unwired foundation.

OTHER BASIC EQUIPMENT
One-time expense, $250 and up
- Zipper-veil bee suit and helmet
- Boot bands
- Gloves, plastic-coated canvas
- 7-inch stainless steel smoker with shield
- Hive tool
- Frame grips
- Bee brush
- Spur embedder for wiring frames
- Embedding wire

BEES & OTHER EXPENSES
- 3 pounds of bees, plus queen, about $130 to $200, plus shipping (per hive)
- 1 gallon exterior latex paint or Auro natural stain
- Outdoor wood glue (Elmer's or Gorilla)
- Cinder blocks or wood for a base

RESOURCES

BEEKEEPING BOOKS
The following titles are available at www.motherearthnews.com/store.
The Backyard Beekeeper 4th Edition
  by Kim Flottum
The Thinking Beekeeper
  by Christy Hemenway
Beekeeper's Lab by Kim Lehman
Keeping Bees With a Smile
  by Fedor Lazutin
Keeping Bees in Towns and Cities
  by Luke Dixon

BEEKEEPING MAGAZINES
Subscription discount certificates are often available for bee clubs.
American Bee Journal:
  www.americanbeejournal.com;
  217-847-3324
Bee Culture: www.beeculture.com;
Grit's Guide to Backyard Bees and Honey:
  search for current year's edition at www.motherearthnews.com/store.

ONLINE RESOURCES
Honey Bee World: a moderated beekeeping forum; www.honeybeeworld.com/forum
Keeping Backyard Bees: a beekeeping blogging community; www.keepingbackyardbees.com

---

active, healthy bees. Begin preparations for colder weather by installing a windbreak and a mouse guard at the entrance. Throughout the entire season, whenever pollen or nectar levels are low, you'll need to provide protein supplements to stand in for pollen, and sugar water in place of nectar. Just as you would never let your cows go without hay or your hens go without feed, you should never let your bees go hungry.

THE SWEETEST REWARD

Your colony probably won't produce enough honey for a harvest the first year, and your focus should remain on learning the ways of the hive.

In the second year, however, and in years thereafter, the honey harvest will take place around September. When harvesting honey, you must leave enough to feed your hive through winter. According to Flottum, a colony located in the northern half of the United States should have at least 100 pounds of honey stored for winter; a colony in the southern half will need at least 50 pounds.

Depending on the depth of your hive design and the number of frames used, your hive should weigh between 150 and 200 pounds total — including the bottom, boxes, frames, bees, brood, and honey — at the beginning of winter. Use a handheld spring scale to weigh your hive, and if it weighs more than this amount, you can remove the excess honey for your use.

Honey is ripe for gathering when a frame has at least two-thirds of its cells filled with honey and capped with wax.

A simple harvesting technique is "brushing." This involves holding a ripe frame over the hive and gently brushing as many bees as possible back into the hive before placing the mostly deserted frame into a separate box. To extract the honey from the comb, just cut away the wax capping with a knife and then remove the honey from the wax comb either by manually crushing and straining the comb or by using a mechanical extractor.

Apiary management is an activity that most everyone in your family can enjoy. In addition to savoring the sweet golden elixir and useful beeswax, you'll all appreciate the increased garden harvests and marvel at the hustling hive's diligence. 🐝

SAVE THE BEES?

The causes of colony collapse disorder (CCD) have been hotly debated in the news for years, yet honeybee populations continue to decline. Bees pollinate many fruits and vegetables, so their absence is alarming not only for farmers and beekeepers, but also for agricultural regions suffering billions of dollars in lost revenue. The latest research indicates that chronic exposure to neonicotinoid pesticides is a prime culprit in bee die-offs. These pesticides and others, such as Roundup, also indirectly contribute to bee loss by weakening immunities to mites and viruses, and hampering hive recoveries after winter. Home beekeepers are having better luck than commercial operations, so if you want to help protect bees, eliminating pesticides and starting a hive or two in your yard are good options. For more news on bees and CCD, go to bit.ly/2gYSvqC.

How to Become a Beekeeper

A certified beekeeper offers a checklist for beginners.

By Lindsay Williamson

This flower's color attracts one of the far-ranging honeybees.

Recent weather was unseasonably warm and it made my spirits soar to see how busy my bees were. I also saw a lot of pollen being brought into the hive, which is another sign that things are on track for the busy season.

Beekeeping is such wonderful hobby and rewarding in more ways than one. I almost didn't take the leap into it and I certainly wouldn't have if I had weighed the pros and cons in my honeybee-ignorant mind. The reason I'm telling you this is because I'm speaking to all of you who think beekeeping sounds like an interesting or worthwhile hobby. I'm not saying to jump right in without doing your research, and (more importantly) connecting with some experienced beekeepers, but I am encouraging you to get busy checking off your beginner beekeeper to-do list.

TO-DO LIST

The truth is that if you're hoping to have some hives this year, if it's spring, then

you're already behind. It's not impossible to get caught up at this point, though, so here's my recommended to-do list:

1 Read! There is so much wonderful information out there about all things beekeeping. Read about hive design, check out books from your library, and read what beekeepers are posting on beekeeping forums. Also, many local beekeeping associations have a library that you can borrow from.

2 Get in touch with your local beekeeping association. Start attending regular meetings. It's a wonderful source for local connections and you will certainly meet some beekeeping veterans who are generous with their time and knowledge. I don't think my bees would've made it through my first season had it not been for the kindness and experience of a local beekeeper I met through the association.

Busy worker bees take a moment just outside the hive before they take off or go inside to deposit pollen.

3 If you decide you're going to take the plunge, it's time to order bees! Many, if not most places are sold out of nucs and packages by the time February rolls around. You can still find them but you definitely want packages no later than halfway through April and nucs no later than the beginning of May.

4 When shopping around for bees, ask the supplier where their bees come from, if they've successfully overwintered and, most importantly, if they're coming off of pollination. Sometimes, large apiaries will take bees that are weak and unhealthy, coming off of pollination, and combine them into packages or nucs and sell them for what may seem like a good price.

Believe me, you get what you pay for with bees and equipment.

5 Consider asking a beekeeper you know if she would be willing to mentor you during your first season. No matter how many YouTube videos you watch showing you how to install a package or nuc, it is really valuable to have someone with a good bit of experience alongside you.

6 Keep records! It's important to always check for certain things during hive inspections and make sure that you write them down. Do you see eggs, larvae, and capped brood? If so, how is the laying pattern? Did you spot the queen? Did you see any bees or brood that look sickly? Were there any weird or bad smells? How are their food stores?

I'm not a fan of feeding bees sugar syrup, and for that reason, I always leave them with more than enough honey, but sometimes there is just no avoiding it.

After installing most nucs and definitely with packages, you will need to provide some sugar syrup for your bees until they can build

A beekeeper scrapes off the wax covering on the honeycomb cells before harvesting honey.

adequate stores, but keep in mind that sugar syrup can be hard on their systems and may cause nosema.

If you find you have no choice, check out one of my blog posts, *A Better Sugar Syrup Recipe* (search for the title on www.motherearthnews.com); it's a great recipe that adds essential nutrients and alters the pH of the syrup, making it a more nutritious and more easily digested food for our beloved friends.

WHEN TO EXPECT YOUR FIRST HARVEST

The last thing I want to tell you is not to expect to harvest any honey your first season. It's not unheard of to have a beginner start out with a crazy successful colony that produces more than they need to overwinter, but it's definitely not the norm. At the very least, even if you feel they have produced plenty, wait until close to fall to decide, because in most areas, your bees will go through a significant amount of the stores just making it through the late part of summer when there is not as much nectar available but still a ton of mouths to feed.

Enjoy your hives. Bees are such noble and amazing creatures. Naturally, I expected to learn some things when I started keeping bees, but they have taught me so much more than I could have anticipated.

What's All the Buzz?

Bees have played an important role in pollination, nutrition, and culture throughout the ages.

By Terri Schlichenmeyer

When it comes to your garden, you've always had a good Plan A, and a halfway decent Plan B. But without Plan Bee, you might as well throw away the seeds and burst any thought bubbles that include hauling a huge basketful of fruits and vegetables out of the garden come summertime.

You really have to wonder what a dinosaur thought, some 130 million years ago, when confronted by a honeybee. Maybe he was glad he had a thick hide because, really, what kind of threat is a stinger on dino-hide? He might've batted the bug away, but he should've been more careful. Much like some mammals developed hooves and horns, bees evolved to do what bees do better than most any other creature on the planet: pollinate plants. Dinosaurs eventually went extinct, but it didn't take long for the proficient pollinators to migrate all over Africa and the Eurasian landmass.

You can almost imagine how humans stumbled upon the other thing bees do: Chances are, they saw some rascally animal raid the hive and figured that sticky stuff had to be pretty tasty. Rock art in Africa and Spain shows that early humans knew how

to hunt honey, Ice Age humans knew that smoke calmed bees, and Egyptians learned to keep bees in central locations. Many moons later, bees were brought to North America by beekeepers looking to relocate both home and hive.

Much like a miniature castle of old, each beehive centers on a queen. Despite the fact that most of the 50,000 to 200,000 bees in the hive are female, she is the only one allowed to lay eggs. The queen is pampered and fed and required to do no worker-bee drudgery. She doesn't even have to take care of any squalling brat-bees. In fact, when there become too many mouths to feed, she swarms and flies off with some of her retinue—but not before allowing at least one of her eggs to become a new queen with a new colony. That new queen will ruthlessly kill all other newborn queens in the hive until she, alone, is left to rule. Unlike her subjects, the queen bee can use her stinger over and over without being killed by its use.

INDEED, IT'S GOOD TO BE QUEEN

When it's time for a queen bee to mate, she leaves the hive—one of the few times in her life that she does so—with the drones, or male bees, in hot pursuit of her Highness. She mates over and over in midair, and then flies back to the colony able to lay fertile eggs throughout her lifetime. The male bees, having lived a mere week and having done their only duty in life, die, which proves that it's a drone to be a drone.

Of her eggs—and a queen bee can lay a million eggs in her lifetime—the vast majority will become female worker bees.

Although a hive lives and dies for its queen, worker bees are an absolute necessity for honey-making and bee birthing. Worker bees graduate from job to job based on their age. Experienced worker bees forage for nectar, pollen, and water, while younger bees make the wax combs and process the nectar to make honey. There are attendants to the queen, as well as nurse bees, housekeepers, and even bees that work as little bee funeral directors. Still others tend to the queen's eggs because, when she's ready for retirement, they'll have to start feeding the heir apparent, and the cycle begins again.

If you want to have a hive of your own, you have a lot of decision-making to do. There are somewhere around 22,000 species of bee, the smallest being the *Perdita minima*, which is just about microscopic, and the largest, the *Chalicodoma pluto*, which can reach nearly 2 inches (females typically 39 mm) in length. Bees can survive both cold (they've been found in the Himalayas) and hot (some live in the desert) climates. There are bees that dig, and some that create a kind of cement. The ones you probably see in your garden are bumblebees, honeybees, mason bees, leafcutter bees, and possibly digger bees, which should make your decision a little easier.

Basically, what all bees have in common is that they collect nectar to feed their young (and you), and they have those cute little furry bodies (to differing degrees). Bees can fly up to 15 miles per hour, handy because a worker bee could visit as many as 2,000 flowers each day to produce about $\frac{1}{12}$ of a teaspoon of honey in her lifetime. She'll do it largely by scent, because bees see every color but red, including some that we can't.

Oh, and bees sting. A honeybee, if her nest is threatened, will chase interlopers for quite awhile and is not one bit afraid to sting. Once she does, though, she's a goner because she leaves her stinger in your skin, which also rips apart her abdomen. If you've ever been stung, you can understand why bees were used as weapons in ancient times.

But really, you shouldn't worry too much. Bee stings are somewhat uncommon, and bees are wonderful to watch and interact with. We need them to pollinate crops, flowers, and other plants, and we use bees for their pollen, honey, wax, and royal jelly. These creatures, throughout the ages, have contributed to human health, beauty, and food in huge and irreplaceable ways.

So next time you give your honey some honey, you should both bee very thankful.

> You really have to wonder what a dinosaur thought, some 130 million years ago, when confronted by a honeybee. ... Much like some mammals developed hooves and horns, bees evolved with bodies to help them do what bees do (best): pollinate plants. Dinosaurs eventually went extinct, but it didn't take long for the proficient pollinators to migrate all over Africa and the Eurasian landmass.

To Bee or Not to Bee

Ten compelling reasons to encourage your inner beekeeper.

By Linda Rountree Grove

Labor costs can eat up meager earnings on the farm, but imagine the benefit of signing up thousands of workers who will literally pay for the privilege of pollinating your crops. I'm not talking about the latest scheme for taking advantage of your fellow humans; I'm talking about creating a hive of activity at your place with bees. Given the right environment, bees will work hard to add to your bottom line with increased yields — and if you treat them right, they'll pay you rent in the form of sweet, delicious, healthful honey and wax, which you can easily convert to cold cash.

Beekeeping may be the best small-farm business you've never considered. Read on for 10 compelling reasons to recruit a buzzing labor force to your farm.

1 Some farming activities need large amounts of physical strength for heavy lifting, or endurance for long, strenuous hours of activity, but beekeeping is different and democratic. It can be accomplished by men or women. Youngsters, under adult supervision, make excellent beekeepers. Seniors find that beekeeping makes an excellent hobby. The most physically demanding part of beekeeping is lifting honey-filled supers (the boxes that hold the frames on which the bees build the honeycombs) from the hive.

2 Beekeeping is an activity that can be enjoyed anywhere in the United States. Hives can be kept in cold Northern states, the desert, and in the hot and humid South.

A local beekeeping group can be an invaluable resource for assessing specific regional strategies for beekeeping.

If you live where there are flowering plants, shrubs or trees, you can keep bees. You can find hives in the city as well as the country. Country beekeepers, however, enjoy fewer restrictions. City dwellers will want to check local ordinances regarding rules or restrictions for beekeeping.

3 Bees do not require daily feeding, watering or milking like many kinds of livestock. They generally need supplemental feeding in the spring and fall, which requires checking food reserves in the hives every few days.

During the summer, you might check your bees every week or so for health of the colony, condition of the hive, and

progress of honey production. Late summer or fall involves removing surplus honey from the hive, which can generally be done in a day if you only have one or two hives. Winter involves no work for the beekeeper. It is a time to read up on the latest beekeeping information and make plans for next year's honey crop. The practice can easily be done with other daily farm chores or with a full-time job away from the farm.

4 Beekeeping has benefits for those who garden, maintain orchards or vineyards, or who raise row crops. Honeybees are the leading pollinator of all plants. Increased fruit, vegetable, and flower production make beekeeping a real asset.

Pollination increases can be enjoyed by neighbors as well, since bees can travel up to three miles from the hive looking for food sources. Some beekeepers rent hives to other farmers for pollination purposes.

5 Home-produced honey is delicious. Drizzled on top of biscuits or added to a cup of hot tea is just the beginning. Baking with honey creates moist muffins, cakes, and cupcakes.

Many who suffer from seasonal allergies swear by local raw honey's ability to

From hives to flowers, honeybees gather the pollen and create the honey that beekeepers harvest and the rest of us enjoy at our meals.

Beekeeping Basics   **23**

help alleviate allergy symptoms without the need for costly prescriptions or over-the-counter medications.

Honey and honey products make great gifts that are always welcomed by family and friends.

6 Bees produce items other than honey. Wax, propolis (a sticky resin-type substance), and royal jelly all have retail possibilities. Beeswax makes beautiful candles. Beeswax candles are valued for their cleaner burn and mild, sweet fragrance. Honey and beeswax are frequent additions in handmade soap, lotions, and lip balms. Milk and honey soap is a perennial favorite, and farmers with dairy cows, goats, or sheep often find it a good use of extra milk.

7 Working with bees can be a great stress reducer. Tending the hive requires concentration and smooth, deliberate movements so as to not provoke the bees. This ability to focus only on the task at hand allows the other stressors of the day to melt away. Observing the industry of the colony and listening to the hum can be very relaxing.

8 Compared with other farm startup costs, beekeeping is an inexpensive proposition. Most beekeeping suppliers offer beginner kits in the $165 to $450 range. These kits generally include a hive, basic tools, smoker, gloves, and basic protective garments like a veiled hat, as well as an introduction to beekeeping book. Bees are purchased by the package or a nuc (pronounced nuke and short for nuclear hive). A package will include worker bees, drone bees, and a queen

A beekeeper in full safety gear works his hives. The tool in his right hand is called a "hive tool," which is used to pry frames from the hive and scrape away beeswax.

bee, which will be in a separate cage within the package of bees. A nuc consists of workers, drones, a queen and brood. Expect to pay at least $100 for bees shipped to your place.

A beekeeper with protective gloves lifts a frame from one of his hives.

9 Beekeeping is a fun hobby with the perk of extra income. In a good year, one hive can produce about 100 pounds of surplus honey, which can more than pay for startup costs. Many beginning beekeepers start with two hives so they can compare the progress of the two. Add in the additional income that could be earned by making value-added items such as candles, soaps, lotions, and lip balm, or selling wax, pollen, and propolis, and beekeeping contributes nicely to the bottom line; not to mention the increased profits from fruits and vegetables due to improved pollination.

10 Small-scale beekeeping may well keep this important labor force alive. Bees all over the country are suffering from the devastating effects of Colony Collapse Disorder (CCD). A proliferation of smaller, isolated colonies can help keep our honey-making helpers alive long enough to learn how to combat CCD.

Honeybees could be a productive part of many farms, but there are caveats. Beekeeping is not recommended for those who have a severe allergic reaction to bee stings (or whose family members are severely allergic to bee stings). Severe reactions can result in the onset of anaphylactic shock and rapid death without immediate

HOW TO MINIMIZE THE CHANCES OF BEE STINGS

Bee stings are the No. 1 concern of new beekeepers, as well as their family and friends. Generally speaking, bee stings are a rare occurrence even with the presence of hives on the property. Unless you are dealing with Africanized honeybees, most varieties of honeybees are generally more concerned about their tasks than stinging. This is especially true when the bees are away from the hive gathering food.

- Back at the hive, they may try to defend their honey stores. Unless you are extremely comfortable around bees, it is recommended that you wear long sleeves and pants, as well as gloves and a protective hat with veil when opening the hive.
- Common sense would dictate locating the hive away from frequently traveled walkways, recreation areas, or relaxation areas of humans or animals.
- You also will encounter fewer bees at the hive between 10 a.m. and 5 p.m. on nice days since they are out gathering nectar and pollen. Cold, rainy and extremely windy weather tends to keep bees at the hive, which means there are more to deal with if you open the hive.
- Keep the clothing you wear for beekeeping laundered. The venom from previous stings can be detected by the bees, setting off alarm throughout the colony. Do not wear heavy perfumes or strong smelling hair and body products. Bees also tend to react negatively to body odor.
- Light-colored clothing without a heavy texture is always a good choice. There are some people who believe bees may associate dark colors and heavily textured fabric with fur, and bears, skunks and other animals have been known to raid beehives for honey.
- Resist the urge to swat at the bees. They are curious by nature and will often land and walk on your hands, clothing and equipment as you work the hive. If you must move a bee, gently brush it aside.
- Work carefully so as to not squash any bees. Squashed bees can release a scent that alerts other bees to danger and the need for defense of the hive.

A natural honeycomb from the interior of a Turkish hive of a special type of bee called "Karakovan."

SUPPLIERS OF BEEKEEPING EQUIPMENT

The following websites specialize in beekeeping supplies and offer free or online catalogs, and all offer beginner hive kits to get you started.

Betterbee
www.betterbee.com
800-632-3379

Dadant
www.dadant.com
888-922-1293

Mann Lake Ltd.
www.mannlakeltd.com
800-880-7694

Kelley Beekeeping
www.kelleybees.com
800-233-2899

Brushy Mountain Bee Farm
www.brushymountainbeefarm.com
800-233-7929

epinephrine treatment. Consult your family physician if you have any concerns.

Also, some people have an extreme fear of stinging insects. Obviously beekeeping would not be enjoyable for those individuals. For the beekeeper, however, the possibility of an occasional bee sting does not outweigh the enjoyment and income of maintaining a beehive.

Still on the fence about whether to try your hand at beekeeping? Here is an awesome 11th reason to consider. Beekeepers are some of the friendliest, most helpful people you'll ever meet. Beekeeping can be a great way to meet new people, make new friends and build community.

A grandfather passing along his beekeeping experience.

Remembering a Honeybee Hive

A trip for honey turns into a lifelong fascination with the buzzing makers of the sweet treat.

By Heidi Overson

My father had an insatiable hankering for honey, and he knew where to get the best honey in the whole state of Wisconsin: Ingman Nelson's house. Ingman was in his late 60s and lived deep in the woods of rural Coon Valley, in southwestern Wisconsin. He and my father had grown up together and were good friends. While my father left the area and traveled the world, Ingman stayed and never married, making a living doing manual labor and umpiring the small town's baseball games. My father returned from his travels and bought a farm close to Ingman's house, and that is how they rekindled their friendship.

Dad had sampled honey from different areas of the world, and he felt that Ingman's honey was the absolute best. He loved Ingman's honey so much that he often referred to Ingman as "The King of Bees." Being a daily honey eater, he'd go to Ingman's house often to replenish his supply.

One day, he took me along for the first time. I was excited: I'd never seen a real king before. The quest for Ingman's honey started out with a bumpy ride in my

father's 1956 Chevy pickup truck. I was 10 years old and loved riding by Dad's side as he drove the gray beast up and down the gravel back roads to Ingman's driveway, a narrow lane that led to a glorified shack at the top of a hill. The King of Bees stood outside, waiting for us.

To my disappointment, he didn't look like a king at all. He was small, with a slightly hunched back and a pronounced limp, due to a bad hip. He wore old, tan pants that were slightly dirty and a checkered oxford shirt. No crown sat on his bald head, and he squinted through scratched and smudgy spectacles. Ingman's two mammoth-sized dogs barked excitedly when we arrived, waiting to inspect the new visitors.

"Stay there!" Ingman snarled at us as he limped to the front steps of his porch to get the plastic, bulbed turkey baster filled with water. He kept this weapon on hand for times like these. Squirting the dogs with streams of water from the baster, he motioned for us to come forward. The dogs whimpered and backed away—they hated getting wet. We walked as quickly as we could toward the house, and Ingman continued to bombard the dogs with water until we were on the crooked, wooden front porch. There, my father and Ingman talked, while I watched the dogs carefully. Every time they came closer, more streams of water came out of the baster, and another round of profanity, directed at the dogs, came out of Ingman's mouth.

"I've come for honey," my father said over the ruckus.

"Yes, that is what I thought," Ingman responded. He then tossed the baster on the front porch and led us inside his humble house.

INSIDE THE PALACE

Ingman's house was witness to a lonesome bachelorhood: newspapers strewn everywhere, dirty dishes and clothes left here and there. He was hospitable and offered us bottles of fizzy soda pop. I accepted the unexpected treat with delight—drinking soda was forbidden at my house. I savored each sip as Ingman and Dad talked and finally got around to the reason for our visit: the honey.

Not only did we fetch our honey in old Ball glass jars, we got to see Ingman's bees in action. In the living room—amidst the clutter and old newspapers, glasses, and empty soda bottles—taking precedence over any other thing in the entire house, stood a double-sided bee colony case made out of glass. Ingman managed to produce a small smile for me, as he knew that I would be utterly fascinated by his bee shrine.

As though coming upon a great treasure, I reverently walked to the case, put down my soda, and gawked. There were hundreds and hundreds of bees, all busily crawling around their hive, making the delicious honey. I could lean in as close as I wanted to, with no fear of any bees hurting me. I stared for minutes on end, not minding how long Ingman and my father talked. To me, it was miraculous how these little bees could stay so busy and content in their glass case, all of them on a mission and happy with their little lives and purpose.

A CHANGED MAN

"Can you find the queen bee, Heidi?" Ingman asked. I tried and tried, my eyes burning, looking for the telltale sign that one of those bees was the queen. I could not figure it out. Ingman stopped talking to my father and limped over to me. When he was beside that case with me, all of his scariness and snarl faded away. His weathered face softened as he shared his passion with me, pointing an old and gnarled finger to the grandest and most worshiped bee of all.

"There she is," he said softly. "There she is." Together, we quietly gazed at the queen. To me, she looked like any of the other bees, yet, she was the chosen one; she was the center of the bees' universe.

> (Ingman) gave me an understanding and respect for bees I still have today. I learned that one man's passion can be contagious—when that passion is offered, shared and accepted, differences melt away. (We) rested in the contentment of quiet observation, and during that time, we understood much about each other.

I was intrigued by how Ingman's passion and my fascination for the bees erased our age difference. Ingman was an old man often misunderstood by those who did not know about his bees or honey. He hadn't aged well. Many hours of working hard under a hot sun had taken its toll. Crooked back, skinny arms and legs, worn and wrinkled face, barely much to smile about—his life had turned him into an apparently grumpy old man. But the bees had brought joy and purpose to his days. He knew bees.

When he stood with me in front of his colony, all his eccentricities and bitterness over a hard life melted away and we connected. I sensed his love for his bees, and suddenly, he became my friend. He gave me an understanding and respect for bees I still have today. I learned that one man's passion can be contagious—when that passion is offered, shared, and accepted, differences melt away. Ingman and I rested in the contentment of quiet observation, and during that time, we understood much about each other.

It took a long time for my father to tear me away from the case, but I knew that when our honey was gone, we would return and get more. The King of Bees would be waiting for us, turkey baster and all. Wading through Ingman's mess, we headed back out to the porch and the waiting dogs, watched another round of water-squirting, and listened to more disgusted outbursts from Ingman. Dad and I jumped back into the truck and backed out of the long driveway. I looked back to see Ingman and his dogs, and I waved. He offered a small gesture of goodbye and hobbled back toward his house. I felt a small twinge of sadness as I wondered what he did after we left. I imagined that as any good king would do, he went back to be with his queen.

His weathered face softened as he shared his passion with me, pointing an old and gnarled finger to the grandest and most worshiped bee of all.

BUYING BEES

"In the mid-1800s, (the Rev. L.L.) Langstroth discovered he could employ bee space (space neither large enough or small enough to encourage bees to build comb or seal with propolis) to make it easy to remove his hives' covers and to remove the hives' comb-filled frames with ease. Langstroth also discovered that it was possible to increase honey yields in healthy hives by stacking several boxes of frames atop one another, while restraining the queen in the lowest with a device called a 'queen excluder' that allowed workers to pass, but not the queen."
— Oscar H. Will III, "The Reverend Langstroth's Beehive," Page 41

Setting Up a Beehive

Maintaining a beehive is not nearly as complicated or scary as some people believe.

By Ed Robinson

Whether you have one hive or a dozen, keeping calm is key to becoming a well-versed beekeeper.

We didn't decide to have bees until we had laying hens, chickens to eat, goats, pigs, and — of course — our garden all producing.

As I look back, I believe it was my father who got us interested in the idea of keeping bees. Actually, he didn't know anything about beekeeping, but, every time he visited us, he brought along a jar of honey. He liked honey so much and believed it to be so much healthier than sugar, he got us interested in producing our own.

STARTING A BEEHIVE

We've found out that doctors do recognize that honey is the perfect sweet — it's easier to digest, furnishes a quick source of energy, and, unlike processed sugar, contains minerals.

About this time, we were reading a book called *The Farm Primer* in which the author says that a hive or two of bees will increase the fruit yield by 30 percent and even make the fruit taste better. Moreover, he pointed out that a hive of bees requires only eight hours of care per year and gives about 75 pounds of honey. Seventy-five pounds per hive seemed a lot, but I've since heard of single hives producing as high as 500 pounds. Of course, it's unlikely a novice will get as much as that.

One lunch hour in New York, I went down to a bee equipment place. All I meant to do was buy a booklet called *Starting Right With Bees*, which I was going to read first, then get the bees later. I asked them about the equipment necessary to have one beehive. They said, "Right now we have only one complete amateur outfit left."

Obviously, if I were going to have bees, then I'd best sign up for them right then and there. So, I wrote out a check for the works.

Incidentally, somewhat later on in talking to C.C. Whitehead, one of the best amateur beekeepers in Connecticut, I found it was his opinion that the only way to learn about bees is to get up your courage and order a complete beginner's outfit, as I did, and then you'll just have to learn or else.

One of the nice things about bees is that if you sign up for a beginner's outfit in January to March, you'll learn a good deal before the bees arrive.

That's because your outfit arrives in two shipments. The first shipment is equipment. Later, sometime in April, depending on the weather, the queen and three pounds of bees — about 15,000 of them — arrive.

In the first shipment, you get a smoker, bee feeder, hive tool, bee veil,

a booklet of directions, a year's subscription to a bee magazine, wax foundation, plus a hive, a deep super, and two shallow supers, knockdown.

We spent about three evenings assembling the beehive and supers. Unassembled, the 200-odd pieces look like a jigsaw puzzle — each piece is so perfectly cut, it's fun putting them together.

The hive is simply a box-like structure. At the bottom is a stand with an alighting platform. Set on top of this is the bottom of the hive — three or four boards cleated together to make a floor. Upon this rests a large oblong box without top or bottom. This is called the hive body or brood chamber. In it are hung 10 wooden frames, each one holding a patterned sheet of wax. The bees draw these sheets of wax into cells. In the cells, the young bees are hatched.

On top of this large box, you eventually place a shallow box, maybe two or three. These are called supers and, like the hive body, each holds 10 frames. The honey stored by the bees in the hive body must be left with the bees for winter food. But the honey stored in the supers can be taken away and extracted.

A queen excluder is placed between the hive body and the supers to keep the queen from laying eggs in the supers. On top of the supers is an inside cover. Then over all is the tin-topped wooden cover that telescopes down over inner cover and top super to make the hive waterproof.

All the above — hive, supers, bottom, inner cover, frames, and sheets of wax — are sent in pieces, which you then put together. Very complete directions are provided. We had a little difficulty putting the hive together because our playful kitten chewed up the directions, but we still made out all right.

By the time you get the hive together and painted, you'll understand a little something about the art of beekeeping. You'll also have a chance to study up on what to do when the bees arrive.

Let me tell you, you'll get a real thrill when you come home some day and find the second part of your order — a screened box about one square foot crammed full of 15,000 buzzing bees.

I'd read that anyone can handle bees, if they do it properly, and not get stung. But I'll admit I had my doubts the evening my wife, Carolyn, took me into the garage, pointed to the cage of buzzing bees the expressman had brought and said, "Well, do you want to put the bees in the hive now or after supper? Remember, that's your department!"

I confess I postponed putting the bees into the hives until after supper. I also sneaked upstairs for a last reading of the chapter "How to Install Bees in a Hive."

After supper, I set up the hive and carried the caged bees out to the uncovered hive. I wore the bee veil, but no gloves. It wasn't that I was being brave, I just couldn't find a pair of leather ones.

In opening the cage, I spilled the syrup can that goes along with the bees — spilled it all over my hand and about 3,000 bees tumbled out after it. Before I knew it, my hand was covered with crawling bees. For about 10 seconds I stood perfectly still. Then, suddenly I realized I was not being stung!

When you order an entire beginner's outfit, the first step is putting together the hive.

The author describes one method of collecting a swarm of bees. Another is to build a wooden trap to hold the swarm until you can relocate them to a new hive.

The bees were happily lapping the sugar syrup off my hand—that is, the 2,000 or 3,000 that could get a lick in. I began to think again and remembered to put the opened cage inside the hive. Then, somehow, I brushed the bees off my hand into the hive, released the queen, put the cover over the hive, and went to the house.

My wife had been watching me from the kitchen window. I came in, undid my veil and tossed it onto a chair.

"Didn't you get stung?" she asked. "Of course not—why should I?" I replied, shrugging my shoulders.

Right then and there I did get stung. It seems that one lone bee had crawled from my hand, up my arm, and when I shrugged my shoulders, I pinched her—and she let me have it.

I've dwelt at some length on the way I felt handling bees for the first time because so many people are missing the real benefits they can have keeping bees because they are afraid of being stung.

All the rest of the year, I was stung only twice. Both stings were due to my own carelessness. For example, one day I had been working hard in the garden in the hot sun. In fact, it was so hot that I wore only dungarees. Suddenly, I remembered I should feed the bees some sugar water. I carried it over to the hive, not stopping to put my veil on or even a shirt. I opened the hive, flipped off the cover, bent over to pick up the Boardman bee feeder and had no sooner straightened up when I was stung by three bees. That was my fault for being so brisk and blowing my hot breath on the bees.

Buying Bees

One other time, I pinched a bee and she stung me. But by then I'd learned to rub, not pull the stinger out. And by getting the stinger out fast, the sting was hardly more than a mosquito bite. With my veil and gloves, and handling the bees properly, I don't get stung.

For quite some time — from the middle of April when the bees arrived until the first nectar flow in June — I fed the bees a mixture of sugar and water. This is fed through the bee feeder, which holds an inverted Mason jar with its zinc top perforated.

After the clover blossoms, the first real nectar flow is on and the bees make their own honey. You'd think it might be smart not to get your bees until the nectar flow started so you wouldn't need to feed them sugar-water. But the reverse is true.

Although 15,000 bees sound like a lot of bees, they're just the nucleus of the hive. A strong hive builds up to three or four times this size. A few days after your bees arrive, the queen should begin producing eggs — at the rate of 2,000 to 3,000 a day. These eggs are attended by the 15,000 bees, and the eggs begin to hatch 16 to 18 days later. So, if you get your bees in April, your colony should be built up to a fair size when the first nectar flow starts in June.

For the first two or three months after our bees arrived, the only help we had was from our books. I well remember one line in a book that proved comforting again and again — "The amateur is apt to err by giving the bees too much attention." So, whenever I was in doubt about doing this or that, I didn't do it.

The sight and sound of swarming bees is something you will remember for a long time.

The industrious bees get right to work as soon as they are installed in a new hive.

This system worked fine until one evening when I arrived at 6:42. Mrs. R. said, "Well, a phenomenon of nature took place today."

I didn't like the way she said it. "What do you mean?"

"You guess," she replied.

"Jackie has started to talk."

"No."

"One of the geese laid a golden egg."

"No — your bees have swarmed."

Sure enough, in our backyard, way at the top of the highest tree, was a huge swarm of bees. My wife said she'd heard them come out of the hive around noon — they sounded like a squadron of high-flying airplanes, and after flying around a bit, they'd clustered at the top of the tree.

It so happened that very morning a fellow commuter had told me about a neighbor of his, Mr. Whitehead, who was an expert beekeeper. All I knew about swarming was that bees don't usually stay around long after they swarm — sometimes only a half-hour. So, I telephoned Mr. Whitehead.

Mr. Whitehead calmed me down and told me he'd lend me another hive. Then said that I should take a ladder, climb the tree, cut the branch on which the bees clustered, take it down and hang the bees on a clothesline overnight. All this I did—incidentally without getting stung. The cluster was a foot in diameter and 3 feet long.

The next morning I got up at 5:30 a.m., spread a sheet on the ground in front of the newly set up hive, shook the bees off the branch and watched them stream into the new hive.

Two hours later, the last of them were marching into the hive and I now had two hives of bees, for there was quite a colony still left in my original hive.

Right here, I'd like to say that Mr. Whitehead has since taught me a lot about bees. Incidentally, one of the real pleasures of beekeeping is getting acquainted with other folks who keep bees.

If you're really interested in starting in with bees, visit a beekeeper in your locality—tell him you're thinking of getting a hive of bees and see if he won't invite you over to his place to watch him open his hives. If you can, spend a few hours with a beekeeper and if you read *First Lessons in Beekeeping*, you should get along fine.

It wasn't until sometime after we got our bees that we found out we could not expect much honey from them the first year particularly because we let them swarm. The reason for this is simply that the bees have all they can do to draw the wax foundation into cells plus raising the young bees and storing enough honey for themselves. Our bees had stored up more than 60 pounds of honey their first year, which we left them to eat over the winter. We took only four or five pounds for our own use. The second year we had about 60 pounds of honey for our own use.

Bees are one of the most fascinating things you can have. They require only a few feet of space, gather their own food, and need only eight hours care per hive a year. You can have bees even if you live in the city; I know of a beekeeper who lives in Brooklyn.

Most beekeepers, novice or experienced, will say meeting others in the same line of work is one of the best parts of keeping bees.

Buying Bees

Find Your Favorite Honeybee

A guide to the top backyard producers and pollinators.

By Caleb D. Regan

If you're like me, when it comes to adding livestock — or any animal for that matter — to your home, you relish the research. It's fun to flip through literature and find the breed, species, or whatever the subspecies (also called ecotypes) may be called that jumps out at you and finds its way into your heart and onto your land.

With bees, it's no different. In the case of the honeybee, there are four main European ecotypes (called bee races) of the western honeybee that were introduced to the New World.

The important thing to consider, as always, is for what purpose do you want this creature? The most profitable use is most often contracting with agriculture producers for pollination purposes. And some honey production is usually important to the

backyard beekeeper. With the different races of the western honeybee, you can have both. For the rural or urban apiarist, a good mix of honey production and pollination probably is the most desirable use, but you also want to find a gentle bee. If you get a hive that is "hot" or "sparky," you'll most likely have to remove the hive or requeen, and it will take some time to restore production.

It's also worth noting that with bees, there is a large amount of crossbreeding between races. Simply put, it's far more difficult to isolate and control breeding among them than it is with dogs, cattle, or chickens. Crossbreeding has created more and more of a melting pot over time, and that's not necessarily a bad thing. So, while there's no guarantee of race-specific characteristics, research can't hurt. One tip for finding a gentle hive is to scour websites and find reputable beekeeping operations, take note of those that tout gentle hives, and keep an eye out for images of sellers working their hives with minimal equipment.

The first four races listed were brought to the New World. Finding them in pure form is virtually impossible, since hybridization is rampant. Moving down the list we see more hybrids like the Russian and Buckfast, and when you buy Italian Honeybees to start your hive, you too are more than likely getting a hybrid whose seller has hopefully selected for desirable characteristics. While it is a melting pot, your bees are still descendants of the following subspecies. Understanding the races no doubt gives you a better understanding of the creatures you're bringing to your property.

From top: Caucasian honeybees produce more propolis; an Italian bee pollinates an avocado blossom; Russian bees are more resistant to mites (this hive's queen is identified by the blue dot).

Italian Honeybee (*Apis mellifera ligustica*) — This is the standard in the United States, the most commonly available, and the honeybee most often recommended for beginners. It was imported to the New World in 1859. The bee is adapted to a Mediterranean climate, so this is the variety best suited to the warmer climates common to much of the United States. The color of workers and drones is bright yellow, so queens are easy to identify because they are darker in color. The Italian has a moderately low tendency to swarm, and they are good producers of honey. Drawbacks are that they can be difficult to keep alive in cooler climates, and they are susceptible to the tracheal mite and the varroa mite.

Carniolan Honeybee (*A. mellifera carnica*) — Otherwise known as the Gray Bee, the "Carni" comes from Slovenia as well as neighboring Carinthia and countries east to Romania and Bulgaria. Its chitinous abdominal rings are dark with light gray-yellowish hairs. This honeybee is second to the Italian in terms of worldwide economic impact. It's cold hardy and well adapted to the mountains. Some say this bee is gentler than the Italian. Carnis are prone to swarm.

German or Black Bee (*A. mellifera mellifera*) — This race is extremely hard to find today. It was probably one of the first to be introduced into the Americas, but lost favor due to defensiveness, and because beekeepers

usually prefer lighter-colored honeybees. The short-tongued German Bee is often susceptible to disease.

Caucasian Honeybee (*A. mellifera caucasica*)—The Caucasian is known to be cold hardy and gentle, but collects a lot of propolis, gumming up the hive and making it a little more difficult to work. The Caucasian is similar in shape and size to the Carni. Chitin appears dark with brown spots at different times of year, and hair color is lead-gray. The Caucasian has a longer tongue than most races, so it can take advantage of more nectar sources.

Russian Honeybee—This honeybee is not a subspecies per se, but rather a hybrid created by the U.S. Department of Agriculture Honey Bee Research Laboratory in Baton Rouge, Louisiana, for the purpose of showing resiliency to varroa and tracheal mites. The bee comes from stock located in the Primorski region of the Sea of Japan, where it had been exposed to the mites for about 150 years. Russians are twice as resistant to varroa mites as other honeybees and highly resistant to tracheal mites, but they can be a little on the aggressive side. They are moderate honey producers and collect a fair amount of propolis.

Buckfast Honeybee—Another hybrid, this honeybee exhibits good hygienic behavior and strong resistance to tracheal mites. It was created by Brother Adam of the Buckfast Abbey, who spent a large portion of his life crossing races in hopes of creating a superior subspecies. These bees can be defensive, so make sure you find a gentle hive. Can be more difficult to find than other races, but does well in cool, damp temperatures.

BEEKEEPING BEHAVIOR AND INDICATIONS

Understanding bee behavior makes a better beekeeper.

Why are there lots of bees piled on the outside of my hive? This is known as bearding, and most often occurs when the bees are hot. It can also be caused by congestion and lack of ventilation. Take immediate steps to do what you can, but then accept it. Humans sweat; bees beard up. Top and bottom ventilation helps cool them.

Why are my bees dancing? Many believe these repetitive movements can communicate information about food sources. Dr. Karl von Frisch won a Nobel Prize for his study in the 1920s and '30s on dancing bees. He concluded that through dancing, bees communicate four things about their food supply: quality, quantity, direction, and distance.

Why are there dead bees outside the hive? Don't panic. With the queen laying between 1,000 and 3,000 eggs per day, and bees living only about six weeks, there are always going to be some dead bees right outside the entrance of the hive. If you start seeing bucket loads or larger piles, then it's time to start worrying about other causes—pesticide poisoning, mites, or some other problem.

Why are my bees spread on the surface of the box, moving up and down and seemingly cleaning it? This is known as washboarding, and it's common in warmer weather. It looks like the bees are scrubbing the hive front and moving back and forth. We really don't know why, apart from guessing it's some sort of cleaning behavior. Other than being a little hypnotic to the beekeeper, there's no known harm in this behavior.

The Reverend Langstroth's Beehive

Nineteenth-century invention is still on the job.

By Oscar H. Will III

Every cloud has its silver lining. The Rev. L.L. Langstroth's silver lining was that he found bees and beekeeping to be an effective antidote to nearly debilitating clouds of malaise. As a meticulous student of the hive, the Philadelphia clergyman and private school principal discovered a way to use bee space to great advantage and designed what amounts to the modern beehive — the modular boxlike structures seen wherever bees are raised throughout much of the world.

Bee space — defined as the space that is neither large enough or small enough to encourage bees to build comb or seal with propolis — was discovered by European apiarists prior to Langstroth's putting it to work. Langstroth discovered that he could use this approximately ⅜ of an inch to make working the hive and collecting honey a relatively simple proposition.

In the years leading to Langstroth's discoveries, European bees had been typically sheltered in fairly elaborate bee houses, open-chamber boxes, crude dome-shaped skeps, or hollowed logs. With all of these structures, the comb was sealed to the hive with wax, and hive components were sealed to one another with propolis, making it difficult to work the hives and collect honey without disturbing the bees to the point that they would go on the attack. In the United States, the open-chamber box hive had reached some level of popularity, but the beekeeping enterprise was depressed, in general.

In the mid-1800s, Langstroth discovered he could employ bee space to make it easy to remove his hives' covers and to remove the hives' comb-filled frames with ease. Langstroth also discovered that it was possible to increase honey

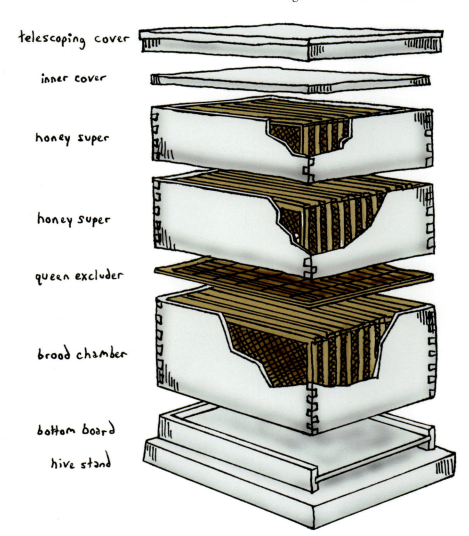

Buying Bees 41

Well-tended Langstroth-style beehives await the beekeeper's next visit.

Bees return via the porch-like structure of their Langstroth hive.

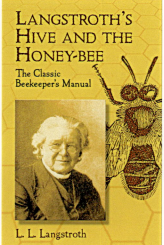

For more on the hives designed by the Rev. L.L. Langstroth, read his book, *Langstroth's Hive and the Honey-Bee*.

yields in healthy hives by stacking several boxes of frames atop one another, while restraining the queen in the lowest with a device called a "queen excluder" that allowed workers to pass, but not the queen.

Portability, removable frames, and modular construction with available materials made Langstroth's hives a big hit when he began selling them after patenting the design in 1852. His four-sided removable frames saved bees' lives (they didn't get riled when you took out the comb) and increased their honey production because it was possible to harvest the honey without destroying the comb — meaning the bees no longer had to expend energy and consume honey to create new wax.

Langstroth never profited from his patent, as it proved too difficult to defend, and its popularity led to many "tweaked" designs that were themselves patentable. Nonetheless, Langstroth is still referred to as the Father of American Beekeeping. His legacy is evident in orchards and backyards, on urban rooftops and flatbed semis moving from one pollinating job to another, and in the faces of beekeeping enthusiasts and bee club members around the world.

The Key is Location, Location, Location

Take a look around your property and decide where to place your new beehives.

By Julia Miller,
FiveFelineFarm.com

Take the time to consider where you want to locate your beehives, and how you want to arrange them in the bee yard.

So you have decided to invest in a colony of honeybees. Your package bee order is set to arrive in the spring at just the right time for your location. Your new Langstroth-style hive is assembled and waiting at the back door.

Now where do you put this new livestock?

One of the first considerations is access. A perfect location may be available but not easily accessible. You will be visiting the hive every week or so to check on the bees. For a new package installation, you will be visiting more often in those early weeks to provide sugar water. In the late summer and fall will be the honey harvest. Supers full of honey are heavy. Access with a truck, utility vehicle (we use a Kawasaki Mule), or at the very least a wagon to pull is critical.

CONSIDER WATER

Look around for a good water source within a reasonable flight for the bees. They tend to like water that has some organic matter in it. A farm pond, creek, stream, stock tank, or even a goldfish pond will give your bees access to the water they need.

Most areas will have nectar and pollen nearby, but make sure your bees have something to forage. Bees can fly up to three miles for pollen and nectar, but more time in flight equals less nectar in the hive. Closer supplies mean more honey.

CONSIDER SUN EXPOSURE

Next look for a site that has full sun. Bees are active from sunup to sundown so locating your hives where there is maximum sun exposure will allow your bees to

benefit from a full day's work. Hives should ideally face south. This gives the bees the earliest start in the morning when the sun warms the entrance. Even though bees like sun, they also need a bit of protection from wind. For a windbreak, you can locate the hives against a building, a few feet from a fence row, a line of trees, or you can build a windbreak. Strong winds can topple a hive or blow off an outer cover despite your best efforts to weight it down. An open or toppled hive is a sure way to lose your colony.

Try to choose a location with a slight slope to allow for drainage. At a minimum, ensure that the ground is not prone to flooding. Bees do not thrive in damp locations, and you need to ensure there is no risk that water will run or seep into the bottom of the hive. If your location is otherwise good, you can accommodate this factor by raising the hives on a stand or concrete blocks.

Flowering trees and shrubs, plus plenty of colorful blooms, make an ideal area for foraging.

CONSIDER DISTANCE

At Five Feline Farm, the apiary or "bee yard" is a short distance from the house accessible by either truck or UTV. This gives some space between the bees and the house, but allows for easy access. The UTV is particularly helpful when transporting supers or brood boxes and bee equipment as well as when harvesting honey. If we are just doing a quick inspection however, it is easy to grab a tool and walk to the hives.

Our hives are located in a tall meadow with native flowers and brambles. A few wild olives have been allowed to grow and flourish as the bees like nectar from these invasive plants. These brushy trees, tall flowers, and brambles provide a natural wind break for the hives.

One year, we experienced a late spring snow that threatened the health of the colonies. The bees had already broken cluster with temperatures in the 60s, so we offered additional insulation and wind protection during the storm. Even with a polar vortex like that in recent memory, keep thinking about spring and getting started in beekeeping.

Many beekeepers site their hives near a field full of wonderful blooms; take into account the distance from your home.

Buying Bees

Hive Pros and Cons

Breaking down the top-bar design with an experienced apiarist.

By Lindsay Williamson

I love our top-bar hives, but like any other hive design, they are prone to certain problems. This doesn't mean I'm going to throw in the towel and stop using them; I just want to make a few modifications I think will correct these problems. To give you an idea of my overall experience working with my own top-bar hives, I'm going to offer a quick list of pros and cons, and then go into more detail about the ways I'm going to modify them. Perhaps these insights will give you some ideas about how you will (hopefully) build or choose your own top-bar hives.

TOP-BAR PROS

My top-bar bees are without a doubt the calmest both in the yard and during hive inspections. This is especially appreciated by someone like me who has children and close neighbors. The more docile, the better.

Hive inspections are a breeze as long as you pay adequate attention to comb attachment during comb-building season (nectar flow). You don't have to tear the whole hive apart at once, which can be stressful to the bees. You're literally just moving one bar at a time and replacing it. It's so much less disruptive and quicker to get through than with conventional box-style hives.

No heavy lifting is an especially big deal to someone who has back problems. Langstroth supers full of honey are heavy (40 to 60 pounds) and can be cumbersome to deal with. I've heard stories of beekeepers who were no longer able to keep bees in their Langstroth hives due to physical problems or injuries so they switched

One nice thing about the top-bar hive is when inspecting the comb building and the health of the hive, there's no need to completely disassemble the wooden structure.

With a top-bar model of hive, a beekeeper can harvest one bar of honey and comb at a time.

Healthy workers are busy sealing up cells within the honeycomb. The hives in the author's backyard are calm indeed.

to top-bar hives. Also, you can build or stand your hive at your perfect working height, avoiding back strain, and because there are no supers, this height will not change.

I love the flexibility where harvesting honey is concerned. You can do one or five bars at a time. In other hive designs, there is typically one harvest a year, and it's a long, hard, messy day. Top-bar design allows you the flexibility of harvesting honey specific to the time of year and what type of nectar they are bringing in, which I really like.

With a top-bar hive, there is little or no equipment to store through the winter. If you keep bees in Langstroth hives, you can fully appreciate this. No supers full of drawn comb to figure out how to freeze and then keep safe from those tenacious wax moths. Also, those empty supers take up an amazing amount of space that I really don't have to spare.

CONS

Because you harvest the comb along with the honey, you will typically not harvest as much honey each season as you would with a Langstroth hive, where the comb is reused. This doesn't really bother me because I also use the wax, but if you're in it for maximum honey production, this might be something to consider.

Small hive beetles — I really hate these things. I saw a bigger problem with the small hive beetle in our top-bar hives (compared to my Langstroth or Warre hives) in recent years, and believe it is because the bottom is solid wood (unlike the screened bottom boards on the others hives). This makes it more difficult for the bees to get rid of the small hive beetles. Also, I realized a bit late that the pests love to hide out in the knots or imperfections in the wood.

You're going to need to do more frequent inspections during the spring when the colony is building most of the wax in a top-bar hive. For a new colony, I'd recommend getting into your top-bar hive twice a week to stay on top of any comb that may be getting attached to more than one bar. You don't want to find out later by ripping brood apart.

There are no extractors for top bar hives, so extracting the honey from the comb can be a little more work. It requires crushing and straining the comb as opposed to just uncapping and flinging as you can do with a Langstroth frame. Cutting out chunks of the comb and including it in the honey you sell, though, will fetch a higher price.

Of all the cons listed above, the only thing that's a deal-breaker for us is the problem with small hive beetles, so that's what we had in the front of our minds when designing our new and improved version of the hive.

After several discussions and sketches,

we got in touch with an acquaintance and local woodworker who has an interest in beekeeping to help us produce some modified hive designs.

CHANGES TO TOP-BAR HIVES

We're taking off the solid bottom board and replacing it with a screened bottom using No. 8 hardware cloth, which is small enough to keep out robber bees, wasps, and small animals, but large enough that small hive beetles and varroa mites will fall through.

Below the new screened bottom, there will be a pullout tray that can be filled with oil to catch and kill the varroa mites and small hive beetles, ensuring that once the bees find and toss the pests, they will not make their way back. The tray will be completely removable to help ventilate the hive during hot weather, but it will also slide right back in during winter or to ward off the pests should they start to become a problem.

Also, we will seal any imperfections in the wood (pits, screw holes, knots, etc.) with beeswax prior to installing a new package or swarm (much easier that way). This will deny any pests a place to hide.

I feel confident that these new and improved versions of our top-bar hives will make a major difference in our chemical-free apiary, and I look forward to reporting back at the end of the season.

Inspecting the top-bar hive involves minimal disturbance to the bees and the hive, and the beekeeper even gets a little closer look than with conventional-style box hives.

The Difference Between Hives

Beekeeper details the pros and cons of the three top beehive designs: Top-Bar, Warre, and Langstroth.

By Jennifer Poindexter, MorningChores.com

In the past few years, the popularity of and interest in beekeeping has soared. Whether it is due to the rise in the number of people involved in homesteading or concern for the alarming decline in the bee population, more and more people are raising bees. So where do you start?

First of all, you need a home for your bees, and there are three types to choose from: the top-bar, Warre, and Langstroth beehive. Each type of hive has its own strengths and weaknesses, and the one you choose depends on your needs and preferences.

TOP-BAR BEEHIVES

The top-bar hive has been around for centuries. It is a simple concept, taking a wooden trench or tub and lining the top opening with wooden slats or bars. Once the honeybees take residence, they begin building their combs from the underside of those bars, working their way down into the tub. For a closer look at the honeycomb from a top-bar hive, turn to the previous article on Page 46.

PROS

- Top-bar hives have a simple design. You can build them yourself out of any materials you like, taking advantage of recycled materials, with whatever dimensions you need, all of which help cut down on cost. For a variety of plans, go to www.morningchores.com/beehive-plans.
- As with some hives, you won't require hundreds of dollars worth of equipment and accessories to maintain a top-bar hive. All you essentially need is the hive itself and a sharp knife.
- Top-bar hives are foundation-less, so the combs you end up with are completely natural, devoid of any of the pesticides or chemicals that may come in purchased wax or plastic foundations.
- Because of its horizontal design, top-bar hives don't require any heavy lifting, save for the lid and the combs themselves. Also, the height can be adjusted to the beekeeper's preference, adding convenience and ease-of-use all around.
- Your bees will be less agitated. Lifting one slat at a time to harvest allows the rest of the hive to remain undisturbed, keeping the bees' stress level down and reducing your risk of being stung by an anxious bee.

CONS

- The only way to harvest honey is to crush and strain the combs, meaning that the bees will have to rebuild new combs from scratch. As a result, top-bars are said to produce less honey than other hives.
- More inspections are required to make sure that bees continue to have plenty of space for honey storage.

> Top-bar hives don't require any heavy lifting, save for the lid and the combs themselves. Also, the height can be adjusted ...

The top-bar beehive, below, looks quite a bit different from the Langstroth-style hives at left.

Buying Bees 51

Warre beehives are, in many respects, a interesting blend of the Langstroth and top-bar hives.

> The Warre hive ... requires minimal inspection, leaving the bees to their work and, as a result, keeping them undisturbed and happy.

- Top-bar hives are not standardized, so if you're looking for accessories, chances are you'll have to build them yourself.

WARRE BEEHIVES

The Warre hive was designed by a French monk named Abbé Émile Warré. He wanted a hive that closely resembled what nature intended, requiring minimal interference from beekeepers. It has wooden slats similar to that of the top-bar hive, but it stacks vertically much like a Langstroth hive. However, you add new boxes to the bottom of the hive rather than the top. The idea here is to allow bees to work and build from the top down as they do in nature.

PROS

- The Warre hive is extremely low maintenance, aside from harvesting. It requires minimal inspection, leaving the bees to their work and, as a result, keeping them undisturbed and happy.
- This hive has a layer of insulation in a small box just under the roof. It is lined with cloth and filled with sawdust to keep condensation down, resulting in a much healthier hive. In addition, this extra layer makes the Warre hive much more suitable to colder climates.
- If you have the tools and know-how, you can build this hive yourself and cut back on costs.

CONS

- You'll have to do a bit of heavy lifting with the Warre hive. When it comes time to add a new box, the top ones need to be lifted. Given the smaller size, they aren't nearly as heavy as their Langstroth counterparts, but you can expect to hoist anywhere from 30 to 50 pounds.
- With the "minimal interference" concept that comes with a Warre hive, it can be difficult to assess hive activity or add accessories such as bee feeders.
- Extra, unused boxes will take up storage space.

LANGSTROTH BEEHIVES

Even if you're new to beekeeping, chances are you've seen a Langstroth hive, the most common hives used in the United States, especially for commercial purposes. Langstroth hives are vertically stacked wooden boxes filled with frames upon which the bees build their combs. When a new box, otherwise known as a super, is needed, it is added to the top of the hive.

PROS

- Langstroth hives are standardized, so you will find that replacement parts or accessories are readily available. Also, there's a huge amount of resources for beginner beekeepers.

- These hives have a high production rate. When harvesting, only a portion of the comb is cut as the honey is spun out. Bees don't have to start building new combs from scratch, resulting in more honey.
- You can choose whether or not to use a foundation.
- You have a choice between an eight-frame Langstroth (which will prove to be much lighter) or the more traditional 10-frame hive.

CONS
- Langstroth hives require accessories such as extractors and smokers, and costs like that can add up.
- Expect to do some very heavy lifting. Some supers can weigh up to 100 pounds, which just may not be an option for some people.
- The Langstroth hive causes the most stress for bees. You'll have to open the main box to harvest or inspect, exposing the bees' home and riling them up. Not only that, but when you go to stack the boxes again, it can be difficult not to crush some of your bees.
- Most Langstroth users opt for foundations, and these can contain pesticides or chemicals. Also, they offer unnatural comb shapes that could result in an unhealthy hive. For these reasons, going foundationless is growing in popularity.
- Parts for the eight-frame and 10-frame hives are not interchangeable, so sticking with one size is the way to go.

You have a lot to consider before acquiring a hive and bees and becoming a beekeeper. There's no wrong choice, really, you just need to think about what your goals are and which hive will best serve those goals.

A major advantage to a Langstroth hive is the readily available parts.

Building a Beehive

Create your own bee condo and save money in the process.

By Keith Rawlinson

- Outer cover
- Inner cover
- Shallow super
- Frame
- Deep super
- Queen excluder
- Deep super
- Bottom board

Keeping bees is a good, sure way to put some extra money in your pocket, pollinate your crops, and stock your pantry with honey. While you can purchase all the equipment you'll need, hands-on folks may prefer to build their own hives. Not only will this save you some cash, it'll also give you an understanding of the inner workings of the place your bees will call home. (See diagrams at right of the supers and covers, and bottom board.)

- All items within this set of plans are built with ¾-inch boards and plywood. The type of wood is really not important, so I generally use the cheapest I can find, as long as the wood is solid and without cracks.
- It is extremely important to make sure all eight corners of each super are matched up before driving any nails. After glue is applied and the joints are slipped together, match up each corner, one by one, and drive in the nail closest to the matched corner to hold it in place while you nail the remainder of the joint. This is especially necessary if working with slightly warped or cupped boards. Straight boards are no problem.
- When nailing the top corners of the supers, be sure to place the corner nail down low enough so that it does not go into the rabbet joint instead of the wood itself.
- Remember, it is always a good idea to use plenty of waterproof wood glue when assembling beekeeping equipment. It's better to use too much rather than too little; you can wipe off excess, so be generous!
- The deep and shallow supers are put together with what I call a "tab joint" (really a modified box joint). It's nearly as strong as the finger joints used on commercially made equipment, but is much easier to make and requires no special tools.
- It may appear at first glance that some of the dimensions are not called out in the plans. However, any that are not directly marked can be calculated from those that are.
- Paint the equipment with exterior latex paint. White is most common since a light-colored hive tends to stay cooler during summer. Spend the extra money and get a high-quality paint. It'll pay you back in equipment longevity. Apply at least two coats, preferably three or four.
- You can shield the outer cover with some sort of sheet metal if you wish, but with adequate paint, the extra covering becomes optional.

Deep Super
Perspective view

Shallow Super
Perspective view

Covers and Bottom Board

All material is ¾" pine. Glue all joints and nail as shown in perspective. Pre-drill all nail holes to prevent splitting. Make four handles, one for each side. Assemble with waterproof wood glue and 4D 1½" box nails. Install kick-up frame rests in rabbets of both short sides if using ¾" rabbet. Otherwise, use 90-degree rests.

Fold thin aluminum or galvanized metal over top of outer cover and 1 inch down sides for weatherproofing. All material is ¾" pine, except inner cover, which is ½" plywood. Assemble bottom board with nails only, no glue.

Buying Bees

Beginning With Honeybees

Questions and answers help beginning beekeepers learn more about their hives.

By Pat Stone

You can keep bees anywhere enough nectar-bearing flowers grow. If other people are keeping bees in your area, you probably can, too. If no one is (unless you live in an untapped suburb or city), there's probably not enough forage available.

WHERE DO YOU PUT COLONIES?

Many urban beekeepers put their hives on their rooftops, out of the way of pedestrians. People with hives in crowded neighborhoods keep them out of sight, preferably behind a bush or barrier so the insects will have to fly up a few feet to head out foraging.

Other hints for backyarders: Keep a gentle breed (called "race") of bees; make sure they have a water source on your property; work hard to reduce swarming; and after your first harvest, take your neighbors some gifts of honey and explain to them how innocuous your bees have been.

In a rural area, choose a site that has some ventilation (no muggy frost pockets, but no windy hilltops either). Ideally, it should be exposed to the sun in the morning (to get the bees going) but shaded in the afternoon (so they can spend less energy cooling).

Also, put your first hives where you can observe them easily – you'll learn and enjoy a lot more that way.

HOW MUCH TIME DOES BEEKEEPING TAKE?

Once you know what you're doing, you can maintain a few healthy, established hives in just a few hours a year. Or, you may find yourself smitten with a severe case of bee fever and want to spend every spare minute in your bee yard.

The busiest times are spring, when you try to make sure your hive is strong but not about to swarm, and harvest, which takes place at the end of your area's main honeyflows.

Other than those busy times, an occasional inspection or trip to add more supers should be just about all that your bees will need.

HOW DO YOU HARVEST HONEY?

To get it away from the bees, you can just brush them off each frame you're after. A soft, no-animal-hair brush — like an artist's drafting brush — is best.

At the hobby level, the best way to go is to set a bee escape (a dandy one-way exit that you can put in the oval hole of the inner cover) under the supers you want to harvest, go away for a day or two, and then come back to an almost completely bee-free harvest.

Two cautions: Tape any cracks above the escape, or other bees may well harvest the honey before you do. And bee escapes don't work well in very hot weather.

Commercial beekeepers use blower guns or chemical repellents to evict bees from supers. Don't bother.

As a novice apiarist, keep in mind contact with experienced beekeepers is a great way of meeting people and learning your new craft.

Covered in pollen, this bee looks for her next meal in a sunflower.

HOW DO YOU GET THE HONEY OUT OF THE HIVE FRAMES?

Get the honey out in one of two ways: Either cut the honey out in comb chunks with a pocketknife, or scrape just the caps off all the sealed cells and spin the liquid honey out in a special centrifuge called a honey extractor. Extractors do increase yields because they leave the honey cells intact. But they also cost $375 and up — more than the rest of your start-up expenses put together. So you probably won't be able to start out with one. (Go to www.motherearthnews.com and search for "honey extractor" for plans to build to build one yourself.)

Instead, just cut comb sections out with a sharp knife, and carve off thin slivers of those to spread on toast, biscuits, and pancakes. This is the most delicious way to enjoy honey. If you want some liquid-with-no-beeswax honey, too, cut out the comb, then "pop" all the cells by slicing with a mandolin (or kraut cutter), and set the squashings up in a sieve to drain out your harvest. Heat and cool the remaining glob in a double boiler, and it will separate into solid wax (which you can use or sell) and some additional honey.

NOTE: Since extracting puts stress on bee equipment, if you do want to extract, you'll have to use special thick-wired foundation in your frames. On the other hand, since you want to be able to eat comb honey, you start that off on thin, nonwired foundation.

HOW MUCH HONEY WILL YOU GET?

If you're in a good beekeeping area, if the weather's great that year, and if your bees do well, you can get 100 to 200 pounds (30 to 60 gallons) or even more from one hive.

Not me, however. Where I live — an area where woodland trees are the main nectar sources — my hives probably average 50 pounds each, which, by the way, is the national average. (That includes the really lousy year when I may not get any.) In most places, two hives, a good number to start with, should give you all the honey you can use and some extra to give away or sell.

HOW DO YOU PREVENT SWARMING?

Swarming — the departure of many or most of a colony's bees with the old queen, leaving behind the other bees and some new queen cells — can cripple a hive's honey production, but it's the way colonies reproduce. You can't prevent it. There are scores of intricate methods for reducing swarming.

> In most places, two hives, a good number to start with, should give you all the honey you can use and some extra to give away or sell.

Raise Backyard Bees

In essence, though, colonies that are overcrowded or have older queens are more likely to swarm. So give your colonies plenty of space in the spring. And consider requeening your hives every other year—it cuts swarming in half. Requeening entails killing the old monarch and, a day later, installing a caged, new—probably mail-ordered—one. It's a bit tricky, but not too tricky.

WHAT IF YOU HAVE A MEAN HIVE OF BEES?

It happens. Some colonies are more aggressive than others. Often, the meanest bees gather the biggest harvests, so you may choose to frown and bear it.

If they bother you (or your neighbors) too much, you can solve the problem in one fell swoop, by requeening. A more docile queen will lay more docile eggs, and in six weeks you'll have an entire hive of more docile bees. The one hitch to this scheme is you'll have to work your way down through the brood chamber of your nasty colony so you can find the old queen and kill her. (Bundle up.)

WHAT ARE SOME COMMON PROBLEMS?

Pesticides. A lot of people lose bees because farmers or gardeners spray the flowers of crops that bees work. Educate your neighbors to spray only in the late afternoon (or not use pesticides on any blooms): What's good for your flying pollinators is good for the crops. (Sevin is a common bee killer; Bt is safe.)

Diseases. Today there are quite a few honeybee ailments, including American Foulbrood, a bacterial disease. (Your bees have this larval fungus if the hive smells foul and a matchstick poked into a brood cell comes out gooey, as if there were gum on it, instead of clean.) You have to destroy infested colonies—it's the law—to keep the disease from infecting other hives. To avoid the problem, buy only inspected, clean bees and equipment. There are some antibiotic preventives available, but don't use them unless you've had a prior Foulbrood problem.

Other problems include varroa mites, tracheal mites, chalkbrood and colony collapse disorder (CCD). (Turn to Chapter 5 for more on keeping your bees healthy.)

Winterkills. A good number of colonies starve each winter, primarily because their owners didn't leave enough honey in the hive to last until the following spring flows (not until the end of winter; lots of colonies starve in March). So don't get greedy. Always leave plenty of honey—30 to 90 pounds, depending on winter length—for the bees. You'll save yourself a lot of sorrow or, at the least, time and hassle syrup-feeding your bees.

Allergy. Most people develop an immunity to venom after repeated periodic "exposure." (The sting itself still smarts.) A few go the other way and develop serious nonlocal reactions. If you become highly allergic to bee venom, you may be risking your life the next time you're stung. See an allergist for immunotherapy (it costs, but it works) or find honey from some other local source.

These bees have likely been calmed with smoke before the frame was lifted from the hive.

Buying Bees 59

WHAT TO DO THE FIRST YEAR

"Suppose there was a way you could get your bees for free? I'm not talking about inheriting established hives, which can also mean inheriting problems like parasites and diseases. No, I'm talking about catching honeybee swarms. Honeybee colonies reproduce by swarming. When a colony runs out of room in its hive, it will split in two, each with its own queen. A colony that's strong enough to swarm is a sign of good health and vigor."

—Andrew Weidman, "Harness a Swarm," Page 100

Buzz-Worthy Plants

Attract native bees by transforming your backyard into a sanctuary filled with nectar-rich flowers, insect hotels, and more.

By Barbara Pleasant

The planet's best pollinators are in big trouble. Wildflower meadows where native bees once gathered nectar and pollen have turned into shopping malls, and dead trees where these ancient insects nest are getting harder to find. The native bees that do manage to survive are imperiled by Big Ag's pesticides — unless they can find safe haven in diversified organic gardens.

Gardeners can reap huge benefits from hosting helpful pollinators, which tend to stay put when given food and a place to live. Native bees — including bumblebees, sweat bees, mining bees and others — pollinate many crops more efficiently and completely than honeybees do, with strawberries, blueberries, and the entire squash family reliant on local pollinators to produce their best crops. Tomatoes visited by bumblebees bear bigger fruits, because the big bees' buzzing action shakes loose more pollen than wind alone. Strawberries pollinated by multiple types of bees yield fewer misshapen berries, and pumpkins pollinated by native squash bees produce larger pumpkins. Pollinators play a significant role in producing 150 food crops in the United States and, according to the Xerces Society (a nonprofit wildlife conservation group), one in three mouthfuls of our food and drink requires their work.

From left: Squash bees collect only cucurbit pollen; bumblebees pollinate legumes; sweat bees prefer strawberries and blueberries; mason bees can help ensure a good harvest of many tree fruits.

THE BEES' NEEDS

For about 70 percent of the 4,000 bee species native to North America, home is a secure spot tunneled into the ground (ground nesters). The other 30 percent nest in dead trees and stems (wood nesters). Almost all native bees live alone, not in colonies. Passive by nature, bees won't usually sting unless squashed or pinched.

Young adult bees emerge from their nests at various times during the year, usually in sync with the blooming period of their favorite crops. Females quickly mate and select good nesting sites, which are often within 1,000 feet of desirable flowering plants (see "Best Plants for Attracting Native Bees," Page 64).

After making a few short flights to learn their new addresses, most ground-nesting bees immediately start working to excavate a nest and stock it with eggs. Gathering the necessary pollen, nectar, and sometimes mud requires

What to Do the First Year

thousands of trips between flowers and the nest. The closer the flowers are to the bees' nest, the less energy the bees must expend in flight.

TYPES OF NATIVE BEES

The following five types of native bees provide pollination for gardens and orchards.

Bumblebees are the largest native bees, and they also tend to fly the farthest in search of food. Active from spring to fall, they pollinate a wide range of plants and are especially important to legumes. Bumblebees usually nest in the ground or in cavities in trees. Bumblebees are the only native bees that are truly social.

Mason bees are also called "orchard bees" because they often appear in fruit orchards in spring. These stout, bristly little bees may be black or metallic blue or green. Mason bees use mud to pack their well-provisioned eggs into the hollows of twigs and branches. They frequently accept manmade nesting blocks.

Mining bees look like miniature honeybees but have long, wasp-like wings. Active early in the year, they are important pollinators of fruit trees. Although mining bees are solitary ground nesters, numerous closely spaced nests may appear in hospitable spots.

Squash bees are the small black and yellow bees found in cucurbit blossoms, including those of cucumbers, summer squash, and pumpkins. These solitary ground nesters do not emerge until early summer.

Sweat bees are small and often have metallic backs. You'll spy them pollinating strawberries, blueberries, and a wide range of flowers. Different species are active early and late in the year. They prefer to stay within a quarter-mile of their nests and they live alone.

BEE SANCTUARIES

Most ground-nesting bees are quite small and rely on secrecy to ensure their survival. Their entry holes in bare ground are difficult to spot and resemble those made by ants and solitary wasps.

Close observation is the only way to determine whether areas on your property have been inhabited by ground-nesting bees.

"When they emerge from their nests as adults, they tend to start new nests near where they were reared, so preserving the area bees use one year is likely to lead to continuous use of the nesting area," says T'ai Roulston, curator of the State Arboretum of Virginia.

"My best suggestion for maintaining ground-nesting bees is to provide areas with substantial bare soil or gaps in vegetation that will not get tilled."

Sunny, south-facing slopes are preferable, though some ground nesters look for vertical banks.

Bumblebees' shelters are usually well-hidden and equipped with long entry tunnels. If habitat is in short supply, though, some bumblebees may take up residence too close for comfort (right next to the front door, for instance). Two to three days of intermittent soaking with a hose will usually persuade the bees to move.

You can invite bees to your backyard by setting a low wooden frame around a pile of dirt mixed with sand, then topping it off with a couple of rotting logs. Only allow clumping grasses to grow on the mound, and provide a diversity of bee-beckoning plants nearby.

Some of the best bees for pollinating early-blooming fruits are wood-nesting mason bees. They nest in the soft centers of semi-hollow twigs (such as those of

---

BEST PLANTS FOR ATTRACTING NATIVE BEES

Annual flowers: bachelor's button, cosmos, cuphea, larkspur, poppy, sunflower, zinnia

Perennial flowers: achillea (yarrow), agastache (hyssop), black-eyed Susan, caryopteris (blue mist shrub), coreopsis, echinacea (coneflower), foxglove, hollyhock (single-flowered), lamb's ear, monarda (bee balm), ornamental alliums, penstemon, Russian sage

Vegetables: artichoke and cardoon, beans, cucumber, peas, squash

Herbs: basil, borage, catnip, comfrey, coriander, dandelion, dill, fennel, lavender, low-growing clover, mint, oregano, rosemary

Fruits: apple, blackberry, blueberry, currant, melon, raspberry, strawberry

For an extensive list of great plants for backyard bee sanctuaries, check out "Organic Pest Control: The Best Plants to Attract Beneficial Insects and Bees" at goo.gl/rfQEi. —MOTHER

To build an insect hotel, stack wooden pallets and fill with stems and logs with holes drilled in them.

bramble fruits) or in holes made in dead trees by beetles or other small insects. Other wood-nesting bees prefer rotting stumps or logs.

If your garden is near open woods that include standing dead trees and rotting logs, you may already have a good population of mason bees and other wood-nesting species. I

If there are no dead trees around, you can use fence posts or logs as substitutes. Use a drill to make a number of deep holes in the south side of a fence post or stump. Because different species prefer different sizes of holes, drill them ranging from $3/32$ of an inch (2 millimeters) to $5/16$ of an inch (8 millimeters) wide. Drilling at a slight upward angle will keep water from entering the holes.

In Europe, many urban parks include insect hotels, which are free-standing structures stocked with habitat for wood-nesting bees and other insects.

Envision a deep box artfully filled with hollow stems, and logs with holes drilled in them. A simple way to make an insect hotel is to stack several wooden pallets together, and then slip stems and logs with holes drilled in them into the openings.

ATTRACTIVE POLLINATORS

Many types of bees emerge at just the right time to gather pollen and nectar from specific crops (from blueberries in spring or from squash in summer, for example). They may only forage for a few weeks, so having different flowers coming into bloom all summer long is important.

Recent studies have found that many native bees are more attracted to a diversity of plants than they are to large plantings of a single flower crop. Backyard gardeners can help by planted a variety of blooms.

Native bees coevolved with native plants, so growing native plant species will naturally attract local pollinators.

Many vegetables and herbs attract native bees, as do easy-to-grow annual and perennial flowers, flowering shrubs, and trees. Look closely and you'll discover that many plants in your garden are natural magnets for these winged wonders.

When you find good bee plants — lo and *bee*-hold — grow more of them! That's the best way to give native bees the help they so desperately need.

What to Do the First Year

A Bounty to Buzz About

The art of attracting nature's pollinators to your garden.

By Mary Pellerito

Growing fruits and vegetables takes more than quality soil, well-timed moisture, and sufficiently mild temperatures. The unsung heroes of the garden patch are the pollinators that help ensure proper fruit development and that precious crop of viable seed for next year. Put it all together and you have a self-perpetuating system that will supply you with good food into the future and look great to boot.

For those who share a love and passion for gardening or crop farming, sowing a diverse group of plants is the quickest way to entice pollinators and ensure successful bounties for years to come.

POLLINATORS

When we first think of pollinators, it's easy to think of bees and, in particular, honeybees, though honeybees are not native to North America. European settlers brought the honeybee to the New World around the turn of the 17th century, along with a bevy of plants that the "white man's fly" (so called by Native Americans) pollinated.

Honeybees may be the most prolific pollinators, but with around 4,000 species of bees in North America, and the honeybee being only one of them, you'd be remiss to focus solely on the honeybee in attracting pollinators to your backyard garden or orchard.

Bumblebees also do their fair share of pollinating, as do digger bees, mining bees, orchard bees, and a host of other natives, and for the most part these smaller, often solitary, creatures have a quality about them that might make a bald person thankful that they aren't evaluated on how much pollen they can carry back to the nest — they are hairy.

Although these native bees don't produce and store honey, they are invaluable to our food supply — be it pollinating a 1,000-acre monoculture or a quarter-acre backyard garden.

Native bees in New Jersey and Pennsylvania have been known to effectively pollinate watermelon farms, without the help of honeybees. Native bees also are efficient pollinators of pumpkins, tomatoes, apples and berries.

There are plenty of pollinators besides bees, although most of them aren't quite as effective. Flies — hoverflies in particular — are good pollinators you might find hanging around flowers of various plants. Wasps do some pollinating, while also helping backyard gardens by occasionally stinging an intruding herbivore.

Butterflies and moths are better at pollinating wildflowers than food crops, but they are still a welcome addition to a garden; after all, anything that leads to a more diverse group of flowers will help biodiversity and pollination across all plant species. Not to mention, beekeepers should especially welcome butterflies and moths, since the flavor of wildflowers add that special flavor to honey.

Bats and hummingbirds also can be effective pollinators for the garden.

You also may see other more traditional birds, predatory beetles — such as

> Honeybees may be the most prolific pollinators, but with around 4,000 species of bees in North America, you'd be remiss to focus solely on the honeybee.

ladybugs and lightning bugs—lacewings, and parasitic wasps in your garden. They might not focus solely on pollination, but they do feed extensively on crop pests.

To attract these pollinators and beneficial insects to a backyard garden, it is essential to provide a diverse plant habitat in which all can thrive.

WHAT POLLINATORS NEED

With bees being your best pollinator, it's important to know they require pollen and nectar in order to live.

Nectar is composed of sugars and water, and it provides adult bees with the energy they need to fly, build nests, collect pollen, and lay eggs. Pollen provides the protein necessary for the growth of young bees into adults, as well as brooding a new queen.

> It might surprise those long-removed from biology class that the rose family means a heck of a lot more than the pretty red rose young—and hopefully older—lads pick for the women they adore.

Lavender is a member of the mint family, and can actually produce a profitable harvest while also attracting large numbers of beneficial insects.

But not all flowers provide the pollen and nectar that bees need. When selecting flowers for your garden, use heirloom or native flowering plants. Hybridized plants may be sterile, and sterile plants are often useless to bees.

And avoid "pollenless" varieties of sunflowers and other flowers.

WHAT AND HOW TO PLANT

Some plant families that typically do very well at attracting bees are the rose family (Rosaceae), mint family (Lamiaceae), and the aster family (Asteraceae).

It might surprise those long-removed from biology class that the rose family means a heck of a lot more than the pretty red rose young—and hopefully older—lads pick for the women they adore. The largest genus of the rose family is *Prunus*, with includes plums, cherries, peaches, apricots, and almonds, among a multitude of others.

Strawberries and many of the fruits in the family are edible, so do some taxonomic homework and find plants that you and your family will enjoy to help attract those bees.

Butterflies are beautiful and also beneficial as pollinators.

A ruby-throated hummingbird feeds on the perennial Turk's-cap and pollinates in the process.

What to Do the First Year **69**

GOOD BORDER FLOWERS

- Aster
- Goldenrod
- English Lavender
- Coreopsis
- Cosmos
- Blue Lobelia
- Daisy
- Joe Pye Weed
- Milkweed
- Poppy
- Purple and Yellow Coneflowers
- Sage
- Sunflower
- Sedum
- Zinnia

Planting a flower bed with diverse flower color, shape, blooming time, and biological makeup attracts more pollinators.

Mint family plants that attract effective pollinators include some favorite culinary herbs: basil, rosemary, sage, savory, marjoram, oregano, thyme, lavender, and obviously mint. Hyssop is another good herb to plant.

Forgotten among a lot of backyard gardens, or farmstead gardens for that matter, is the need to plant flowers for bees and other pollinators like the butterfly and those mentioned earlier.

Flowers planted to attract bees should be all different colors, different shapes, blooming throughout the entire gardening season, planted in clumps of the same species, and planted out of the way of strong winds.

As a lot of what you plant to attract pollinators is region-specific, you can learn what pollinator-friendly plants will grow well in your part of the country from the North American Pollinator Protection Campaign (NAPPC, pollinator.org/nappc), which is also part of the Pollinator Partnership (pollinator.org).

THERE'S MORE

Further methods for attracting some of those other pollinators are installing bat houses and bee nesting blocks. Birds and all beneficial insects need a place to live, so if there's space to do so, consider creating a hedgerow or treeline—you can use it to separate your gardens—or a garden border with trees (fruit trees and conifers), flowering shrubs, perennials, more flowers, you name it.

It's better to treat garden borders as a perennial space; weeding is good, but tilling might destroy the homes of beneficial insects that live in the ground.

Include plants in this border that bloom from early spring through fall to attract pollinators all season long, and make them tall and short. Taller, flowering perennials provide food for nectar-loving birds and insects. Shorter plants provide cover for ground beetles and protected areas where lacewings can lay eggs.

If you ever thought about installing a backyard waterway, there's no better time than before the next gardening season, as a source of fresh water will also help attract pollinators. And next time there's a tree limb or dead tree in a wooded area next to your garden, consider leaving it as a potential nesting spot.

And last but certainly not least, if possible, avoid the use of pesticides since, although

A bee box attached to a fence is also suitable for other insects.

MAKING HOMES FOR WILD BEES

Solitary cavity-nesting species such as mason bees are attracted to logs and dead trees, as well as to hollow branches such as bamboo or sumac. Wild bees will also make their home in a suitable handmade dwelling, in a dead tree trunk, in a block of wood, or in a bundle of tubes. Here are three easy-to-make bee homes:

BUNDLED STICKS

Bundle together a dozen or so 10-inch-long pieces of half-inch-diameter bamboo or sumac that have been hollowed out at one end with a drill or awl. Stuff the bundle into a coffee can or a piece of PVC pipe, then wire it securely onto a tree branch or fence post.

BEE STUMP

Drill into an existing tall tree stump, making 6-inch-deep, ⅜-inch holes that are spaced 2 inches apart on the south and east sides of the stump.

NESTING BLOCK

Start with an 8-inch-long piece of untreated 4-by-6 or 6-by-6 wood post, or use a short log. Drill ⅜-inch holes, 6 to 7 inches deep and at least 1 inch apart. Blacken the front of the block by placing it in a fire for a minute or two. Attach the block to a post or tree branch.

GENERAL TIPS

A secure entrance is crucial, so holes ⅜ inch in diameter are best. The tube-shaped holes also should be at least 6 inches deep, so you will need an extension bit for your drill.

Several species can control the gender of their offspring, and they like to place female eggs deep in their burrows, with male eggs closer to the entrance. That way, males will be waiting when the females emerge. The holes should be closed at one end to ensure the safety of the eggs, too.

Early spring is the best time to put out new bee nesting blocks; that's when females are seeking new homes. Locate the nests at least 3 feet off the ground in a place where they will get warm morning sun, and attach securely so they won't shake in the wind. Make the holes slope slightly downward to prevent rainwater from running into the holes. As summer progresses, you know you have tenants if the holes or tubes become plugged with mud or debris.

— *Barbara Pleasant*

designed to kill pests, the chemicals often kill plants and animals that aren't pests. Pesticides can and do kill pollinators as well as some of the plants on which they depend.

POLLINATION INDICATORS

Plants such as beans, peas, strawberries, and tomatoes generally have flowers that are self-fertile—containing both male and female parts, and the pollen produced by the flower can fertilize the ovum of the same flower.

Some self-pollinating crops will fertilize themselves before their flowers open (beans and peas), but others (strawberries and tomatoes) rely on vibrations caused by wind or by visiting bees to facilitate pollen transfer. Some native bees, especially bumblebees, can vibrate their wing muscles (called sonication) to release pollen from flowers (tomatoes, blueberries)—something honeybees cannot do—and when bumblebees move on, they transfer more pollen per visit than honeybees, says Julianna Tuell, tree fruit integrated pest management outreach specialist in the Department of Entomology at Michigan State University.

When bees move between the same kinds of flowers, the result is cross-pollination—the movement of pollen from one plant to another—and for many plants this means larger and better quality fruits.

Plants such as squash, melons, and cucumbers have separate male and female flowers on the same plant (synchronously monoecious). Bees move pollen from male flowers to female flowers—sometimes on the same plant (self-pollination) and other times on different plants (cross-pollination).

A plant is effectively pollinated when, after several days, the female flower dies and the tiny fruitlike swelling (ovule) beneath the flower, whether it is a squash, tomato, or bean pod, begins to grow. If pollination did not occur, the ovule generally shrivels and dies.

Plant a diverse group of flowers, herbs, shrubs, trees, and other plants, install a little extra cover and structure, and you'll sustain your resident pollinator population that will in turn sustain your vegetable garden. 🐝

Providing a bat box somewhere along the perimeter of your property can encourage more pollination for your plants.

Let Your Bees Do the Gardening

Work in tandem with native bees for a bountiful, beautiful garden.

By Barbara Pleasant

If you've never equated those big, juicy homegrown tomatoes—or lack thereof—with bees, it's time to grab some wood (literally). From Alkali bees to Shaggy Fuzzyfoot bees, you'll harvest more and bigger fruits and vegetables if you have enough of these pollinating bees visiting your garden. By planting bee-loving plants and offering wild-bee habitat, your garden bounty will ripen faster and taste better. I bet you're thinking "gardening is sounding a whole lot easier right about now …."

Cornell University researchers have found that bee-assisted pollination of strawberries can increase fruit size up to 40 percent. Other crops that depend upon native bees for pollination include tomatoes, peppers, eggplants, pumpkins,

squash, and melons, as well as most berries and tree fruits. But heavy reliance on pesticides, loss of habitat, and monoculture crop systems have decimated pollinator populations.

"Monoculture makes it impossible for any bee — native or otherwise — to keep year-round populations sufficient for pollination," says David Green, who maintains the native bee website Pollinator.com. "A modern orchard has such a flush of bloom in spring that the pollination task is overwhelming. The rest of the year, it's starvation or even a toxic environment."

Besides avoiding pesticides, you can support native bee populations by protecting natural areas on your property, leaving field and road borders unmowed to provide habitat for ground-nesting bees, and planting or preserving stands of native flowering plants (that the bees use for food) in pastures and hedgerows. A diverse selection of flowering plants and food crops ensures that pollinators have a steady supply of nectar and pollen throughout the growing season.

Take a close look at the flowers in your garden and you will quickly see that honeybees, which are native to Europe, have plenty of company, including numerous native bee species with specialized talents. But while honeybees are commonly protected by a beekeeper, native bees have no human guardians. This is why it's important to help increase native bee populations in your own area.

Herbs are a great addition to any garden, both for pollinators and the gardener.

BEE SPECIES

Like honeybees, native bees feed on nectar while gathering pollen to take back to their nests as food for their young. In the process, they pollinate flowers, often doing a better job than honeybees on certain crops such as apples, berries, alfalfa, and almonds. Bumblebees are the preferred pollinators for greenhouse-grown tomatoes, and pumpkin growers from Wisconsin to Alabama are recognizing the value of squash bees — a short-lived native species that often outnumber

BEE-WORTHY PLANTS

Consider planting an herb or ornamental garden just for the bees. Install a hedge of boxwood around the edge to protect pollinators from wind, and plant in clusters — an arrangement bees prefer. Select specimens from this bee-loved list:

- **Lavender** (*Lavandula* spp.). An aromatherapy classic, this perennial flower is tough and drought-resistant once it established.
- **Basil** (*Ocimum basilicum*). Tuck a few of these tender, fragrant plants into your garden, and the bees will come. Use both green- and purple-leafed varieties.
- **Butterfly weed** (*Asclepias tuberosa*). Draw in the bees and butterflies with this trouble-free, hardy perennial native with its bright-orange flowers.
- **Thyme** (*Thymus vulgaris*). This creeping perennial ground cover is a favorite of bees. It comes in many forms and can naturalize.
- **Rosemary** (*Rosmarinus officinalis*). This fragrant perennial herb must be brought indoors for the winter in colder climates.

honeybees visiting squash blossoms, even when honeybee hives are nearby. In areas where cool temperatures limit honeybee activity during the spring blooming of fruit trees, native mason bees do the job because they are better adapted to cool weather.

Pollination in some crops is a collective effort among different species, however. Researchers at Ohio State University found that 18 species of native bees were doing most of the pollinating work in nearby strawberry fields.

These native bees don't produce honey, and they can't be reared in managed hives. But when they are given even small patches of suitable habitat, such as a fencerow or diverse garden, some of the 4,000-plus species of native bees will show up.

"In a 20-acre woodland park that includes trees and flowers and that hasn't been sprayed with pesticides, there may be 100 species of native bees present on a summer day," says Jim Cane, research entomologist at the U.S. Department of Agriculture's Pollinating Insects Research Unit (Bee Lab) in Logan, Utah.

According to the National Sustainable Agriculture Information Service, the following native bees are particularly good pollinators of certain crops, although they pollinate other flowering plants as well:

- **Alkali bees:** onions, clover, mint, and celery;
- **Bumblebees:** blueberries, tomatoes, eggplants, peppers, melons, raspberries, blackberries, strawberries, and cranberries;

A bumblebee embraces this blossom's bounty.

- **Feverfew** (*Tanacetum parthenium*). Hardy and cheerful, this perennial has white, daisy-like flowers and grows 2 to 3 feet tall, with dwarf varieties available as well.
- **Sunflower** (*Helianthus annuus*). Tall annuals for the back of the garden, the ray flowers come in a wide variety of bright, even gaudy, colors.
- **Oregano** (*Origanum* spp.). These fragrant herbs are low-growing summer bloomers, and they are almost as useful in the landscape as in the kitchen.
- **St. John's wort** (*Hypericum perforatum*). This carefree, hardy perennial has golden-yellow flowers and shiny, dark green leaves. It blooms in late spring to early summer.
- **Yarrow** (*Achillea* spp.). Perennial and dependable, native yarrow's flat flowers are available in various colors, including soft yellow, red, and white.
- **Black cohosh** (*Cimicifuga racemosa*). These tall, beautiful plants can be seen so covered with bumblebees that the late-spring and early-summer white flowers seem to disappear.
- **Russian sage** (*Perovskia atriplicifolia*). The soft blue-purple blossoms and finely cut silvery leaves of perennial Russian sage add a lovely, airy look. This hardy perennial plant is drought- and heat-tolerant, and a beautiful foil for larger, more substantial flowers nearby.
- **Anise hyssop** (*Agastache foeniculum*). This perennial flowers in midsummer, attracting bees and other pollinators.
- **Bee balm** (*Monarda* spp.). Bees seek out the tubular pink, red, or white flowers on its rounded flower heads.
- **Borage** (*Borago officinalis*). Easy to grow and reseeds readily; bees love its bright blue blooms throughout summer.
- **Catmint** (*Nepeta racemosa*). Spikes of tiny purple flowers are loved by honeybees in late spring.
- **Greek mullein** (*Verbascum olympicum*). The tall flower stems attract bees, and the plant readily reseeds.
- **Purple coneflower** (*Echinacea purpurea*). This flower provides pollen for many honeybees and bumblebees.

— *Kathleen Halloran and Jean English*

DOS AND DON'TS

When it comes to encouraging and protecting bees around your place ...

DO
- Handpick pests off plants or spray a soap-and-water solution
- Grow flowering native plants in a variety of colors, shapes and species
- Provide nesting spots

DON'T
- Spray pesticides
- Destroy any hives — nuisance or not; find a beekeeper to move it
- Grow a monoculture

— Karen K. Will

- **Carpenter bees:** passion fruit, blackberries, canola, corn, peppers, and beans;
- **Leafcutter bees:** legumes, especially alfalfa, and carrots;
- **Mason bees:** almonds, apples, cherries, pears, plums, and blueberries;
- **Shaggy fuzzyfoot bees:** blueberries and apples;
- **Squash bees:** squash, gourds, and pumpkins.

It's also important to understand that male bees can't sting (a bee stinger is a modified egg-laying organ), and females won't sting unless they are provoked.

"They have no honey to protect, so they are not built to defend themselves from mammalian predators," Cane says.

If you find that you like sharing the company of native bees, or you want to enlist their help to pollinate your plants, some species will accept human invitations in the form of nesting boxes.

THE SECRET LIFE OF BEES

Big, fuzzy, black-and-yellow bumblebees and a few types of small sweat bees are the only native bees that live in colonies. Most other species live alone and associate with others only long enough to mate.

Mason bees, carpenter bees, and leafcutter bees are called cavity nesters because they make their nests in the holes of trees, fence posts, firewood, hollow plant stems, or handmade bee-nesting blocks. More numerous ground-dwelling bees dig tubular burrows no larger than a drinking straw. Bumblebees often make their home in underground burrows vacated by rodents.

Like honeybees, bumblebees are general feeders that visit a broad range of host plants. But many wild bees have restrictive tastes and stick close to the plants they were born to serve.

Squash bees, for example, followed early strains of squash as native people moved the crop northward from Central America. Females emerge in early summer and only fly in the morning when squash blossoms are open. In the afternoon, you often can find males curled up asleep in closed squash flowers (yes, bees do sleep).

Cane recently worked with the specialist bee that pollinates only rabbiteye blueberries — and does so with amazing efficiency. The adult life of a specialist bee is quite short, but in only a few weeks, just one of them often out-pollinates 100 honeybees.

Because specialist bees need pollen from specific plants, they tend to stay close to home and forage in smaller plantings, says James Tew of Ohio State University's Honey Bee Lab in Wooster. Most native bees pose no problem for plants, though leafcutter bees do harvest rounded leaf pieces from roses, ash trees, and several other plants, which they use to build their nests.

"The small amount of leaf material taken is a bargain when the pollination activities of leafcutter bees are considered," Tew says.

Various species of leafcutter bee have

Selecting a squash blossom, these bees decide to take a rest.

been found to be much better pollinators of alfalfa, blueberries, carrots, sunflowers, and onions than honeybees. For example, in an enclosed greenhouse where carrots were being grown for seed, researchers found that 150 leafcutter bees could do the work of 3,000 honeybees. One non-native species, the alfalfa leafcutter bee, is now reared by the millions because it does such an outstanding job pollinating alfalfa grown for seed.

THE NATIVE EDGE

Particular characteristics contribute to native bees' pollination talents. Many native bees are quite hairy, and tufts of hair (such as those on the abdomens of female leafcutter bees) serve as soft brushes that gently transfer pollen from a flower's stamens to its stigma (the female part that connects to the ovary).

The buzz factor also is important because some flowers, such as blueberries and most members of the tomato family, need to be vibrated to shake the pollen loose from the stamens. Scientists call this process "sonication," but Arizona entomologist Stephen Buchmann (co-author of *The Forgotten Pollinators*)

A bumblebee explores a flower on its hunt for nectar.

After collecting pollen from a spring daisy, a bumblebee takes flight en route to its nest.

A carpenter bee engaged in a little floral foraging.

came up with another phrase: "buzz pollination." Bumblebees, digger bees, and several other native bees are great buzz pollinators.

The diversity of native bees matches the diversity of native plants. With the help of his camera, David Gordon, a professor of zoology at Pittsburg State University in Kansas, has seen that some native bees have long tongues, so they can lap nectar from tubular flowers, while others have shorter tongues more suited to flat blossoms. Native bees also vary in size from ½-inch iridescent sweat bees to 1½-inch carpenter bees.

Tiny bees can access the smallest flowers for pollination purposes while bigger bees buzz blossoms, tramping pollen from place to place with their feet, and sometimes accidentally improving pollination by chasing honeybees across the faces of sunflowers and other big-blossomed plants.

A GARDEN TO CALL HOME

Native bees seldom travel more than a quarter mile from their nests, so improving bee habitat can have a very direct benefit in your garden. The Xerces Society, a

A native bee in Arizona takes a siesta in a wildflower blossom.

nonprofit insect preservation group based in Portland, Oregon, suggests simple ways to make your property more hospitable to native bees:

- Minimize the use of pesticides and avoid spraying botanical or biological insecticides in the morning, when native bees are most active;
- Grow a diverse selection of flowering plants — including as many native species as possible (see "Bee-worthy Plants" on Page 74);
- Grow crops such as squash, sunflowers, blueberries, and strawberries every year to maintain resident populations of the specialist bees that serve them;
- Leave some areas of your yard or garden uncultivated so you don't disturb bees that nest in the ground.

The same plants that attract butterflies and beneficial insects often attract native bees; both insect groups are most numerous where plants bloom over a long season.

For example, early spring-blooming willows and redbuds can be followed by fruit trees, brambles, and red clover before your summer vegetables and flowers take over as primary host plants. Then keep the pollen flowing into fall by growing late-blooming asters and allowing goldenrod to flourish along fencerows.

With a solid food supply nailed down, you can further encourage native bees by providing attractive nesting sites.

For ground-nesting bees, a patch of uncultivated, well-drained soil that gets morning sun will work well, as long as you avoid disturbing it with vehicles and tractors. You also can make a sandpile or sandpit — or simply fill a planter with sand and place it on a warm, south-facing slope.

If you see bumblebees buzzing around the roots of a tree, leave them alone. They probably have established a colony in a burrow vacated by mice or voles.

Improved crop pollination aside, good food and habitat for native bees have a ripple effect in the natural world.

Native bees pollinate forest trees and wildflowers, which in turn provide food for wildlife.

Cane says that because wild bees are vegetarians, they'll never ruin your barbecue by buzzing around your burgers.

"Sit down and enjoy the bees," he says. "They are great fun to watch."

A bumblebee coming in for a perfect six-point landing.

What to Do the First Year 79

Wise Pairings

Plant a profusion of fragrant flowers among your edible plants to help control pests, boost pollination, and provide eye-pleasing pops of color.

By Rosalind Creasy

In the 1970s, when I was a budding landscape designer, I attended the garden opening of one of my clients. As I walked around anonymously, wine glass in hand, I overheard many guests exclaiming, "Do you see that? She put flowers in the vegetable garden!"

In the United States, segregating vegetables from flowers still seems like such a hard-and-fast rule that when I lecture on edible landscaping, one of the first things I mention is that I've checked the Constitution, and planting flowers in a vegetable garden is not forbidden. Not only *can* you put flowers in with vegetables, you *should*.

I admit that, in the '70s, I first intermixed my flowers and vegetables because I was gardening in the front yard of my suburban home and hoped the neighbors wouldn't notice or complain as long as the veggies were surrounded by flowers. Soon, however, I discovered I had fewer pest problems, I saw more and more birds, and my crops were thriving.

It turns out that flowers are an essential ingredient in establishing a healthy garden because they attract beneficial insects and birds, which control pests and pollinate crops. Most gardeners understand this on some level. They may even know that pollen and nectar are food for insects, and that seed heads provide food for birds.

What some may not realize is just how many of our wild meadows and native plants have disappeared under acres of lawn, inedible shrubs, and industrial agriculture's fields of monocultures, leaving fewer food sources for beneficial critters. With bees and other pollinators under a chemical siege these days and their populations in drastic decline, offering chemical-free food sources and safe havens is crucial. Plus, giving beneficial insects supplemental food sources of pollen and nectar throughout the season means they'll stick around for when pests show up.

THINK INTEGRATION, NOT SEGREGATION

One of the cornerstones of edible landscaping is that gardens should be beautiful as well as bountiful. Mixing flowers and vegetables so that both are an integral part of the garden's design is another key. Let's say you have a shady backyard, so you decide to put a vegetable garden in the sunny front yard. Many folks would install a rectangular bed or wooden boxes, and plant long rows of vegetables, maybe placing a few marigolds in the corners, or planting a separate flower border. In either case,

> Not only *can* you plant plenty of flowers amid the vegetables in your home garden, you *should*.

Short on space? Pack pretty pots with flower and vegetable companions on your patio (far left). Play with colors and textures as the author does in her central California garden (below).

the gardener will have added plants offering a bit of much-needed pollen and nectar.

Integrating an abundance of flowers *among* the vegetables, however, would impart visual grace while also helping beneficial insects accomplish more. Plentiful food sources will allow the insects to healthily reproduce. Plus, most of their larvae have limited mobility. For example, if a female lady beetle or green lacewing lays her eggs next to the aphids on your violas, the slow-moving, carnivorous larvae won't be able to easily crawl all the way across the yard to also help manage the aphids chowing down on your broccoli.

In addition to bringing in more "good guys" to munch pests, flowers will give you more control because they can act as a useful barrier—a *physical* barrier as opposed to the chemical barriers created in non-organic systems. The hornworms on your tomato plant, for instance, won't readily migrate to a neighboring tomato plant if there's a tall, "stinky" marigold blocking the way.

CREATE COOL COMBOS

To begin establishing your edible landscape, you should plant flowers with a variety of colors and textures, different sizes and shapes, and an overall appealing aesthetic. After you've shed the notion that flowers and vegetables must be separated, a surprising number of crop-and-flower combinations will naturally emerge, especially if you keep in mind the following six guidelines.

1 Stagger sizes. Pay attention to the eventual height and width of each flower and food plant (check seed packets and

Tuck petite flowers between plants. Here, bright violas peek up through the big, silver-purple leaves of these cabbages.

10 POLLEN-RICH FLOWERS FOR YOUR FOOD GARDEN

I usually choose heirloom annuals because they're versatile and add substance and height to my plantings. Many popular modern flower varieties are short, so they only work well in front of a border. Plus, some modern varieties—sunflowers, for example—have actually been bred for decreased pollen production so they won't shed on your tablecloth. (What a terrible breeding project, from the bees' perspective!) While heirloom flowers tend to work wonderfully in edible landscapes, they're not always conveniently available at the nearest big-box store. Thankfully, several mail-order sources offer heirloom varieties (see "Flower Seed Sources" on Page 85), and these plants are usually easy to grow from seed.

So where should you start? After 40-plus years of creating and evaluating edible landscaping combos, I recommend these common flowering plants that provide pollen and nectar for beneficials, plus a few suggested edible companions for each.

Alyssum. These plants spread along the ground and produce hundreds of tiny flowers that bloom all season. Combine the purple and pink varieties with eggplants and purple varieties of basil, bush beans, lettuce, and sprouting broccoli. The white varieties will give a frilly setting for stiff, dark kales, chards, bok choys, and red-leafed beets, and fill in nicely between chives, leeks, onions, and shallots.

Calendulas. Orange, yellow, and apricot calendula flowers brighten cool-season vegetable beds filled with beets, broccoli, bush peas, cabbage, carrots, collards, lettuce, kale, and parsnips. The tall heirloom varieties grow to 18 inches and are less prone to mildew than the 6-inch dwarf varieties. Bonus: You can save calendula petals for use in teas and natural body care products.

Coreopsis. This endearing plant is a perennial native to the North American prairie that furnishes a season full of sunny yellow flowers held well above its foliage. I give these flowering plants a permanent home near the edge of trellises built for beans, cucumbers, and tomatoes. Again, I gravitate toward the tall, native variety sold as *Coreopsis grandiflora*, which I typically stake. The shorter varieties work well in small areas near basil, endive, eggplants, kale, peppers, and other short edibles.

Cosmos. There are two common types of cosmos: *Cosmos bipinnatus*, the familiar pink and white varieties, such as the old-time 'Sensation' mix, and *C. sulphureus*, which comes in orange, red, and yellow. Both attract beneficials and, if you let the flowers go to seed, flocks of yellow finches. I combine the 4-foot-tall 'Sensation' cosmos with artichokes and cardoons, and plant the 2- to 3-foot-tall *sulphureus* varieties, such as 'Diablo,' in front of tomatoes and okra, and next to trellises of cucumbers and beans.

nursery tags), and place them accordingly. Tall plants, for the most part, belong in back. They'll still be visible, but they won't block the smaller plants from view or from sunshine. A good rule is to put the taller plants on the north and east sides of your garden, and the shorter ones on the south and west sides.

2 Consider proportions. A 6-foot-tall sunflower planted next to an 18-inch-tall cabbage would look lopsided. Instead, place plants of graduated heights from tallest to shortest so your eye will travel naturally from one location to the next.

3 Experiment with complementary colors. Use the hues of your edibles—red tomatoes and peppers, yellow squash flowers, purple cabbage and basil—as a starting point. Look for flowers that will highlight those shades, such as bright yellows or soft purples, or choose a hue on the opposite side of the color wheel to provide an unexpected pop. For foliage, experiment with different shades of green to give your landscape more depth.

4 Play with textures and shapes. Pair a sprawling squash with more upright basils. Partner thick-leaved plants with those that don delicate leaves. Surround a straight-edged tipi of runner beans with a bed of rounded dwarf marigolds.

5 Plant for all seasons. Grow plants with a range of different blooming times so something will always be in flower from early spring to late fall. Not only will this mean a feast of colors to enjoy all year, but, more importantly, it will yield a steady source of pollen and nectar for beneficial insects.

6 View your garden holistically. An ideal landscape draws

Mix contrasting colors, such as bright green summer squash, orange marigolds, and purple basil.

Echinacea. A native plant prized for its healing properties and a favorite with bees, this perennial forms clumps of upright leaves and pink-purple, daisy-like blooms off and on all summer. The plant can grow to 4 feet tall and comes in numerous varieties. I plant echinacea at the end of mixed vegetable-and-herb beds, and combine the plants with tall herbs, such as dill, fennel, lovage, and sage.

Marigolds. These annual flowers come in shades of yellow, orange, and reddish-brown, and bloom from spring through fall. The tall, older varieties grow to 4 feet, and I use these in front of a trellis full of tomatoes, beans, cucumbers, and other climbers. The dwarf marigold varieties range from 6 to 18 inches, and these are ideal for creating a compact flowering hedge to border a bed of bush beans or peppers, for interspersing among kale and other greens, and for surrounding a squash plant or two. My favorite dwarf marigolds are the 'Gem' series, which have fine, citrus-smelling foliage and small edible flowers.

Sage. The stately sages, such as 'Victoria' and other non-edible natives, bear spikes of either red or blue flowers that are especially enticing to bees and hummingbirds. Varieties range from 18 inches to 3 feet tall. While some are perennial, some native sages common to home gardens are often treated as annuals. Interplant them with okra, tall pepper varieties, and shorter tomato varieties.

Sunflowers. These cheerful, towering plants attract many beneficials and several varieties offer edible seeds for you, too. Some varieties reach 8 feet and pair well with a patch of corn or behind a planting of large winter squash. The dwarf varieties can be used behind large zucchini plants or a bed of bush beans or soybeans. When choosing varieties, skip any that have been bred to produce little or no pollen.

Violas. You can really paint your garden with this family of edible, cool-season annual flowers. Violas come in a pleasing palette of purples, blues, and yellows, and their whiskered, up-facing, flat blooms make perfect fillers among members of the cabbage family (see photo above). They can also accent a geometric bed of lettuces and shine in colorful containers.

Zinnias. Butterflies adore the blooms of this family of annual flowers, which come in an array of sizes and colors, making them suitable for almost any vegetable combination. Try the dwarf 'Mexican' varieties in a bed of chiles, and pair the tall, pastel varieties with artichokes, Brussels sprouts, or fennel. Edge a planting of edamame with a mix of dwarf zinnias, and combine these petite varieties in a large container with a mix of basil plants.

The height of perfection: Shorter feverfew plants play a foreground role to taller zinnias and peppers.

you in with its diversity, and also with repeating elements, whether those elements are plants, shapes, types of containers or beds, colors, or textures. Browse gardening magazines, books, and websites for landscapes you like, and substitute some of your favorite edibles for some of the ornamentals. An article on foliage plants might show a container of ornamental coleus, and that same composition may work just as well if you swap in some crimson chard or curly, chartreuse kale. A feature on flowering vines might inspire you to add scarlet runner beans to the mix.

PICK THE BEST BLOOMS

Choosing the right flowers for your space is at once simple and complex. It's simple because there's a lot of research out there about flowers that attract birds, bees, butterflies, and beneficial insects. It's complex because dozens of flowers appear on those lists, and pinpointing the ones that will work best in your climate and with your vegetables and your overall garden design may take some time.

Keep in mind that different insects are attracted to different flower characteristics, such as color, scent, and blossom shape. The more diverse range of flowers you offer them, the more diverse the insect population in your garden will be. Try some plants in the daisy (*Asteraceae*) family, such as black-eyed Susans, coneflowers, cosmos,

PLAN YOUR PLOT!

Map out your garden with effective edible-landscaping combos using our Grow Planner app, which we've released in an updated version with a sleek, new design. This app, now available for iPhone and iPad, puts growing guides, crop spacing requirements, planting dates for your exact location, and more planning tools right at your fingertips. Go to www.motherearthnews.com/grow-planner.

The display gardens at Seed Savers Exchange in Decorah, Iowa, give prominence to plenty of flowers.

Clockwise from left: Runner beans, basil, and yellow zukes are centerpieces to colorful borders of marigolds, zinnias, portulaca, and geraniums.

marigolds, sunflowers, and zinnias. Also consider the parsley (Apiaceae) family, especially carrots, cilantro, dill, and parsley; the mustard (Brassicaceae) family, including nasturtiums and sweet alyssum; and the mint (Lamiaceae) family, with basil, sage, Victoria salvia, and, of course, mint. For a much more comprehensive list of insect-coaxing flowers, see "The Best Plants to Attract Beneficial Insects and Bees" online at goo.gl/YK3YcT.

Plants native to your area will naturally attract the insects and birds vital to your ecosystem, so seek out native plants. Try heirloom flowers, too, as they're often packed with nectar and pollen, and some are wonderfully fragrant. If choosing modern hybrids, look for varieties with those same characteristics. For more flower choices, see "10 Pollen-Rich Flowers for Your Food Garden" on Page 82.

After you've enticed plenty of beneficial insects and birds to your garden, you'll want to keep them there. To do so, first place shallow water sources, such as small birdbaths, around your garden. Second, allow flowers to grow and spread to provide shelter. Third, don't be too quick to clean things up. Let a few of your herbs, such as basil and parsley, and vegetables, such as broccoli and lettuce, mature to their flowering stage to attract insects. Finally, trust nature to keep things in balance rather than jumping in with controls and chemicals. Be patient, allowing the interactions among flowers, insects, and crops time to play out.

I'd like to say that I had an "Aha!" moment when I realized how effectively and elegantly all of this worked. Actually, though, it took a while before I finally understood that, when it comes to flora, what we compartmentalize as "edible" and "ornamental" are in fact an interconnected system, and if you take out the flowers, you've removed a critical part. Growing flowers and vegetables together isn't just a pleasing way to garden—it's an essential way to garden.

FLOWER SEED SOURCES

Mother's Seed and Plant Finder: Locate sources for specific flower varieties at www.motherearthnews.com/find-seeds-plants.

Baker Creek Heirloom Seeds: www.rareseeds.com; 417-924-8917

Burpee: www.burpee.com; 800-888-1447

Renee's Garden Seeds: www.reneesgarden.com; 888-880-7228

Seed Savers Exchange: www.seedsavers.org; 563-382-5990

Select Seeds: www.selectseeds.com; 800-684-0395

Go Native With Wild Bees

The humble little orchard mason bee is the best-kept (pollinator) secret.

By Lisa Tiffin

Not seeing that old familiar friend the honeybee buzzing around much? Well, it's not your imagination. Because of colony collapse disorder, mites, and lost habitats, the honeybee population has dwindled over the last several years. And gardeners and growers have suffered right along with the friendly bees.

That's the bad news. The good news is that there's an undersung permanent resident ready to take up the charge. The orchard mason bee is a native North American bee that has been around longer than the imported European honeybee and—although it doesn't produce honey—has been pollinating fruit trees and flowers steadily for years; thousands of years, in fact.

AMERICA'S OWN POLLINATOR

Never heard of the mason bee? No surprise there. This little black bee works humbly in obscurity, quietly pollinating and laying eggs in old beetle holes, broken reeds or other gaps made by man or nature. Lisa Novich, owner of Knox Cellars Native Pollinating Bees in Washington state, explains that mason bees are simple, non-aggressive bees that spend their days pollinating and laying eggs.

Because they have nothing to protect (unlike honeybees who store all their food and eggs in one place), mason bees only sting if truly provoked. Novich, whose father, Brian Griffin, literally wrote the book on mason bees, says, "They're nonaggressive, so you can have a colony in your backyard. They're not zoned out of neighborhoods like honeybees sometimes are. And they're easy to raise in your home garden."

EARLY BIRD GETS THE WORM

The biggest advantage in raising orchard mason bees is that they are early spring pollinators. This means they start flying and pollinating as early as February or March in many parts of the country. In fact, as soon as daytime temperatures reach 50 degrees with some consistency, mason bees will begin to fly.

Orchard bees will fly in colder, wetter weather because their dark color helps them absorb the heat of the sun. And because they tend to lay their eggs on warm, sunny walls, Novich says,

Gordon Cyr has made a business out of making mason bee homes; www.masonbeecentral.com.

HOW TO MAKE BEE BOXES: DO-IT-YOURSELF HOMES FOR ORCHARD MASON BEES

A bee box is a place where bees can find cover and create the next generation. You can make them quite easily, or if you'd rather, you can buy them.

The orchard mason bee, unlike other types of bees, does not live in a nest or hive; instead, it lives in holes in blocks. Other insects drill holes for themselves, sometimes destroying the wood in the process, but not so with orchard mason bees. They find holes that already exist and use them.

BUILDING A BEE HOUSE:

- Find some scrap lumber (be sure your wood is untreated) and your drill. Using drill bits of various sizes (mason bees seem to like 5/16 inch best), drill holes 3 to 5 inches deep. Do not drill all the way through the wood. (For example, if you're using a 5-by-5, drill holes that are 4½ inches deep.) If there are birds to keep away, cover the holes with chicken wire.
- Now take your box and attach it to a building, fence post or tree—on the south side.
- Also take some bee boxes to other places in your community. Another location may have many bees, which you can capture and move to your place.
- Once your bee house is in place, it is best to not move it until late fall (November).
- Be careful not to spray any insecticides around your bee boxes.

—*Grit staff*

The white tuft on the head of the orchard mason bee indicates it is male.

they can warm up in the sun, fly out and pollinate your fruit trees, and still have energy to fly back to that warm, sunny wall.

ATTRACTING MASON BEES

Novich notes that the mason bee will not bore its own holes, so, she says, it is very important to provide nesting material in order to attract the bees to your yard.

This can take the form of wooden bee blocks with a series of holes drilled to accommodate bee eggs, replaceable cardboard tubes or other suitable holes (see "How to Make Bee Boxes" on Page 87).

Whatever type of nesting holes you choose, the most important thing to remember is to mount materials on the sunny side of a building. For most parts of the country, this means the south-facing side of a house or barn.

Buildings are key because they tend to absorb heat (from inside and out), and they are stable. Fences and decks are bad choices because they shimmy and shake with wind and human interaction, often shaking loose the newly laid bee eggs.

Once you've put out suitable nesting material, you should start to see your little black friends buzzing in and out, pollinating, and laying eggs.

If you do not have a native population in your area, it is easy to purchase tubes of dormant bees, shipped in the winter and held in your refrigerator until spring arrives.

NEW USE FOR MAIL TOTES

One of the principal ways to promote a healthy population of native bees around your place is to offer them places to nest. Nesting spots can be as simple as a bundle of paper drinking straws placed in a strategic location. But it is important to protect those straws from the elements. The corrugated plastic totes used in mail handling are perfect for just that.

Agricultural Research Service scientist James H. Cane says female wild bees will readily use a properly placed, nicely furnished tote as a shelter for their nests. Turned on their long side, the totes can be held firmly in place on a wooden or metal post by means of a lightweight steel chain and a metal support frame.

Folks who want wild bees to live near and work in their fields, gardens and orchards can use the totes to house nesting materials. Wild female bees like the blue orchard bee, *Osmia lignaria*, can use the straws as homes for a new generation of pollinators. A single tote can accommodate as many as 3,000 young, which would be sufficient to pollinate a small orchard.

— Oscar H. "Hank" Will III

COLONY CARE

Caring for your bee colony is easy. Simply provide nesting places, and you will increase your colony.

"In a good spring, you can get a five- or six-fold increase in your bee population," Novich says, but she also warns gardeners not to cultivate too many bees.

A population of about 800 bees will easily be able to pollinate an acre of commercial fruit or an acre of suburban gardens. Any more than that, and you risk weakening the population with lack of food.

Another thing to remember is to put out fresh nesting material each spring. Because the rich pollen and nectar mix seeps into the grain of the wood, old nesting blocks can harbor mites and bacteria that can kill your bee population.

Novich suggests putting a fresh block or empty clean cardboard tubes right next to your current block each spring.

About five weeks or so after your first bee has emerged, you can toss away the old nesting material. This gives the dormant bees time to emerge and begin pollinating, and forces them to use the new nesting holes when it's time to reproduce.

GET BUZZING

With a few easy steps, you will soon be enjoying your very own mason bee colony. And you'll rest easy knowing you have native pollinators on the job increasing your fruit production and beautifying your garden for years to come.

RESOURCES
FOR MORE INFORMATION:

The Orchard Mason Bee, Third Edition, by Brian Griffin, 1999. (Available through Knox Cellars)

TO PURCHASE BEES AND NESTING MATERIAL:

Knox Cellars (bees, blocks, systems)
360-908-0817
www.knoxcellarsmasonbees.com

Mason Bee Homes
www.masonbeecentral.com
info@masonbeecentral.com

This orchard mason bee works its magic in Mayes County, Oklahoma.

Balm for Bees

Herbs have the power to help pollinators. Discover these plant medicines for our busy buddies.

By Jean English

In the two-acre herb Apothecary garden of Avena Botanicals in West Rockport, Maine, at least three kinds of bees can be seen (and heard) collecting pollen from a huge weeping willow tree in late spring. A patch of blue lungwort beneath a flowering magnolia is a favorite stop for honeybees, while a bleeding heart growing against the house is frequented by hummingbirds.

"Might pollinators benefit from the medicinal compounds in herbs, just as we do?"
— Deb Soule, owner of Avena Botanicals

In the beautiful landscape of Avena Botanicals, more than 120 species of medicinal herbs, trees and shrubs grow lush with compost and organic preparations. But the garden does much more than supply raw ingredients for owner Deb Soule's business.

Avena also is an outdoor classroom, a source of seeds, a quiet spot for meditation, and, last but not least, a haven for pollinators.

Visitors often comment the garden hums almost continuously with the sounds of pollinators. Everywhere, honeybees, bumblebees, hummingbirds, and others are abundant and busy—at a time when conventional farmers lament a lack of pollinators in their own gardens and fields.

BEES LOVE TINY FLOWERS

Just as bees and other pollinators find sustenance at Avena, Soule appreciates the pollinators. Her journey to discover "who pollinates what and how" began about 15 years ago, when her echinacea failed to produce viable seed. Reading *The Forgotten Pollinators* by Stephen L. Buchmann and Gary Paul Nabhan, she learned that pollinators are integral to ecosystems, and they're affected by the toxins prevalent in our modern world. After years of study, firsthand observation, and beekeeping, Soule knows very well which medicinal herbs attract pollinators. But she has new questions: Do pollinators get more than nectar, pollen, protein, and carbohydrates from her plants? Might they also benefit from the medicinal compounds in herbs, just as we do?

"Basil, lemon balm, and rosemary flowers are tiny," Soule says, "but the pollinators go for them. Why? In September, our sacred basil is literally covered with bees—their pollen sacs are a beautiful pink-orange, the color of the pollen of sacred basil."

Ross Conrad of Dancing Bee Gardens in Middlebury, Vermont, author of *Natural Beekeeping*, says, "I'm not aware of any studies that have proven honeybees benefit from the compounds in herbs, but some beekeepers have reported that bees foraging on wintergreen and other mints seem better able to withstand the stress caused by tracheal and Varroa mites (suspected as one of the culprits in the decline of bees)." Essential oils from some of these herbs are used to combat the mites, so picking up small amounts of these oils in nectar could help bees deal with the mites, he says.

Tony Jadczak, Maine state apiarist, also doesn't know of any definitive research that shows bees benefit from the compounds in herbs. Jadczak notes high concentrations of menthol and thymol are needed to effectively control mites. For example, beekeepers use a 99-percent menthol preparation in hives—far more than the small percentage of menthol bees would pick up from mint plants. He suggests bees get some other reward from foraging on the small flowers of some herbs: maybe pollen, nectar with quality sugar, trace elements, or some other substance.

BENEFITING POLLINATORS AND GARDENERS

Everyone agrees herbs do provide pollen, nectar, shelter—and perhaps more—for bees and other pollinators. To support these key links in

HOW THE POLLINATORS' PARADISE WAS MADE

Deb Soule founded the herb apothecary business Avena Botanicals in 1985 in a small room in her West Rockport, Maine, home, where she prepared remedies from her garden herbs. In 1995, Avena moved down the street to its current 32-acre farm, where Soule designed and planted her large, organic and biodynamic herb gardens. The plants in the herb gardens supply nearly 70 percent of the herbs that Avena uses in its products, and also support hummingbirds, bees, butterflies, and other visitors—including humans. The artfully designed gardens—some in full sun, others wooded—include stone paths; meditation benches; statuary; and handcrafted arbors, bridges and gates. The gardens are open to the public year-round, free, Monday through Friday. Avena's herbal products are sold at the apothecary adjacent to the gardens, through the Avena catalog and online. For more information, visit avenabotanicals.com.

Healing haven: Herb business Avena Botanicals is home to more than 120 healing species, including mullein, meadowsweet, calendula and coneflower. Pollinators and people make a beeline for the beneficial blooms.

What to Do the First Year **93**

> "The more people think about planting for pollinators—whether in a large garden or simply a hanging pot of nasturtiums and fuchsia—the better. Every little bit really helps."

the ecosystem over a long season, Soule suggests growing the following herbs, in particular.

8 HEALING HERBS FOR PEOPLE AND POLLINATORS

Some, but not all, of these herbs can be used by home growers to make healing teas or other preparations. If a medicinal use is not suggested, look for this herb in its commercially prepared form.

Anise hyssop (*Agastache foeniculum*): This perennial flowers in midsummer, attracting bees and other pollinators. It makes a good tea for the digestive system.

Bee balm (*Monarda* spp.): Soule grows 'Raspberry Wine' bee balm for pollinators in early to midsummer, and dries the species *M. fistulosa* and *M. didyma* for tummy-soothing winter teas. (See illustration on Page 92.)

Black cohosh (*Acetaea racemosa*): The tall, beautiful plants were so covered with bumblebees one August day that Soule could hardly see the white flowers. Commercial preparations are used to treat menopausal symptoms.

Borage (*Borago officinalis*): Easy-to-grow borage reseeds readily, and bees love its

bright blue blooms throughout summer. Use commercially prepared borage seed oil to treat troublesome skin conditions.

Catmint (*Nepeta racemosa*): Spikes of tiny purple flowers are loved by hummingbirds and honeybees in late spring. Its leaves make a tea that nourishes the nervous system.

European meadowsweet (*Filipendula ulmaria*): Its creamy-white flowers are "absolutely covered with a total frenzy of bees" in late July, Soule says. The leaves and flowers make a comforting tea; commercial preparations are used to treat colds, flu, and kidney and bladder problems.

Greek mullein (*Verbascum olympicum*). The tall flower stems attract bees, and the plant reseeds readily. Deb puts the flowers in olive oil to make earache drops. Mullein leaf tea is soothing to dry coughs and sore throats. To dry the leaves, first remove the large midrib. "Harvest and dry the younger leaves of the first-year plant, and let the second-year plant go to flower," she says.

Purple coneflower (*Echinacea purpurea*): The flower provides pollen for many butterflies, honeybees, and bumblebees. Use commercial preparations to stimulate the immune system.

Other medicinal herbs that benefit honeybees include arnica, angelica, basil, calendula (especially ones with simple, bright orange blooms), catnip, dandelion, feverfew, lavender, lemon balm, marshmallow, motherwort, nasturtium, sage, and Solomon's seal.

Soule notes that pollinators seem to prefer hedges or clumps of plants—one reason for the three-dimensional, room-like design of her garden. Several varieties of creeping thyme form the "floor"—a large, central circle—with taller plants around it. Hedges, arbors, trellises, and other "walls" frame her garden and protect it from wind.

HEDGE YOUR HUMMINGBIRD BETS

Not all pollinators are bees. Herb business Avena Botanicals owner Deb Soule's favorite pollinator is the ruby-throated hummingbird. The key to attracting these beautiful migrating birds is to have a mix of their favorite plants in bloom all season, she says. (Although all of these plants are beautiful and beneficial to the hummingbirds, not all of them are used to make medicinal preparations.)

Hummingbirds usually arrive at Avena May 1 to 15, when they feed on apple blossoms and true Solomon's seal, which grows in a bed in part shade.

Another early-season hummingbird favorite is lungwort, which is "a great ground cover below shrubs or trees," Soule says. "The hummingbirds love that little bit of shade."

Hummingbirds also frequent dandelions and coral bells in spring.

In summer, scarlet runner beans provide four to five weeks of blooms that attract hummingbirds, and a hedge of jasmine-scented nicotiana "is fragrant in the evening and morning, and they love that," she says. Hummingbirds visit magenta liatris in August, and in mid- to late summer, bright red cardinal flower (*Lobelia cardinalis*). Other late-season attractions include fall phlox, asters, Mexican sunflowers and hummingbird sage (*Salvia coccinea*).

"For those with small decks or gardens, potted nasturtiums, hanging pots of fuchsia, and vining honeysuckle are fantastic choices for hummingbirds and people," Soule says.

The bright, nectar-filled blooms of tithonia, an annual, draw monarchs in late summer. Butterfly-pollinated flowers tend to be large and showy.

"Hummingbirds, like honeybees, are very species-specific, so if your garden includes plant groupings, they won't have to fly so far," Soule says. (For specific plant choices, see "Hedge Your Hummingbird Bets" on Page 95.) To benefit all pollinators, plant in groups, plant a variety of species, and avoid pesticides, she advises. "The more people think about planting for pollinators — whether in a large garden or simply a hanging pot of nasturtiums and fuchsia — the better. Every little bit really helps a lot."

RESOURCES
BOOKS
Status of Pollinators in North America, bit.ly/2JFmnWi

WEBSITES
The Xerces Society for Invertebrate Conservation, xerces.org
North American Pollinator Protection Campaign, pollinator.org/nappc
Avena Botanicals Blog, www.avenabotanicals.com/blogs/news

SEED COMPANIES
Johnny's Selected Seeds, www.johnnyseeds.com
Fedco Seeds, fedcoseeds.com

Trees for Bees

Landscape with flowering trees and shrubs.

By Laura Dell-Haro

It's old news that beekeepers are struggling to provide diverse, pesticide-free forage for their colonies, as scientists have been voicing alarm about the decline in pollinator populations for more than a decade. But part of the solution to help today's stressed, malnourished bees may be in your own backyard: Consider the incredible quantity of nectar produced by a tree in bloom. Now consider the compounded effect of many trees blooming in strategic sequence throughout the growing season.

David Hughes of Rock Bridge Trees mail-order nursery (www.rockbridgetrees.com) markets a collection of trees that are perfectly suited to pollinators and, most importantly, that bloom successively during most of the growing season. "If you're going to have trees in your landscape, let them be both beautiful and useful," Hughes says. Heavily blooming shade trees top his list of bee-friendly tree species.

Increased diversity and security of nectar and pollen sources benefit honeybees in manifold ways, such as reduced stress, increased life span, heightened immune system response, more precise communication, and, yes, increased honey production.

For diverse bee forage from early spring through late summer, consider the following trees for your property: black locust (*Robinia pseudoacacia*), catalpa (*Catalpa* spp.), linden (*Tilia* spp.), manzanita (*Arctostaphylos* spp.), maple (*Acer* spp.), honey mesquite (*Prosopis glandulosa*), sourwood (*Oxydendrum* spp.), sumac (*Rhus* spp.), tulip poplar (*Liriondendron tulipifera*), and willow (*Salix* spp.).

While all of these trees can provide excellent food for honey bees and many other pollinators, your top choice should always be regionally appropriate. A tree that's comfortable in its environment is much more likely to be a healthy tree. For comprehensive, area-specific advice on bee-friendly trees and bloom times, check out the nonprofit Pollinator Partnership's Planting Guides at www.pollinator.org/guides.

Entomologist and author Doug Tallamy notes in his book *Bringing Nature Home* that "a plant that has fed nothing has not done its job." Raise the bar for what's invited into your landscape, and the benefits will easily outweigh the time and cost of planting some buzz-worthy trees.

13 Drought-Tolerant Plants for the Bees

Try these low-maintenance perennials to attract bees and other pollinators to your garden.

By Stacy Tornio

Bee populations have been on the decline all around the world for the past few decades, and that's a problem. Scientists estimate that nearly one-third of all food grown on Earth is dependent on bees. Without these important pollinators, the future of our food supply could be in trouble. Many factors contribute to bee declines, but nearly all scientists agree that loss of habitat and lack of nutrition are major factors. Fortunately, that means there is something simple every one of us can do to help: Include bee-friendly plants in our gardens. Not only will these plants feed bees, they'll help support birds, butterflies, and beneficial insects, too. Plus, these hardy, drought-tolerant perennials are nearly guaranteed to grow well with very little care, and they'll come back year after year. To protect the health of the pollinators you're aiming to attract, always use plants grown without pesticides.

1 ASTER (*Aster* spp., Zones 3 to 8)
If you like daisies, then you'll love asters. They start blooming in late summer and continue through fall. They offer a great pop of color and a late source of nectar just when other flowers are starting to fade. Plant in a sunny spot.

2 BEE BALM (*Monarda didyma*, Zones 4 to 9)
If you like uniquely shaped flowers, this is the one for you, with its bright color and spiky shape. Also known to attract hummingbirds, you can't go wrong with a plant that already has bee in the name. Bee balm can handle some shade.

3 BLANKET FLOWER (*Gaillardia* spp., Zones 3 to 9)
They don't grow very tall (usually only reaching a foot or two), but blanket flowers pack bold punches of color in varying shades of red, orange, and yellow. Because of their short height, they are perfect for the front of flowerbeds or in containers. Plant in full sun.

4 BUTTERFLY WEED (*Asclepias tuberosa*, Zones 4 to 9)
This is a tough and hardy wildflower that deserves a spot in every sunny garden in North America. It requires almost no maintenance, is very drought-tolerant, and serves as a host plant to monarch butterflies.

5 CATMINT (*Nepeta* spp., Zones 3 to 9)
Catmint is one of the easiest perennials you'll ever grow, and since it has a long blooming time, bees can enjoy it for months. Depending on the variety, catmint can grow several feet tall and wide. If you need to fill an empty space, catmint is an excellent candidate. Grow in full sun.

6 CONEFLOWER (*Echinacea* spp., Zones 3 to 9)
Coneflowers benefit many types of pollinators, attracting butterflies and bees

early on, and then becoming a great seed source for birds once the flower heads dry. You can find dozens of coneflower options on the market today. You'll always have good luck with purple coneflowers, but also be sure to check out native varieties specific to your area—ask for advice at your local garden center. All coneflowers need a sunny spot.

7 GOLDENROD (*Solidago* spp., Zones 4 to 9)

If you've ever seen goldenrod in a backyard garden or in the wild, there's a good chance you saw bees hovering around the blooms, too. This plant has such a good reputation for producing pollen that it has been falsely accused of causing allergy problems. (The pollen from this plant is actually too heavy to travel in the wind, thus it can't cause allergies.) Grow in full sun, and look for native varieties best for your backyard.

8 JOE PYE WEED (*Eutrochium purpureum*, Zones 4 to 9)

This perennial commands attention in the garden, and it can reach more than 7 feet tall. Joe Pye weed prefers moist, even swampy areas, but it holds up surprisingly well in dry and hot weather. The pink blooms are like magnets for bees.

9 LANTANA (*Lantana* spp., Zones 8 to 11)

For many gardeners in the United States, lantana will only grow as an annual—note the small zone range. But this plant is definitely a good choice if you live in a hot weather area, because it's one of the most drought-tolerant options on the market today. Gardeners in the South swear by this resilient plant with tropical-looking blooms. Grow it in your sunniest, hottest spots.

10 PENSTEMON (*Penstemon digitalis*, Zones 3 to 9)

You have to love a plant that goes by the nickname "beardtongue." Penstemon blooms are tubular in shape, and are known for attracting hummingbirds and butterflies. Bees like them, too, and this hardy plant can tolerate a wide range of growing conditions.

11 RUDBECKIA (*Rudbeckia hirta*, Zones 3 to 7)

Also called black-eyed Susan, rudbeckia is remarkably easy to grow. You can throw a couple of plants in your garden, and before you know it, they will have doubled or tripled with little to no care. They're perfect for butterflies, birds, and bees, so try planting a few different varieties in your garden. You won't be sorry you did. Grow in a spot where you get lots of sun.

12 SEDUM (*Sedum* spp., Zones 3 to 9)

Sedum is naturally drought-tolerant because it's in the succulent family. The tiny, star-shaped flowers on short stems attract bees well into fall, which is perfect when summer blooms are starting to fade. Sedum is one of the most reliable plants you can grow.

13 YARROW (*Achillea* spp., Zones 3 to 9)

For years, many people have thought of yarrow as a weed, but don't let that discourage you. Yarrow is actually a perfect backyard plant, and it comes in a variety of shades, including yellow, red, and pink. Grow in full sun, and the butterflies and bees will soon find their way. 🐝

GROWING HERBS FOR BEES

Looking for multipurpose plants? Many herbs we grow to eat also happen to be good for bees. After you've picked their leaves for culinary use, let the plants below keep growing and flower. The bees will love the blooms.

- Borage
- Chives
- Cilantro
- Mint
- Oregano
- Rosemary
- Sage
- Thyme

What to Do the First Year

Harness a Swarm

Honeybees don't have to come at an expensive price. This spring and summer, consider the free alternative.

By Andrew Weidman

"Festooning," a wax-building practice, is a sight to behold.

A lot of homesteaders and do-it-yourselfers are getting into beekeeping these days—and why not? There are lots of benefits, from the ultimate taste in local honey to better crop production through pollination; plus working a hive can be a surprisingly effective stress reliever. Then you have the numerous by-products associated with beeswax, propolis, and more. Like most hobbies, however, there are startup costs to consider. You can expect to spend as much as $500 to get started with one hive; less if you are thrifty and have some do-it-yourself chops. About half of that $500 estimate is safety equipment and tools, so a second hive, which many experienced beekeepers recommend, will add another $250 to $300 per hive. The bees themselves will cost $100 to $150 a colony.

Suppose there was a way you could get your bees for free? I'm not talking about inheriting established hives, which can also mean inheriting problems like parasites and diseases. No, I'm talking about catching honeybee swarms.

SPRING SWARMS

Honeybee colonies reproduce by swarming. When a colony runs out of room in its hive, it will split in two, each with its own queen. A colony that's strong enough to swarm is a sign of good health and vigor.

Swarming season can begin as early as March in the Deep South, and usually starts in mid-May across the northern states. It continues through June and into July, although July swarms often cannot establish themselves in time to survive the coming winter. An old saw claims: "A swarm in May is worth a load of hay,

Clustered swarms have no home or brood to protect, so they're generally in a mellow frame of mind.

a swarm in June is worth a silver spoon, but a swarm in July ain't worth a fly."

July and even August swarms are still worth catching — if you're prepared to give them a little more attention. Use a nucleus hive instead of a full-size hive. Give them a head start by feeding syrup and providing them with drawn comb instead of plain foundation, or feed them syrup through the winter.

Before leaving a hive, the bees gorge themselves on honey to hold them over while they establish themselves in a new home. Typically, the old queen will leave the hive with half of the workers and drones following her, while the virgin queen, who will stay in the hive, prepares for her mating flight.

The swarming queen flies a short distance from the hive before settling on a resting spot. Her followers will cluster around her in a roughly basketball-sized mass. Sentries will head out in search of a new home, on a mission that can last an hour to a few days. This is typically when you spot "wild" hives nestled in trees.

BEE PREPARED

When you see those wild hives in the trees on your property, that's your opportunity for free bees. You just need to provide them with a desirable new home.

How you catch your swarm depends a lot on where it settles. A swarm can settle on a tree branch, inside a bush, on the side of a building, and just about

What to Do the First Year

Keep a look out for swarms; if you can capture the queen, the rest of the swarm will follow her into a hive.

anywhere else. Beekeepers sometimes provide a landing spot by planting a small sacrificial tree in their bee yard, giving swarms a place to settle, and the beekeeper a chance to catch them.

The trick to catching a swarm is being ready (see "Swarm Catching Kit" on Page 103). When I kept bees as a teenager, I always tried to keep an empty hive on hand, ready to catch a swarm at a moment's notice. This can be difficult to manage in the peak of swarm season. A large empty box can work in a pinch, but you'll still need to get your bees moved into a hive within a day of catching them.

CAPTURING THE SWARM

Approaching a swirling, buzzing mass of honeybees may seem like a terrible idea, but at this moment they are at their most mellow frame of mind. They're full of honey, surrounding their queen, and have no hive or brood to defend.

You can safely scoop up a handful of bees in your hands if you want to. That's not to say a bee won't sting you if you crush it; they will still defend themselves if you hurt them.

The key to catching a swarm lies in catching the queen. Wherever she goes, they'll follow. And she's somewhere in the center of that swarm cluster.

Don your complete beekeeping safety suit first. Spread a drop cloth on the ground under the swarm, and position the container either directly beneath the cluster or just uphill from it. Some people prefer to drop the cluster directly into the container, while others say bees that walk into a hive will never leave it.

If the swarm settled within a few feet of the ground, this step is easy. Sometimes they'll settle on a branch 15 feet in the air. I've caught swarms resting at those heights—and lost swarms at the same height—but you lose 100 percent of the swarms you don't try to catch.

There are several ways to get the bees into your container. The simplest way is to give the branch a sharp jerk or two, knocking the cluster free. If you can't reach the branch, toss a weighted rope over it. You may need to make a few pitches until the weight catches securely—don't try tugging until it does. The surest way is to cut the branch free below the cluster, carefully lowering the cluster into place. For bees settled in a bush, prune out branches until you can move the cluster where you want them. Clearly, none of these methods work if the bees have settled on a wall. In that case, use a hand brush with soft bristles to gently sweep them where you want them to go.

SETTLING THE BEES

Once you've placed the bees where you want them, either in the hive or box or in front of it, sit back and watch what they do.

If they hang around the box with their abdomens in the air, fanning their

102 Raise Backyard Bees

wings, they like the new home you've offered them, and the queen is in residence within. That fanning action is the bees sending out pheromones, scent messages calling the rest of the swarm in.

However, if they fly out of the container and cluster around the branch, you know you missed the queen and need to try again, after they've had some time to regroup. Keep in mind, with each unsuccessful attempt, the bees will be a little more anxious and irritated, and more likely to sting.

Once you're sure they've accepted their new home, give them some time to settle in. After dusk, go back and close the container and move them to your bee yard.

If you used a hive, this part is simple: Install the inner cover (hole covered with No. 8 hardware cloth), tack hardware cloth across the entrance to seal the bees inside, and strap the whole thing together with a ratcheting load strap. Using hardware cloth over the entrance and lid allows the bees to breathe. It's ready to transport to your yard now. Once there, set it on its base, remove the strap, and, finally, the entrance block.

A temporarily boxed colony requires a little more attention. Close the lid of the box, and tape the flaps shut. You may want to gently poke some ventilation holes in the box, if you didn't think of it before you caught the swarm. Wrap the drop cloth around the whole thing, and it's ready to move. Once you get it to the bee yard, gently shake or brush the bees into the waiting hive body, making sure you get the queen into the hive.

Allow your colony a few weeks to set up shop in their new hive before you inspect them. Caught early enough in the season, and given a good nectar flow,

SWARM CATCHING KIT

Experienced swarm catchers keep a kit of supplies handy during swarming season — mid spring to early summer — in order to take advantage of the short window of opportunity presented by a clustered swarm. A well-outfitted swarm kit includes the following:

- Empty hive or nucleus body with bottom, lid, and frames. Often, the bottom will be tacked into place with scrap board ends to simplify moving the occupied hive.
- No. 8 hardware cloth entrance block, with tacks.
- Ratchet straps.
- Empty large cardboard box as a backup plan.
- Drop cloth or tarp.
- Pruning saw and pruning shears.
- Whisk or dust brush.
- Light rope, approximately 25 feet long, with weighted end. Baling twine or wash line weighted with a small (½-pound) scrap gear works well.
- Bee veil, for yourself or anyone curious enough to want to watch. One might want to keep an entire beekeeping safety suit at the ready.
- A jar of honey or honey sticks to offer to swarm "donors."

Swarming bees are usually mellow enough to hold in your hand; they have no hive or territory to defend.

What to Do the First Year 103

they should have plenty of time to establish the hive and store up enough honey for winter. Be prepared to feed them sugar syrup, just in case they need a boost.

A HELPING HAND

Knowing how to catch a swarm is all well and good, but how, you may ask, do you find a swarm to catch? It's a fair question, and rather than relying on blind luck, the answer is networking.

Get people to call you to handle their "bee problem." Think like a panicked homeowner facing a honeybee invasion, an event that must seem like a plague of biblical proportion. You want to be the person they call, so volunteer as a swarm catcher. Consider these possibilities: your county agricultural extension office, the area police departments, local beekeepers, or even Craigslist notifications (www.craigslist.org).

Most of your swarm calls will come from suburban settings, bees settling in hedges, front yard trees, even garage walls and jungle gyms. Be prepared to do public relations work, educating people, especially kids, about honeybee swarms and soothing fears of "killer" bees. Even though you know the situation is under control, the homeowner might be less assured.

Explain what's going on, and what you're going to do. Let them know the bees aren't aggressive. Do not cut any branches without the homeowner's permission, no matter how much easier it would make your job. If they show interest, offer to let them watch you, from what they think is a safe distance.

ROLLING THE GENETIC DICE

When you consider the amount of effort that goes into breeding honeybees, swarm catching may seem like a risky business. A lot of swarms come from wild colonies, and unless you live near a beekeeper, you will have no idea from where they came.

Let people know you are willing to gather up swarms of bees, anytime, anywhere.

Breathe easy. Except under extremely unusual circumstances, a colony will only swarm if it is strong, healthy, and has outgrown its hive. Plus, wild colonies often possess genetic traits bred bees do not, giving them new tools to fight off local pests and diseases. Wild genetics may even hold the key to overcoming Colony Collapse Disorder—that infamous condition emptying hives by the thousands across the country. And unless you live in the American Southwest, there is little to no risk of catching a swarm of Africanized bees—the so-called "killer bees."

Beekeeping can be an expensive hobby to get started in, and you should never cut corners with used equipment, but with a little luck and preparation, you can get your bees for free. Keep a catching kit handy, spread the word that you catch swarms, and take advantage of the situation when the moment presents itself.

Build a Nuc Vac

A DIY project to help you gather up and remove swarms.

By Carol J. Alexander

Five years ago, when my son and I took beekeeping classes, we purchased our first nuc of bees for $50. This year, hive nucs are going for $150. With a rapid increase in the number of beekeepers in the nation, demand has driven up the cost of all things necessary for this already pricey hobby—including the bees themselves.

If a person is willing and able to remove swarms though, bees are free for the taking. In fact, some folks will pay you to remove bees from inside their home or on their property.

> If a person is willing and able to remove swarms ... bees are free for the taking. In fact, some folks will pay you to remove bees.

The nuc vac, shown here, includes a hive super between the boxes. Secure everything with ratchet straps.

What to Do the First Year **105**

MATERIALS
- 1 12-foot 1-by-8 pine board
- 1 4-by-8 sheet of ½-inch plywood
- 1 16¼-by-20 piece of ⅛-inch hardware cloth or metal window screen
- 1 shop vac or bucket vacuum with 5-gallon bucket
- 15-30 feet of 2-inch vacuum hose
- 1 10-frame beehive super, with frames and foundation
- 1 ratchet strap
- 1 tube of silicone caulking
- 16 feet of foam window/door insulation strip
- 1 bottle wood glue
- 1 box of 1⅝-inch screws

TOOLS
- Drill with bits
- Circular saw (You may choose to use a miter saw for some cuts)
- Jigsaw

CUT LIST
- From the 12-foot 1-by-8 pine board cut:
  A. 4 boards—1-by-8-by-20 inches
  B. 4 boards—1-by-8-by-14⅝ inches
- From the plywood cut:
  C. 1 sheet for top—16¼ inch-by-20 inch
  D. 1 sheet for inclined plane—14⅝ inch-by-19⅝ inch
  E. 1 sheet for cover—11 inch-by-14¾ inch

But if the bees have entered the ceiling joists through a bathroom vent, as one swarm we removed had, you will need a "bee vacuum" to contain the bees before tearing out the drywall. And a bee vac is another piece of pricey equipment—unless you build your own.

The following bee vac uses a bucket vacuum we purchased new, a hive super we already had, and two more boxes I show how to build here.

To create the boxes that turn your hive super into a bee vac, follow these instructions.

1. CUT THE PARTS
- Using a miter or circular saw, cut boards A and B, and plywood sheets C, D, and E to length following the cut list above.
- For plywood D, bevel both of the 14⅝-inch ends at a 20-degree angle opposing each other.

2. MARK THE LOCATIONS FOR SCREWS
- Along the edge of boards A, draw a line ⅜-inch in from the end.
- On this line, mark 4 or 5 points, evenly spaced for screws.
- To avoid splitting the boards, pre-drill holes using a ⅛-inch bit (Photo A).

3. BUILDING THE BOXES
- You are going to make two boxes with your 8-inch-wide boards.* Arrange two A boards and two B boards on a flat surface, creating a box, with the A boards on the outside.
- Fix with wood glue and clamp.
- Drive 1⅝-inch wood screws through your pre-drilled holes to secure.

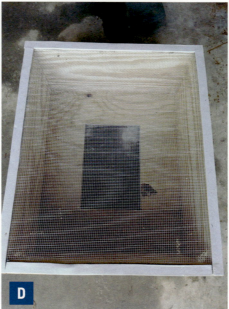

- Repeat with the other four boards. (See photo A)
- With a pencil, label one box for the top and one for the bottom of your vacuum.

*You may choose to purchase one 12-foot 1-by-8, as we did, and make both boxes the same size. Or, you may purchase one 8-foot 1-by-8 and one 8-foot 1-by-4 and make your top box shorter in height. The box will weigh slightly less and be less awkward to carry. We chose to purchase the 12-foot 1-by-8 to save money.

4. ASSEMBLING THE TOP
- Place the C plywood on top of the box you marked "top."
- Mark corners and center of edges for screws.
- Pre-drill with ⅛-inch bit.
- Remove plywood and run a bead of wood glue along the edge of the box where you pre-drilled the holes.
- Replace the plywood, aligning holes, and drive in 1⅝-inch wood screws.

5. FINISHING THE TOP
- Measure in 5 inches from each side of the plywood on your "top" box, drawing lines to create a rectangle in the center.
- Using a large drill bit, drill holes in three of the corners of the center rectangle.
- Using a jigsaw, cut out the rectangle by inserting the jigsaw blade into the pre-drilled holes (Photo B).
- Apply strips of the foam insulation along the edge of the rectangular opening you just created (Photo C).
- Turn the box upside down and apply a bead of caulk to all the cracks on the inside to close any air gaps that would prevent a vacuum from forming.
- Run a thick bead of caulk along the bottom edge of the box. While still wet, lay the piece of screening on to cover the bottom of the box. Press it into the wet caulking.
- When dry, fix with screws or staples and cover with strips of foam insulation (Photo D).

CHOOSE A VACUUM HOSE

Vacuum hose comes in three sizes: 1¼-inch, 2-inch, and 4-inch. We used the smallest size on our first vacuum. In use, it clogged where the hose coiled on the floor. So for this project, we used 2-inch hose—the size used on vacuums found at car washes. 4-inch hose works but is expensive and awkward to handle.

We purchased used vacuum hose from a vacuum repair store in our community. If you find it secondhand, you may need to buy ends for it, too. One end enables you to insert the hose into the box and the other end enables you to attach a wand for longer reach. You can purchase vacuum hose new online but that increases the cost of your project.

For most applications, 15 to 30 feet should be sufficient. You can always add extensions or wands to lengthen.

HIVE REMOVAL SUPPLIES

Swarms frequently enter buildings through small openings like dryer vents or cracks in siding and go unnoticed until they take up residence and begin building comb and storing food. Cutting an established colony out of a building is more complicated than catching a swarm that has landed in a tree—and requires different tools. Once all the bees are safe in your vacuum, locate the comb. Comb left in walls will attract pests or other bees, so you don't want to leave it there. Cut away combs of honey and save for extraction. Cut away any brood comb and secure in empty frames using rubber bands and place in a super. At your bee yard, use this super for the bees' new home rather than an empty one. In addition to your vacuum, protective clothing, and normal hive equipment, the following list includes things you just might want when cutting out a hive.

- Extension cord
- Framing hammer
- Flat bar
- Bee brush
- Duct tape
- Tarp
- Ratchet straps
- Containers for extra comb
- Rubber bands
- Hive super with empty frames—without foundation
- Knife for cutting comb

6. FIXING THE COVER
- Center plywood E over the rectangular cutout in the top.
- Mark a place in the center of each side for the bolts.
- Using a ¼-inch bit, drill through the plywood E cover and the top of the box at each mark. Make sure you are going through both layers of wood but missing the foam insulation.
- Remove cover E and enlarge the holes in the cover with a 9/32-inch bit to make it easier to remove from bolts.
- Thread the carriage bolts up from the underside.
- Replace the cover and secure with wing nuts (Photo E).

7. ATTACHING THE VACUUM
- Assemble your bucket vacuum per manufacturer's instructions.
- Find the center on the end of the "top" box.
- Drill a hole the size of the hose that came with your vacuum (Photo F).
- Insert one end of the hose into the hole.
- Insert the other end into the vacuum.

8. ASSEMBLING THE BOTTOM
- Place plywood D in "bottom" box diagonally from top to bottom. Wedge it in tightly. Screw in place (Photo G).
- Attach strip foam insulation along the edge of the top of the box.
- Mark the center of the end of the box where the interior board slopes to the bottom and drill a hole large enough to accommodate the connector of your long hose—just as you did in the "top" box.
- Cut a small rectangle of plywood large enough to screw over the hole. Cut a slot in it that will slide around a bolt. Fix this cover to the box with one bolt. Drill hole and insert a second bolt opposite the first (Photo H).
- Apply a bead of caulk to all the cracks on the inside to close any air gaps that would prevent a vacuum from forming.

- Attach your long hose.

To use your new bee vacuum, place a hive super with frames between these two boxes and secure the whole thing with a ratchet strap. The bucket vacuum, attached via a hose, creates the suction needed to suck the bees through another hose into the box at the bottom, along an inclined plane, and into the hive super. The top box acts as a barrier to keep the bees out of the vacuum motor.

When you finish vacuuming the bees, remove the top cover to give them ventilation on the ride home. It gets hot inside the vacuum. If the job is taking a long time or you take a break, open the top then, as well.

At home, remove the ratchet strap and transfer your new colony. To do this, set up a bottom board and have a super and lid ready. Remove the super from the vacuum and place on the bottom board. Add the empty super and lid. Leave your vacuum boxes next to the hive until nightfall to give any stragglers time to find their new home. 🐝

> Swarms frequently enter buildings through small openings ... and go unnoticed until they take up residence and begin building comb and storing food. Cutting an established colony out of a building is more complicated than catching a swarm that has landed in a tree — and requires different tools.

Beekeepers in the City

Pittsburgh residents swarm together to keep bees.

By J. Michael Krivyanski

An apiarist allows an onlooker an up-close and personal look at a honeycomb.

With the towering buildings of a city skyline as a backdrop, honeybees seek nectar and gather pollen from flowers growing in apartment gardens and parks—in wealthy areas as well as poor city neighborhoods. When loaded with sustaining cargo, they return to their Pittsburgh hives. These honeybees didn't seek out an urban lifestyle, but they have successfully made the transition, with a little help from an organization known as Burgh Bees.

Apiarists Alex and Meredith Grelli, Jennifer Wood, and Robert Steffes organized Burgh Bees (www.burghbees.com) to bring the pleasure of beekeeping to the urban environment. The four are now directors emeritus of the group.

"Alex and I moved from Chicago to a 'yardless' house in Pittsburgh in 2006. We wanted so badly to keep bees in Pittsburgh and tried to jury-rig all kinds of solutions for our townhouse, but were met with a whole host of issues," Meredith says. "Our house is sandwiched between our neighbors' with about 2 feet of

space between them. We thought of trying (to have a beehive) on our roof, but ultimately decided it didn't seem safe.

"That's when we got hold of Jennifer Wood and Robert Steffes, who've been telling people around town about bees for some time, and we asked if they wanted to team up on this initiative. Despite having 35 acres and a dozen hives of their own, they jumped at the chance of getting urbanites involved."

Since organizing in 2008, Burgh Bees has established four small demonstration apiaries in neighborhoods around the city and one at the Pittsburgh Zoo, in addition to hives in the Mount Washington neighborhood. The demonstration apiaries offer students the opportunity to experience an intensive beekeeper training program sponsored by Burgh Bees. Alex Grelli believes the classes are important to help urban beekeeping grow.

Folks not taking classes also are offered the opportunity to watch each month when the hives are opened for virtually any interested parties. These "Open Apiaries" also enable members of the community to get hands-on beekeeping experience without the need to maintain a hive of their own. One of Burgh Bees' original long-term goals was to develop a group of beekeepers who can maintain a hive where they live or at a community apiary.

In 2009, the group formally organized by adopting bylaws and putting in place a board of directors composed of both new and veteran beekeepers. A new curriculum was formed by Burgh Bees Director and Master Beekeeper Joe Zgurzynski, and classes, such as *Beekeeping 101: Beekeeping in the Classroom* and *Beekeeping 102: Second Year Beekeeping*, have been offered.

Burgh Bees has since trained 175 new beekeepers and established a community apiary in the Homewood section of the city, where a limited number of city residents can own and operate a hive. The Community Apiary—designed with help from Director Emeritus Christina Joy Neumann—came as a result of a lease obtained for a vacant piece of land owned by the city. Currently, it houses 20 hives to be used for education, and the majority are owned by city residents without a place to keep their hives in their own yards. It is believed to be the first community apiary in the United States.

Many apiarists believe that an urban environment may be more beneficial to the health of honeybees than the rural environment. This is due in part to the widespread use of pesticides and agricultural monoculture in rural settings compared with the wide variety of plant life found in a city. Urban apiarists believe that plant diversity is important for maintaining a healthy bee immune system.

"Anyone living in an urban area has to know that some communities have laws about bees. They'd want to keep gentle bees in their hives, and remember that it's important to place a hive where it's secluded and there is plenty of open space," says Pennsylvania Beekeepers Association President Lee Miller. "Bees can fly straight up 17 feet, so it's important they have a clear path."

The efforts of Burgh Bees to increase interest and awareness of honeybees around the city seem to be meeting with success. As of this writing, 40 people are signed up for the next Beekeeping 101 class, and the number of active Burgh Bee volunteers is in the hundreds. More than 150 people are dues-paying members, and monthly newsletters are emailed to more than 500 people interested in Burgh Bees. The organization also played a role in the planning and

Apiarists advise caution around honeybees.

Opposite: Alex Grelli watches as members of Burgh Bees remove honeycombs.

Zan Asha works her rooftop beehives; turn to Page 114 for her beekeeping story.

What to Do the First Year **113**

Opposite: Burgh Bees members calm a number of bees using a smoker.

implementation of Pittsburgh's new Urban Agriculture Ordinance, helping to make beekeeping a permitted activity within city limits.

Many class participants express an interest in starting hives of their own. Check in your area for organizations that help establish honeybee hives within cities.

The increasing success and interest in honeybees that is occurring in the urban world could change its entire landscape. In the future, honeybee hives may become as common a sight in many cities as its squirrels and pigeons.

10 EASY STEPS TO BECOMING AN URBAN BEEKEEPER

As a third-generation beekeeper, I can attest to the many fun and rewarding aspects of beekeeping. As an urban New Yorker, I also can tell you that you can keep bees, even in the city. Just follow these steps, and you'll be well on your way to beekeeping bliss!

1 Make sure it's legal to keep bees in your area. Although places like Detroit, Chicago, and New York City allow for bees, not all urban areas are bee friendly. Double-check your city ordinances to make sure you are cleared to keep bees. Otherwise, you can be heavily fined. And, yes, it does happen—we know of one Brooklyn woman who was fined $2,000 for having two hives on her roof before it became legal to have bees! If you don't own your own property, make sure you have the landlord's permission to keep bees. Our bees are our landlady's project for urban honey production, so we lucked out.

2 Research your new hobby. While bees aren't classified as pets, they are still animals, and it's probably good to have some idea of their basic care before you jump in as a keeper. While this sounds obvious, I've heard of young, new keepers getting bees because they are the new, trendy, green thing, with no idea how to actually care for them. I've been lucky to have my mother's beekeeping advice, but I also have turned to other sources, and there are plenty of books, beekeeping classes, and even YouTube videos to show you everything from bee behavior to harvesting honey.

3 Make sure you have the proper space for your bees. Once we had permission to start keeping bees, it was time to find the proper spot to place the hives. Like their country cousins, urban hives should be situated near a water source (or be in a spot where a source can be provided), ideally underneath a shady area, and with a windbreak.

In our case, because we had so little backyard space, we decided to put our hives on the roof. We were lucky that our landlady is a green activist, and we had a green roof installed. Green roofs and light-colored roofs deflect heat, which create a far better environment for your bees. Tar applications on most city roofs and black-topped roofs, conversely, can reach temperatures of up to 120 degrees F, which is uncomfortable for the bees.

4 Be a good neighbor. Once we figured out where we wanted our bees, we told our most immediate neighbors of our plans.

Unfortunately, most people only associate bees with stings, so it's up to you to let your immediate neighbors know about your new insect project. If you are so inclined, you can leave pamphlets for them, or politely let them know about your project. Some people promise gifts of honey and candles at the end of harvest season to (literally) sweeten the deal.

5 Order what you need before you get your bees. Once we got our logistics together, it was time to order equipment and hives. Like so much in life, beekeeping works better when you're prepared. You'll want to have your hive in place and the equipment to work your bees in your possession before the bees actually arrive, so you can easily introduce them to their home. Go online, read up, and check out catalogs that specialize in beekeeping.

6 Order your bees. What could be so hard about that? Plenty. Since beekeeping has become so popular recently, most apiaries that specialize in selling bees often sell out early in the year. The best time to order from apiaries is January or February. Any later than that and—believe it or not—you may not be able to get bees, or you'll get them so late in the year they won't have time to properly harvest enough pollen and nectar for their winter honey supply. This actually happened to us. We ended up getting our two hives of bees late, which meant we did not get to harvest honey that first year, as we left the bees' honey for them to survive on during the winter.

7 Decide if you want to go solo or if you want help. The beauty of the city is you can cooperatively work your bees. In fact, if you have space to keep bees, you will find many hopefuls to help, in order to learn keeping, since they may not be allowed to keep bees in their buildings. I was lucky that a neighbor became my partner, and this helps in case something happens with your bees while you are out and about in the city.

Also, cooperative help comes in handy for events such as harvesting your honey. The equipment to harvest can be expensive, but often cities have cooperative "honey houses," so you might want to research your options. We were lucky; we had an urban farm friend who allowed us to use her equipment during our harvest season.

8 Get your bees and start caring for them. How you care for

your bees is up to you. I tend to find each beekeeper has her own methods for bee care. You will need to figure out how often you want to inspect your bees for health, progress, and signs of disease. You also will need to determine if you want to care for your bees naturally, or if you want to apply chemical medications. In any case, it is imperative that your bees have immediate water sources, or they will wander to your neighbors to look for it. (This happened during the hottest part of summer last year, and it was not fun for our next-door neighbor to find several bees at his hose spigot!)

Our philosophy ran off my grandfather's natural beekeeping approach. For the most part, we inspected once a month, and used organic and minimal medical applications. Here, we felt that bothering the bees less made for more productivity on their end.

9 Be prepared for "busy season." By this I mean there are a few times a year when you will be hopping with your bees. Primarily, this is swarm season and honey harvesting. The first year of hiving, bees tend not to swarm, but during and after their second season, bees usually swarm in the spring. Swarming is actually a natural act that happens when there are too many bees produced in the hive, and a portion of them leave with the original queen in search of a new home. What this means for you, though, is that you may have to deal with several fearful residents, in case your bees decide to swarm in a low-lying area in the neighborhood. We spent much of last summer wowing our neighbors by collecting bees off trees, wearing our white suits, and carrying around smokers and cardboard boxes.

The next "busy season" falls later in summer, when you will spend a few hours collecting frames of honey and then sending it for harvesting. Set aside time during each season to deal with each issue as it happens.

10 Enjoy your bees! Bees are fascinating creatures that can teach you a lot about caring for them through their specific social structures and behaviors. The old adage is true: "Remember, you don't keep the bees, the bees keep YOU."

—Zan Asha

For more information from Zan, visit her websites at www.therenegadefarmer.com and beyondvagabond.blogspot.com.

What to Do the First Year

HARVEST HONEY

"Bees also unload their pollen into cells within the honeycomb. The mass of pollen in a comb cell is called bee bread and is the major source of protein, oils, vitamins, and minerals for the bees. Pollen is essential for the development of young bees. During the gathering and placing of nectar in cells in the comb, smaller amounts of pollen end up in the nectar cells and therefore in the final honey."
— Chris Colby, "Nectars in Nature," Page 118

Nectars in Nature

What's your favorite type of honey? Learn what all plays into honing the best-tasting honey.

By Chris Colby

The 1970s and '80s saw a spike in generic food. Many supermarkets sold food (or "food") in white containers labeled with only the name of the food. These days, consumers are more aware of where their food comes from, how it is processed, and the varieties available. Recently I learned that there is a wide variety of honeys out there, and each may be processed in different ways. To understand why different varieties of honey have different characteristics, and how processing affects these traits, it's best to start with how bees make honey.

WINTER IN THE HIVE

Honeybees are eusocial insects, meaning they have a queen that lays eggs while all the other females in the hive are nonreproductive worker bees. All the worker bees are sisters. During winter, honeybees mostly remain in their hive. The numerous worker bees huddle around the queen, forming a winter cluster. The heat of their metabolic activity, which can be increased by shivering or beating their wings,

keeps the queen and other members of the cluster warm — quite warm, in fact. The queen is kept at 81 degrees Fahrenheit during the coldest days of winter. The fuel for all this heat is the honey produced earlier in the year.

SPRING AND BEYOND

Once the first spring flowers emerge, worker bees collect nectar and pollen.

Nectar is a liquid solution, produced by the plant, containing more than 50 percent water. The main solid dissolved in nectar is sucrose, followed by lesser amounts of fructose, glucose, maltose, and other sugars. Whatever floral compounds responsible for the flower's scent are also present in the nectar. A worker bee collects 50 to 60 milligrams of nectar — about 90 percent of her body weight — before returning to the hive. Much of this nectar is stored in the bee's honey sac (or honey stomach), an outcropping of the digestive system.

Pollen is "plant sperm," and worker bees collect this, too. Worker bees get pollen grains stuck on their "hair" when they visit flowers. They then groom themselves to roll the pollen into balls and move the balls to their pollen basket, a structure on their hind legs. They bring this pollen back to the hive.

Of course, some pollen rubs off the bee whenever she visits a flower, potentially pollinating it, and that is why flowers maintain features to attract bees.

Worker bees use some of the nectar and pollen for their own nutrition. They will also regurgitate it to feed their sisters.

The remaining nectar and pollen, if any, goes toward honey production. In early spring, most of the nectar and pollen is immediately consumed by the workers to restore the health of the hive, fuel hive maintenance activities, and produce new bees. Typically, honey production lags behind the first appearance of flowers by several weeks.

FROM NECTAR TO HONEY

Honey production actually starts inside individual worker bees. The honey sac secretes enzymes into the nectar to begin modifying it.

One of these enzymes is invertase, which splits a sucrose molecule into its two component sugars — fructose and glucose. Another enzyme is glucose oxidase, which begins converting glucose into gluconic acid and hydrogen peroxide. Hydrogen peroxide acts as an anti-bacterial agent, and the bees secrete it to a greater degree in nectars with higher water content — in which bacterial growth is more likely to appear.

Back at the hive, nectar may be regurgitated into other bees or into cells in the comb. Once in the comb, the bees fan the liquid with their wings to dehydrate it. The liquid nectar gradually loses water, and when the liquid content reaches 17 percent, the cell in the honeycomb is capped, sealing in the solution that is now honey. In arid conditions, honey may contain as little as 15 percent water.

From top: A beekeeper inspects a frame covered with bees and wax from a Langstroth-style beehive; lavender honey goes with everything; a honeybee laden with pollen returns to the hive; and a colony of bees swarms before finding a new home.

Harvest Honey

Hives stand at the ready for their winged residents.

Fireweed (*Chamerion angustifolium*) is a favorite flower for honeybees, and the resulting honey has a mild flavor.

The low water content of honey ensures that bacteria cannot reproduce and lead to spoilage.

It also prevents wild yeasts from fermenting the honey. (*Clostridium botulinum* spores, however, can survive in honey, so it is not advisable to feed it to children under the age of 2. Adults will excrete the spores before they can grow and cause a problem. However, in young children, whose guts may not be completely colonized by bacteria, this botulinum-toxin producing bacteria can take hold.)

Honey is sweet, but it is also acidic. Honey gets its acidity mainly from gluconic acid, but may also contain citric acid and malic acid (the most abundant acid in green apples).

Honey can also contain acetic acid (the main acid in vinegar) or butyric acid. Butyric acid is found in some cheeses and is also the acid that causes the distinctive smell of human vomit.

Excessive amounts of either acetic or butyric acid yield off flavors or aromas.

The pH of honey varies, but the median value is 3.9, a value slightly higher than most fruit juices. Most honey is light in color. However, there are some darker varieties, and those honeys typically have higher pH values and levels of sodium and potassium.

Bees also unload their pollen into cells within the honeycomb. The mass of pollen in a comb cell is called bee bread and is the major source of protein, oils, vitamins, and minerals for the bees. Pollen is essential for the development of young bees. During the gathering and placing of nectar in cells in the comb, smaller amounts of pollen end up in the nectar cells and therefore in the final honey.

Wild bees produce sufficient honey to survive the winter and for the bees to restart hive activity in the spring.

Commercial honeybees, however, have been selected to produce a large excess of honey. Beekeepers take honey from commercial hives when it reaches a level at which removing it does not endanger the safety of hive.

So, in short, bees take liquid nectar from flowers, break down the sucrose in it and evaporate much of the water to leave a stable form of nutrition for the hive. Honey contains not only the sugar from the nectar, but also the aroma compounds of the flowers from which the nectar was harvested.

Raw honey also contains stray pollen grains and bee parts (wings, legs, etc.), wax from the comb, propolis (a resin bees use to seal their hive), and airborne contaminants such as wild yeast and bacteria. Consumers can buy honey in many forms, ranging from honeycombs to the popular liquid honey. In addition to the different forms of honey, there are different varieties of honey—determined by the type of nectar used to produce it.

FORMS OF HONEY

Honey can be purchased raw, but most commercial honey is processed in one or more ways.

Honey may be filtered, pasteurized, or creamed, and each process alters the honey with the goal of making it more desirable to consumers. Increasingly, however, folks are becoming aware of the health benefits of raw honey.

PASTEURIZATION AND CRYSTALLIZATION

Many foods are pasteurized. However, the water content in raw honey is low enough that the growth of microorganisms is suppressed. So why is some honey pasteurized?

Honey is pasteurized to slow the formation of crystals. In raw honey, particles floating in the honey—pollen, bits of wax, etc.—serve as the nucleation site for a crystal. Crystallization does not harm honey—simply heating it melts the crystal back into a liquid—but it can be unsightly. Pasteurization does not harm the honey, but some of the more delicate aromas may be destroyed. Also, small amounts of caramelization may occur.

From top: While gathering pollen, honeybees also help with pollination; buying honey locally is a good idea, helping allergy sufferers and the area beekeepers.

Some people consider bee pollen to be a healthy food supplement.

FILTRATION

Most commercially available honey is filtered. Although raw honey is perfectly safe to eat, it may not appeal to consumers. Honey can be filtered to various degrees.

Some raw honeys undergo a coarse filtration that really only removes wings and "chunks" large enough to be seen with the naked eye. Most commercial honey, however, is filtered to remove particles down to 0.1 to 10 micrometers. This filtration is tight enough to not only remove macroscopic contaminants, but most pollen as well.

Another, even tighter form of filtration is ultrafiltration, which separates out particles as small as 0.001 to 0.1 micrometers. In order for honey to be ultrafiltered, it must first be watered down. The filtered liquid is used in the food industry as a sweetener, but is not considered a honey because its water content exceeds 20 percent.

CREAMED HONEY

Creamed honey is honey that has been whipped to break down any existing crystals in the honey to a very small size. This retards the quick formation of large crystals. The result is a honey that is somewhat granulated.

HOW WE GET DIFFERENT HONEY VARIETIES

Although the distribution of sugars and acids varies among honeys, the primary difference between honey varieties comes from the flavor and aroma of the nectar. The USDA allows honey producers to label their honey as a variety if more than 50 percent of the honey was made from that flower's nectar. So, different honey varieties smell and taste like the nectar from which they were produced.

For many plants, the nectar has a similar flavor to the fruit. For example, raspberry blossom honey has a flavor and aroma reminiscent of raspberries.

Here is a list of popular and prized honey varieties. It is not exhaustive—there are potentially as many varieties of honey as there are varieties of flowers that produce nectar.

HONEYDEW HONEY

Honeydew is made when a bee colony collects the sticky, sugary secretion of aphids (called honeydew) instead of nectar from flowers. It produces a strongly flavored honey that is prized in some parts of Europe and Asia, but this type of honey is not seen often in North America.

CLOVER HONEY

In North America, clover honey is one of the most popular varieties. Clover honey from a single source of clover may be strongly flavored. In practice, however, clover honey from large suppliers is frequently blended for consistency, and becomes generally mildly flavored. Clover honey works great as an all-purpose sweetener, but it isn't the most exciting variety of honey.

RASPBERRY BLOSSOM AND BLUEBERRY BLOSSOM HONEY

These two honeys have aromas and flavors reminiscent of their namesake fruit. Raspberry honey makes excellent mead. Blueberry blossom honey, which is amber in color, is popular in the regions where it is made: New England and Michigan.

FIREWEED HONEY

Fireweed is a perennial herb that grows in the Pacific Northwest. Its nectar produces a mildly flavored, lightly aromatic honey.

ORANGE BLOSSOM HONEY

Orange blossom honey is made from the nectar of various citrus trees—not strictly oranges—in California, Florida, and, to a lesser extent, Texas. It is light in color and has a wonderful aroma, reminiscent

RAW HONEY

Many honey producers also sell raw honey.

Raw honey is usually lightly filtered — just enough to remove the large bits. Raw honey will crystallize, but can be reheated to dissolve the crystals. Because it is not pasteurized, the aroma of the honey will not be diminished.

Raw honey may be slightly more nutritious than filtered honey because of the small amount of protein found in the pollen grains.

Mead makers — the folks who make honey wine — view raw honey as the highest quality honey. Compared to other forms of honey, raw honey just smells and tastes better. Some claim honey harvested earlier in the season is generally preferable to honey harvested later.

Raw honey is generally sold as a liquid, although it may be crystallized on the store shelf. Some sources also sell chunks of honeycomb. This is, of course, as raw as honey gets — but it also takes more work to get the honey you want if you need to drain it from the comb.

Beekeepers often remove the raw honeycomb before harvesting the honey.

of the many citrus fruits. It is one of the most highly prized varieties for mead making, although the quality varies.

TUPELO HONEY

Produced in Florida, tupelo honey is made from the nectar of the white tupelo tree (also called the river lime tree), which grows in northern Florida and produces the Ogeechee lime. The honey is light in color, has a distinct flavor, and is very aromatic. This is another variety of honey favored by mead makers.

BUCKWHEAT HONEY

Produced in Minnesota, Wisconsin, Ohio, Pennsylvania, New York, and eastern Canada, buckwheat is one of the darkest honeys and also one of the strongest smelling and tasting. Buckwheat honey is incredibly rich in antioxidants.

ALFALFA HONEY

Lightly colored with a delicate aroma and not as strongly flavored, alfalfa honey is a good choice if you want a sweetener without a lot of varietal character.

WILDFLOWER HONEY

Wildflower honey is made from the nectar of an unspecified mix of wildflowers, and the mixture and flavor vary depending on geographic location and time of year. As such, it's basically a crapshoot. If you find a wildflower honey you really like, make note of the producer (and maybe even the time of year it was packaged, if that information is available), because another wildflower honey from another producer may be completely different.

SAGE HONEY

Made in California, sage honey is light in color, flavor, and aroma, and it is also slow to form crystals.

LEATHERWOOD HONEY

Made from the leatherwood tree (a eucalyptus tree), this is the most widely produced honey in Australia. It has a strong and distinctively "spicy" flavor.

OTHERS

A nearly endless number of honey varieties exist. For local and regional honeys, check with your local honey producers for varieties produced from crops or wildflowers in your area.

For example, I live in Texas, and two of the local varieties are huajillo honey (made from the desert huajillo bush, sometimes spelled *guajillo*) and mesquite honey.

Measure Moisture Before Honey Harvest

Using a refractometer can increase your honey production; learn how it works and how to use one.

By David Burns,
Long Lane
Honey Bee Farms

Let's examine the importance of using a refractometer. A refractometer is used to measure the moisture level in honey. Beekeepers need to become more aware of what the moisture content is in the honey they are harvesting. Harvest it too soon, and the excess moisture content will cause the honey to go bad or ferment, and when it does, you'll be seeing customers bringing your honey back wanting a refund and spreading around bad news about your honey to others. You don't want that.

So let's look at: 1) How using a refractometer can increase your honey production, 2) how a refractometer works, and 3) how to use a refractometer.

First, how can a refractometer increase your honey yields? Typically, you should not harvest honey from the hive until all the frames are capped over, meaning all of the cells in the honey frames are sealed with the bees' wax cappings. Often the bees fill up the honey cells but do not seal them over, which means the bees cannot store any additional nectar because there is no room. This is especially the case in certain types of climates where the bees may never completely seal the honey comb. Meanwhile, you could have been giving them more frames to fill. What you can do is remove the frames that may still not be completely sealed and place them in an empty super. Then, place the super in a room with a dehumidifier and a fan, and use your refractometer to measure and dry the honey to around 17- to 18-percent moisture. By removing your frames earlier than normal and drying them, you can replace them with empty frames to be filled. This is how a refractometer can help increase your honey yields.

Secondly, just how does a refractometer work? Prisms bend light. A refractometer operates in much the same way, but instead light reacts differently depending on the amount of sugar as the light passes through the honey (sugar), the daylight plate, and the main prism assembly. This reflective light lands on a scale that can then measure the moisture in honey.

HOW TO USE A REFRACTOMETER

First, open the light plate and expose the light blue area. Now take a couple drops of honey so that the honey will cover the blue area completely. If you use too much honey, it will just be messy. You just need enough to cover the blue plate.

Close the light gate firmly to spread the honey evenly over the blue plate. Then simply look into the view finder and take your reading.

To clean your refractometer, use a damp cloth and remove the honey from all areas.

A refractometer is essential to measuring the moisture content in honey.

HOW TO INVEST IN THE RIGHT MODEL

While refractometers are easy to use, I would strongly urge all beekeepers not to purchase the inexpensive refractometers for under $100. These might be accurate, but as many beekeepers have found, they are plagued with problems. In my opinion, save up your money and invest in a solid model.

Mine is not the most expensive model made by Atago, a superior and well-established refractometer company, but the model is designed especially for honey. It is perfect every time, durable, handheld, and affordable with a price tag around $270.

Even though there is the initial investment, you benefit from increased honey yields and the prevention of fermenting honey.

If the bees have not capped the entire honeycomb, remove it and replace it with an empty frame; this helps increase the yield from your hives.

Harvest Honey

Harvesting Honey

One of the most fun parts of beekeeping is harvesting honey.

By Jennifer Ford,
BeesoftheWoods.com

I find that beekeeping is rewarding on so many levels—and one of the more tangible rewards is honey. Thanks to the warm weather and plentiful rain, the bees in our 18-hive apiary have been filling up our honey supers almost as fast as we can put them on.

HONEY SUPERS

A few months ago, we started adding honey supers to our strongest hives. As the spring dandelions and maple trees bloomed, the bees started to make their way out of the hive in search of nectar. Later in the summer, our bees primarily forage on alfalfa and wildflowers.

Now it's time to see if the empty frames have been filled with honey. After smoking the bottom of the hive to calm the bees, we remove the outer and inner covers, and check each frame one by one. We are looking to see if most of the cells in the frames have been filled with honey and capped with beeswax. Our rule of thumb is that at least 90 percent of the cells should be capped. If they aren't, we put the covers back on, and give the girls more time to finish making the honey. This ensures that the bees have had time to "ripen" the honey—removing enough water from the nectar so it will not ferment when stored. If it looks as though most of the cells in the frames are filled and capped, we are ready to move on to the next step.

Step 2 is removing the bees from the frames of capped honey. This takes a little work, because those bees would much rather keep their honey. We can use several ways to remove the honey supers. Some beekeepers pull out the frames one at a time, brush off the bees, and put the frames into an empty, covered box. Other beekeepers use a "fume board"—applying an approved chemical to a felt pad that drives the bees out of the honey super.

I prefer a third method—the escape board. It takes a little more time, but I feel it is less stressful for the bees. An escape board is a thick board that is like a one-way maze—bees can go down through the board pretty easily, but, due to the "maze" on the underside of it, they can't find their way back up. To put it on, we lift up the honey super, put the escape board on top of the hive, and put the honey super back on top with the covers in place. Then, we walk away and leave them alone for a few days.

When we return, most, if not all, of the bees should have moved out of the top super and down into the hive. We give them a few puffs of smoke to calm them down, remove the super, brush off the few remaining bees, and bring the supers back to the honey house—in our case, our kitchen.

If we will not be extracting the honey immediately, we need to store the honey very carefully. The honey supers get stacked in a single stack on a surface that will not be ruined if any honey leaks out, and that pests cannot get into. We have a rubber mat that works well for this. The

Scraping off the beeswax (left) leaves the honeycomb open to allow the honey (below) to be extracted.

Harvest Honey 127

With only a few hives, you may be able to extract the honey using a hand-cranked extractor. For more frames filled with honey, you may want to consider a motor-driven extractor.

heavy boxes sink into the mat so nothing can get in, and the mat is easy to hose off when we are finished. We also make sure the top is secure. An inner cover with the center hole covered with a screen does the trick!

However, we always plan on extracting the honey as soon as possible. Common hive pests such as small hive beetles and wax moths can stow away in equipment. Without worker bees to keep them in check, these pests can potentially ruin the frames of honey. While we have never experienced this, we have heard of it happening to other beekeepers. If you think you will not be able to extract for a long time, it would be better to leave the honey in a strong hive where the worker bees can keep these pests at bay!

Now that the honey is safely stored in our kitchen, it's time for the fun part — getting the honey out of the frames.

EXTRACTING LIQUID GOLD

Once we have our honey supers in the honey house, it's time to extract that golden delicious honey!

First things first — wherever you extract your honey needs to be bee-proof. Honeybees home in on the smell of honey surprisingly quickly, and if it isn't bee-proof you will soon find yourself and your equipment covered in hungry bees. It is also helpful to have access to warm water, and to work on a surface that can be easily cleaned. Extracting right in our kitchen works well for us. It also helps to have the necessary equipment set up ahead of time. Some of the items we use are an uncapping tool, uncapping tank, extractor, filter, honey buckets, and bottles.

Our next step in extracting honey is to remove the protective layer of wax, called the "cappings," from the frame. We use a device called an uncapping plane to do this. Holding the frame of honey in one hand, we draw the heated plane from one end of the frame to the other. The trick is to peel off the wax without going too deep and gouging the honeycomb. It takes a little bit of practice, but once you get the hang of it, the task goes quickly. Other tools do similar job, such as uncapping knives and uncapping forks. I suggest you try out different types to see which one you feel most comfortable with. Workshops, classes, or helping other beekeepers with the harvest are great ways to try out different types of uncapping tools.

> It may be possible to barter with another beekeeper who already has an extractor — maybe they will you extract honey in exchange for your help with their harvest.

We do all of our uncapping over an uncapping tank. An uncapping tank is a large bin with a bar across the top to rest the frame on, and a screen over the bottom. The wax cappings fall from the frame and onto the screen, allowing the excess honey to drain out of the cappings. The honey can then be removed from the bin through a gate at the bottom, and the wax can be saved for other uses.

After we uncap both sides of the frames, they are placed into the basket of an extractor. An extractor spins the frames, pulling the honey out through centrifugal force. Extractors come in many sizes and styles. When selecting an extractor, it is important to consider the size of your apiary, and what you can afford. When we only had a few hives, we bought a used, hand-cranked extractor that could spin two frames of honey at a time. When we started expanding our apiary, we purchased an extractor that is motorized and can spin six frames at a time. If you do not wish to purchase an extractor, other options are available, such as borrowing or renting an extractor through a local bee club. Some bee clubs also hold "extracting parties" where members come together at one person's home to extract honey. It may also be possible to barter with another beekeeper who already has an extractor—maybe they will help you extract honey in exchange for your help with their harvest.

With our extractor, it generally takes 20 minutes to extract honey from the frames. We carefully peek inside the extractor while it is running, and shine a light into it. If we no longer see drops of honey hitting the side of the extractor, it is finished.

At the bottom of the extractor is a gate that can be opened to allow the honey

Several methods can be used to remove the frames from the hive without disturbing the bees.

Fresh honey and fresh honeycomb are the main reasons most beekeepers start working with bees.

to flow out. It is important not to let the honey in the tank get too deep—if it reaches the level of the baskets that the frames sit in, it can burn out the motor in your extractor. Below the gate we position a food-grade 5-gallon bucket that is only used for honey. We prefer buckets with a gate at the bottom to make bottling the honey easier. On the top of the bucket we set a sieve to filter out any particles of wax or other debris. The honey flows out of the extractor, though the sieve, and into the bucket.

When the bucket is full, or when we have extracted all of the honey from the frames, it's time to bottle the honey. We like to let the honey sit in the buckets for at least 24 hours to allow any air bubbles to rise to the surface. The bucket is then lifted onto a table or counter, and the gate is carefully opened, allowing the honey to flow into the bottle held underneath. My husband is actually much better at this than I am—he loses less honey. The type of container we use will depend on what we will be doing with the honey, so we use a variety of containers. One-pound jars—both glass and the plastic "honey bears"—are popular with our customers. We also use half-pound jars as gifts, and 5-pound jars to save for our own use, and for a few customers who prefer to purchase honey in larger volume. Most containers have a mark near the top to let you know when you have filled it with the correct amount of honey. If you don't want to purchase bottles specifically for honey, Mason jars are a popular choice.

If the honey we bottle is for sale, we include a label that lists the amount of honey, our name, phone number, and website.

One of the best parts of honey extraction day is all of the honey we get to sample. After all, it would be wasteful to just wash the spoons and sticky fingers without licking off the honey first!

How to Produce Comb Honey

An experienced apiarist explains why comb honey is such a valuable product of the hive.

By Jennifer Ford,
BeesoftheWoods.com

My husband and I have been extracting honey and collecting beeswax from our hives for quite a few years now. This year, we decided to try something new—producing comb honey. We were lucky enough to be in contact with a beekeeper who has produced large amounts of comb honey, and who was able to guide us through the process. Here is what we have learned.

First, a little background. Comb honey is an amazing product of the hive. It is the most unprocessed form of honey—not extracted, filtered, or heated, and still in the comb. It is great to eat as is, to spread on toast, or to serve on crackers with a mild blue cheese. If you sell your honey, it can be a great product to add to your current offerings.

The first step in producing comb honey is to identify your strongest hives coming out of winter. The bees will have to make both new beeswax comb and fill it with honey before capping. Using only very strong hives ensures that you will have full supers of honeycomb before the end of the season.

You will also need to decide what type of comb honey you will produce. There are

Packaging comb honey for sale takes a bit of time, and can be more than a little messy!

Check out the honey booth next time you visit the farmers market.

several ways to make comb honey, but we decided to make two types—cut comb and Ross Round.

PRODUCING CUT COMB

To produce cut comb honey, you will need a shallow super, with 10 empty shallow frames. You will also need to purchase cut comb honey boxes and covers for the final product. Put the super on one of your strongest hives, above a queen excluder. While this shallow super is on the hive, it is important to not use smoke on the hive, except for just a small bit at the front entrance. If smoke gets into the honeycomb super, your honeycomb may end up with a smoky smell and taste to it. Check the super periodically, and when the frames are completely filled with capped honey, remove the super. Our method of removing the super is to put an escape board underneath the super two days ahead of time. After the two days are up, we go to the bee yard with a couple of spare supers. We pull the frames out one at a time, brush off any remaining bees, and put the frames into the empty super with a cover to keep out any curious bees. When the frames have all been removed, we take off the now empty super and the escape board, replacing it with a new empty super for the bees to begin filling up. Again, we do not use smoke on the comb honey super.

When you have your cut comb frames inside your honey house (or in our case,

our kitchen), it is time to start processing them. We lay the frame of honeycomb on a cutting board, and use a comb cutter to score the beeswax cappings to the correct size to fit in the cut comb boxes.

We then use a sharp knife to cut the comb following the scored lines from the cutter, and place it on a wire rack over a cookie sheet.

Finally, we let the squares drain overnight. The honey from the cells on the sides that were cut open will run out into the cookie sheet. If you skip this step, your honeycomb will be "swimming" in honey, and the boxes may leak. The next day you can gently place the squares of honeycomb in the boxes, and put on the lid.

Gently stack the boxes in a plastic bag—I usually double bag mine—and put them in a freezer for two to three days. This will ensure that any eggs left by pests in the hive (small hive beetles, wax moths, etc.) are destroyed. After two to three days, remove the boxes from the freezer, and allow them to defrost in the plastic bags. This will help minimize condensation on the outside of the boxes. When they are thawed, you are now ready to put on your label, and sell them, give them as gifts, or save to eat yourself.

A variety of bee byproducts can be offered for sale, including comb honey, at far left.

PRODUCING ROSS ROUND HONEYCOMB

To produce these "rounds" of honeycomb, you will need to purchase the Ross Round Comb Super Kit, which can be found at most beekeeping supply companies. The kit (for a 10-frame hive) contains a 4½-inch super, 16 half frames, and 64 rings. Each half frame holds four rings that are snapped together around a piece of foundation. When fully assembled, each frame will yield four comb sections. The foundation, covers, and labels are sold separately. At the end of the season, you can clean and reuse the super and frames for next year, but you will have to purchase additional foundation and rings.

Similar to cut comb, place the 4½-inch super of Ross Rounds on a very strong hive. Again, use a queen excluder underneath the super. Check the super periodically, and when the circles (or rounds) are completely filled with capped honey, you can remove the super. Again, we use an escape board to clear the bees from the super, then remove the frames one at a time. Brush off any bees, and place the frames in an empty super to bring indoors.

Up to this point, producing Ross Round honeycomb is similar to producing cut comb. Processing the Ross Rounds is different. The plastic rings that are filled with honeycomb can now be removed from the frame and placed inside two Ross Round covers. No cutting or draining is required, though you may have to trim excess foundation off the outside of the rings prior to placing them in the covers. The Ross Rounds should then be placed in plastic bags and frozen. After two to three days, they can be removed from the freezer, and allowed to defrost in the bags. At that point, you can add the Ross Round labels, and the honeycomb is ready to sell, give as gifts, or use for yourself.

We have found that both types of honeycomb sell well, and each commands a higher price than an equivalent amount of honey. Our customers also seem to appreciate being able to purchase honeycomb from us. Whatever method you decide to use, we hope you consider giving comb honey a try next season.

> Comb honey is an amazing product of the hive. It is the most unprocessed form of honey—not extracted, filtered, or heated, and still in the comb. ... If you sell your honey, it can be a great product to add to your current offerings.

Harvest Honey

Build Your Own Honey Extractor

You can make an inexpensive honey extractor from simple materials available in your local hardware store.

By Carol Herbert

As animal husbandry costs go, the price of bees and beekeeping supplies is quite a bargain, but setting up an apiary still runs into money if you have many colonies. My husband, Dwayne, and I got into a home honey operation a couple of years ago — it sort of snuck up on us — and from the start, we've tried to reduce expenses by making some of our own equipment.

We've found, for example, that we can save substantially by building our own bee housing. We bought our first hive and super, and Dwayne made the rest using the commercial products for patterns so that the parts of all units are interchangeable. Since we have quite a bit of scrap lumber handy, the only investment was time.

We've also learned to economize by finding substitutes for some conventional equipment. If you camp and have mosquito nets, for instance, they'll work fine as bee veils. If you own a small pry bar, it will do the job of a hive tool.

One recommended item, the honey extractor, which removes honey from the comb, looked like a pretty demanding do-it-yourself project and had no obvious counterparts lying around the house.

So, at first, we thought we would just do without it. Our initial attempt at

harvesting honey, however, showed us our mistake. There just isn't any other practical way to separate a large amount of honey from the wax in which it's stored. The thick fluid can be squeezed out of the cells, but that takes forever and destroys the structure of the comb. An extractor preserves those neat little hexagons, which saves work for the bees — and, in the long run, also saves time and money for their keeper.

It's particularly essential that you have an extractor if you intend to sell honey. Anyone who has a surplus to market has too much to separate by hand ... and in our experience, cut comb honey has a limited market. Most people prefer the product free of wax.

Well, we gave in, checked the prices of extractors, and found the rates higher than we cared to pay: $175 to $370 for a hand-operated machine, and $649 and up for electric models; such equipment comes in various sizes, and the prices vary accordingly. After a bit of thought, Dwayne decided he could build a similar device himself at much less cost. When he got through, he had invested less than $100 and come up with an electrically operated honey separator that works like a charm, and was put together from materials that were on hand or easily obtainable from our local hardware store.

Dwayne started the project by choosing a new 20-gallon metal garbage can to serve as a drum (a food-grade plastic drum also works), and cutting a hole in the bottom near the outer edge. The opening is about an inch in diameter — to let the thick honey run out freely — and is fitted with a valve to cut off the flow.

The rectangular inner basket, which holds the frames of the honey extractor, is 8¼ by 11¼ by 16 inches — the largest size that will fit in the garbage can with spinning room left over. Its maximum load is four small frames (5⅜ by 17⅝ inches), or four medium (6¼ by 17⅝ inches), or two deep (9⅛ by 17⅝ inches), plus any other two smaller frames.

The basket's framework is made of welded angle iron with a center rod on which the container spins. The bottom is perforated sheet metal from the back of an old TV set (other perforated metal options include perforated steel, stainless steel, or aluminum scraps at your local metal recycler). This panel is sturdy enough to support the weight of four frames full of honey, and the openings are large enough to allow the honey to run into the can. The container's sides are made of welded wire mesh that we had on hand. Any similar material could also be used.

The basket works on the same principle as the spinning tub of a washing machine: It turns with enough speed to force the honey out of the comb and fling it against the side of the garbage can, where it runs down the wall and out the bottom drain.

You might be able to get by without an extractor at first, but as your operation grows, it will become a necessity.

The honey extractor uses centrifugal force to throw the honey to the edge of the tub, allowing it to drain out at the bottom.

Harvest Honey

We've found that the necessary rate of spin is about 175 to 200 rpm, depending on the thickness of the liquid.

Across the top of the can, Dwayne built a base for the motor from hardwood crating boards we happened to have around. (Almost any TV or appliance dealer has sturdy packing materials to throw away.)

The motor—a ¼-hp, 1,750-rpm, 110-volt electric—was also scrounged up for free. Such units are common, and you can often find a good one at an auction for only a few dollars.

The biggest expense in the construction of our honey extractor was the 10-to-1 gear reduction, a worm-gear drive train we had to purchase (you can substitute a 2-pulley speed reduction system). A pulley- and-belt arrangement is used to drive the gears, and the pulley size can be changed if necessary to vary the speed of rotation. The parts can be assembled in almost any workable combination.

It's best, however, to keep the device as simple as possible.

Dwayne's final step was to build a heavy-duty stand from more boards. The entire works is fastened to the base so the extractor won't scoot across the room and run us down when it starts spinning.

We're still novices at this beekeeping business, but we've already discovered this much: With some handyman ability and a little extra work, it's possible to run such an operation without investing a lot of money. Furthermore, it's always fun to get out in the shop and tinker until you find a cheaper way of doing things; projects mark progress and are always good to have at your home.

If you're seriously considering a start with bees but have no experience and little cash, don't let that deter you. We began the same way, and we know it can be done. 🐝

Make sure the motor you choose can turn the basket with frames in it at a rate of 200 rpm. Extract the honey and return the empty combs to the hive.

THE SWEETEST HARVEST

You can harvest your honey with the beeswax comb intact (comb honey), or you can use a hot knife to cut the caps from the comb and remove the honey. Extracting the honey and returning the empty comb to the hive is easiest on the bees (they ingest 6 pounds of honey to make 1 pound of wax). Electric extractors quickly spin the honey from combs using centrifugal force, but they are expensive, as noted.

Bee clubs often share an electric extractor and sometimes organize honey harvesting parties. Check your county for a beekeeper's club and get involved.

As frames are replaced, you will harvest more bounty from your bees in the form of beeswax for candles, soaps, and lotion. Should you decide to sell some of your honey, you will find that prices are significantly higher for local, raw honey. Some people buy it for health reasons, including allergy relief, although proof that it works depends on anecdotal evidence. Look to farmers markets for a good starting point in finding a market for your honey.

—M.E.A. McNeil

A Top-Bar Hive Honey Harvest

Honey collection differs as to the type of hive.

By Kirsten Lie-Nielsen, HostileValleyLiving.com

In traditional Langstroth beehives, the honey is extracted via a centrifuge that spins the golden liquid out of the comb and allows it to run into your pot. In a top-bar hive, honey collection is quite different, as is the rest of the top-bar hive beekeeping process.

As the bees build their home in a top-bar hive, they start with brood comb first then begin to make honey. When you are ready to harvest, the bars you want to take will be towards the left of the hive, where all of the newest build should be. From regular inspections, you should have a good idea of what is available.

Do not take uncapped honey as it is not yet ready for harvest. Moving in from the uncapped combs you should find capped honeycombs before you hit the hive's brood area. Remember not to take too much of their winter supply and, if your bees don't have enough honey, be prepared to feed the hive with sugar water during the flowerless months.

It is easy to extract the comb from the hive. Simply cut along the edge of the bar. Bees will linger on the comb, simply brush them off or wait for them to leave. Once you've collected enough bars, it will be time to process your honey.

Unlike Langstroth hives, the honey from a top-bar hive is extracted by crushing it out of the comb. There are a number of ways to do this, and a few good extractors are available from top-bar hive specialists today.

One of the simplest methods I have seen demonstrated is to place the comb in a large bowl and cut it with a knife into very small pieces, allowing the honey to escape from its casings. This mash can then be strained through a mesh bag, leaving it in a warm place over the course of several hours.

Another method is to use a mason jar or similar container and smash the comb into it until the jar is full. A strainer of some kind, such as cheesecloth, can be sealed over the top with a rubber band and the jar can be turned upside down to drain out the honey. Once again, this will take several hours in a warm place.

One option for top-bar hive

Top-bar hive beekeeping has definite advantages over traditional hives, including an easier honey harvest (far right).

honey is to leave it in the comb. You can cut small sections of comb out and keep them in a mason jar or plastic containers, and have the honey freshly dripped out when you are ready to enjoy it.

Once strained, the honey can be poured into whatever container you prefer, and then stored. If left for long periods, it will crystallize and will need to be slowly warmed to return it to its liquid state.

The honey collection system for a top-bar hive is fairly simple and another reason that this beehive style is so popular among hobby farmers today. Not only are the hives easy to keep and more natural for the bees, but the honey is harvested in a simple manner with tools most farmers will have on hand.

Honeycomb placed in jars will eventually release all of the stored honey.

Harvest Honey **139**

The Importance of Nectar Flow

Understanding the nectar flow in your area helps maximize colony health and honey production.

By Betty Taylor

It's late April in Middle Tennessee and our nectar flow is on! In my first year of beekeeping, I made a lot of mistakes because I didn't understand what the nectar flow was or its importance. Since then, I've learned to watch the bees, learn from them, and work with them as the season progresses.

WHAT IS NECTAR FLOW?

The nectar flow is the time of year when the native vegetation is in full bloom. In my area that starts about mid-April, when the trees begin to flower, and continues through May with blooming shrubs like blackberries, honeysuckle, and, yes, even multiflora rose and privet, as well as a multitude of wildflowers. Then at the end of June, the summer dearth begins with few plants blooming other than clover.

In the fall, we usually have another, smaller bloom of asters, goldenrod, and other wildflowers. In dry years, this fall bloom can be minimal.

WHY IS NECTAR FLOW IMPORTANT?

A beekeeper needs to understand how the bees respond to the bloom. Even before the flowers begin to appear in the spring, the trees will begin to produce pollen. At the same time, the queen resumes laying eggs to build up the hive population that will soon collect nectar and make honey. The worker bees bring in the first pollen of the year to feed all the new larvae that will metamorphose into adult worker bees.

By the time the flowers begin to bloom, the population in a healthy hive is exploding, and drone bees also begin to appear in preparation for future swarming.

With the bloom, the bees can build new wax. It takes several times more nectar to make a pound of wax than it does to make a pound of honey, so the bees can't make wax unless they have lots of nectar. As the spring bloom builds, healthy hives may produce queen cells in preparation for swarming, their normal method of making new colonies. The old queen and a large swarm of bees will go off and begin a new hive.

Knowing the specifics of the flow for your geographical location is important in managing your bees to maximize hive health as well as honey production.

If you create artificial swarms or nucleus hives (nucs) when the bees would normally swarm, the bees get to start a new colony and you get to keep more bees. And because you won't lose up to half of your bees, which can happen in a normal swarm, more bees will be left to produce honey.

The original hive will think it has swarmed and settle down to building its stores. The purpose of a spring flow, for the bees, is to provide food for the rest of the year. (Many of my customers are surprised to learn that bees do not make honey all year long and that a beehive isn't a year-round spigot for honey.)

Knowing when the flow ends and the dearth begins also will help you know how much honey to leave in the hives for the bees. Feeding is an unnecessary expense of time and money in a well-managed hive. Nothing you can feed them will be as good for them as their own nutritious honey. Here, the fall honey from asters and goldenrod serve as supplies for the bees to winter on. I may share combs of honey among hives in the fall and winter, giving frames from overstocked hives to lesser prepared hives, but I won't feed them sugar syrup.

Placing hives near gardens and orchards (above and far left) ensures your bees will have plenty to choose from (below).

Harvest Honey 141

Plant early bloomers, like the crocus, as well as late-season blooming plants so your bees have choices.

> City dwellers may have a more prolonged bloom, because people plant and water flowers for an all-summer-long bloom. This can benefit the bees ….

A field of lavender will make for a delicious honey.

Another drawback of artificial feeding is that you can stimulate your bees to behave as if it is spring at the wrong time of the year, causing them to build up and collapse if nectar and pollen are not sufficient for their increased population and abundance of off-season brood.

EFFECTS OF CHANGES

I have described a nectar flow in one particular native environment. City dwellers may have a more prolonged bloom, because people plant and water flowers for an all-summer-long bloom. This can benefit the bees and increase honey harvest for urban beekeepers. On the other hand, if you live in an agricultural area, native vegetation may have been plowed under for row crops. Your bees will have less natural forage and a more feast-or-famine supply, depending on the crops and when they bloom.

After checking all my established hives and adding honey supers to those that needed it, I decided to make more three-frame nucs from the strongest hives. Doing so may cut down a bit on the honey harvest, since I will be taking away more bees from each hive. However, we need to rebuild. Now, during the nectar flow, is the time! 🐝

Honey Business Yields Sweet Rewards

What began as a hobby for her young son turned into a lucrative honey production business for one of our bloggers.

By Alissa Brandemuhl-Zengel

It started with a Christmas present for a curious 9-year-old boy.

My son, Riley, was fascinated with a public television program about the life cycle of bees. We decided it would be a great opportunity to learn about self-sufficiency and get something delicious as a bonus.

Santa brought Riley a complete beehive kit, and we kicked in the membership to the local beekeepers association. A month later, Riley and my husband Clay assisted a master beekeeper in removing a feral bee colony from an empty home. These would become our bees.

The first year we harvested six pounds of honey. The next year, we harvested 116 pounds. We couldn't possibly use all the honey our bees made. We gave away jars to our family and friends throughout the year, and they became our first customers. I found another avenue for sales when talking with the manager of our local wine-making supply store. Mead makers in the area were looking for local honey. I provided samples and our contact information to the wine store, along with how much we had available and our next anticipated harvest date.

I also offered a discount due to the bulk sales. Our costs are considerably lower because we can bottle in jugs instead of the smaller, more expensive, glass jars.

We've been selling honey for six months, and we've already realized a six-percent return on investment. We predict the start-up costs will be paid by the proceeds within the next 18 months as we have bigger sales.

ADVICE FOR BEGINNERS

Start from a place of abundance, both physically and mentally. Don't hesitate to give free samples and share your knowledge. A little goodwill goes a long way in making loyal customers.

Know your bottom line before you talk to people. We told a lot of people we weren't selling honey in the beginning just because we didn't know what to charge. After speaking with other beekeepers, we found the going rate and this helped us figure out a reasonable price.

Networking is for everyone, not just marketers! Sharing your hobby is a great conversation starter, and you never know when you're going to meet your next customer. People are very receptive (and sometimes a little envious) hearing about our adventures.

Watch for Robber Bees

The dearth of summer often brings out robbing behavior in honeybees. An experienced beekeeper discusses what causes it, and what to do about it.

By Betty Taylor

Late summer is the time to be on the lookout for robber bees. Robbing behavior is when foraging bees from one hive enter and rob resources from another, usually weaker, hive. If not prevented, or stopped once robbing has begun, the robber bees can completely empty the stores from the target hive, causing it to starve. Even if the target hive survives, it will be weakened and its remaining bees may become defensive and difficult to manage.

WHY?

Robbing occurs during a dearth of nectar. In Middle Tennessee, that can mean before the flowers begin blooming in the spring, or it can mean in the height of summer, after the spring bloom and before the fall bloom. The bees have little to forage on and are drawn to the smell of honey in neighboring hives. If the bees can successfully challenge and overcome the guard bees, they enter the hive and begin robbing. They will then return to their own hive to recruit more robbers. If not stopped, a frenzy of fighting, killing, and robbing will ensue. Soon you may have piles of dead bees and torn-up wax in front of a doomed hive.

HOW?

You can help prevent robbing by leaving enough honey in all colonies to get them through the times in your area when flowers are not blooming. If you've harvested all of their honey, they will be starving and will be more likely to rob nearby hives. If you open the hives to feed them during a time of dearth, the smell of the sugary syrup or honey can incite robbing. At these times, it's best to minimize your activity in the bee yard, getting into the hives only when absolutely necessary. Using a screen to reduce the entrances can help the guard bees without restricting airflow through the hive in the summer.

Sometimes beekeepers mistake orientation flights or swarming for robbing. In orientation flights, the bees are young, fuzzy bees, and they are numerous but calm in their back-and-forth flights in front of the hive. Robber bees are older, slicker bees, having worn down the "fuzz," and will behave in a frenzied manner, fighting with guard bees on the landing board and in front of the hive. When swarming, bees will be exiting rather than entering the hive and will fly en masse around the queen. Once they leave the hive, most of the activity will be high above the hive and not at the entrance. Swarming takes a matter of minutes whereas robbing can go on all day.

If you see robbing in your bee yard, you'll want to stop it immediately. Cover the hive with a wet sheet (this has worked well for me). Reduce the entrance or screen it up completely for a day or two. Some people suggest taking the top cover off the stronger hive so that the bees will have to stay home and defend their own hive. This seems extreme and I have not tried it; however, I might consider it if I couldn't stop the behavior otherwise. It may be best to combine the hive that has been robbed with another hive before winter. Like other disasters in the apiary, robbing is easier to prevent than to stop. And at the risk of sounding like a broken record, it's another good reason not to harvest so much honey from your bees that you have to feed them.

From Pesky Weed to Wonderful Treat

Tall goldenrod is a fall favorite of the honeybee.

By Julia Miller,
FiveFelineFarm.com

From July through November across the U.S., yellow spikes of flowers on tall, sharp-leafed stems fill ditches and vacant lots. Most people consider goldenrod a weed to be mowed or eradicated in some chemical fashion. At Five Feline Farm, we allow areas of these to grow and mature with a purpose. Tall goldenrod is a fall favorite of the honeybee. Although it is most likely the bees are foraging on a variety of flowers, it is natural to assume the most prevalent flower at any given time is the strongest influence in the honey. Since goldenrod is available in significant quantities at this time of year, this nectar is the primary component of the honey being produced now.

Nectar sourced from goldenrod produces a distinct honey. Fellow beekeepers warned me to not be alarmed when goldenrod is in bloom. Even when opening the hive and before harvesting honey, the smell is markedly different. Without this advance notice, I would have been concerned something was wrong. Some written descriptions categorize this as a spicy smell. Others suggest a faint licorice aroma. The leaves of goldenrod (actually a member of the herb family) do smell a bit like licorice when crushed so perhaps that is a nice way to characterize it. Honestly my best descriptor for the smell of goldenrod honey is "cheesy."

Goldenrod-based honey is a rich amber color, much darker than honey harvested after the bees have foraged on spring flowers such as clover. It is almost as dark as

The goldenrod is a favorite pollen source for honeybees.

maple syrup. There is a slightly spicy taste and, thankfully, nothing cheesy. The honey is truly delicious.

Goldenrod honey tends to crystallize faster than clover or other wildflower honey. Last year, the goldenrod honey crystallized in a matter of weeks while the clover honey stayed liquid for months. Crystallization does not change the flavor or ruin the honey. If liquid honey is desired, it can be gently warmed by placing the container of honey in a bowl of hot water until it liquefies. Never microwave honey. This destroys the nutritional value of the honey and risks scorching. Crystallized honey may also be used "as is." I find that a slightly crystallized honey is easier to spread on toast. If using in hot tea, the crystallization is not a factor, simply spoon and stir.

An unexpected market for Five Feline Farm honey has come from allergy sufferers. Some customers report using local honey to decrease their sensitivity to the pollens that cause seasonal allergies. Taking one to three teaspoons of honey per day is said to decrease allergy symptoms. Obviously we cannot claim that our honey, whether from goldenrod or other flowers, is a treatment for allergies, but there is anecdotal support. Various internet sites also report that regular consumption of local honey is beneficial for seasonal allergy sufferers. As goldenrod is one of the plants in bloom during fall hay fever season, this honey is in such demand that we quickly sold out.

Whether or not goldenrod honey helps allergies, it sure improves a biscuit.

Goldenrod pollen produces a tasty, dark honey, though the honey may crystallize more quickly than others.

HEALTHY BEES

"Honeybees are not native to the Americas and were first brought to North America by English settlers in 1622. Although not native to the American landscape, wild colonies of bees spread quickly as white settlers moved out across the continent. Since the 1940s, the number of managed honeybee colonies in the United States has declined from 5 million to 2.5 million because of various threats — invasive species, diseases, pesticides, and habitat destruction, according to the U.S. Department of Agriculture."
— Andrew Moore, "Saving the Honeybee," Page 158

The Latest Buzz

Honeybees have seen better days, but efforts to boost their populations haven't gone unnoticed.

By Kim Flottum

Almost everyone has heard about the current crisis with our honeybees, so let's take a look at what's going on. Much like you and I and every animal you know of, bees have an average life span. In the summer, once they reach adulthood, their lifespan is only about 4 to 6 weeks because they work harder and wear out; they have more close encounters with lethal enemies, like birds and mantids; and old age. But in the winter it's closer to 2 to 4 months because they spend their time inside the hive where it's safe and warm with no enemies.

That equation has changed recently. Here's the gist of what's going on.

Researchers all over the world have been looking at why that life span has recently become fundamentally shorter—by half or more.

To begin with, they studied what they thought were the obvious problems. Looming large were agricultural pesticides encountered in the big world of food collection by all pollinators. But as persistent and as widespread as agriculture chemicals are, they aren't everywhere. There are also those pesky mites chewing on both adult and baby bees, but they've been around for decades. So why now?

Fortunately, other researchers weren't convinced it was this easy. They kept looking, and what they found has come down to what we call the "four Ps."

Pesticides are part of the problem, for some bees and in a lot of places. Then there are those pesky predatory mites that are now, they've discovered, spreading viruses bees had never seen. Add in a new parasitic disease called *Nosema apis*, with neither symptoms nor a cure, and finally, the one that surprised almost everybody, there simply wasn't enough good food readily available for every bee in the bunch.

Pesticides, predators, parasites, and pasture. It's that simple; and that complicated. Let's look at these a bit closer.

Avoid spraying with fungicides, pesticides, or herbicides. When a bee collects pollen from flowers, it will inadvertently bring the chemicals into the hive. Opt for essential oils when possible.

The pesticide thing got messy fast for a couple of reasons. There are controversial new chemicals being used affecting not only bees, but also most other nontarget insects—soil dwellers, water dwellers, and plant dwellers. They are immediately lethal to those target pests when applied to crops early in the season, but they last the whole time the plant is alive. They seep into all the plant's parts: roots, stems, leaves, flowers, pollen, and nectar. They wash away from the fields and swim with the fish, and they last for years everywhere they go. But in this afterlife they aren't so strong as to be critically lethal.

Sublethal is the term they use. These chemicals challenge immune systems, break down digestive systems, and slowly take their toll. Through consistent use over the past several decades, the residual effects of the pesticides continue in many corn, soybean, and cotton fields.

Another pesticide issue was not new, really, but has been looked at from a different perspective. Fungicides have forever been classified as "not a problem" for pollinators or the environment. But

Beekeepers will sometimes supplement their bees' diets with sugar water (above) or pollen or a protein substitute (below) when there are not enough flowers in close proximity.

the effects of these newly crafted fungicides, applied directly to blooming plants, affect bee growth and colony health. Baby bees grow slowly and die young. Queens fed these chemicals go missing. Drones don't mate.

Beekeepers apply these pesticides in their hives with the hopes of putting a stop to predatory mites, but what it essentially comes down to is poison in a beehive.

Who would have thought that would ever happen? These "miticides" do kill mites while sparing the bees, but they damage queens and drones, and are absorbed by the wax inside. Soon, a beehive can be inadvertently soaked in sublethal chemicals, while the beekeeper had only the best intentions. Controlling mites with nontoxic, organic acids has been shown to be effective while leaving out the other ill effects.

Viruses have always been around, and with bees it's no different. But until the mites and the pesticides came along, viruses hadn't been much of an issue.

When combined, pesticides provide a path for viruses to challenge a honeybee's immune system, making their bodies less resistant. The viruses go from bee to bee when they are feeding babies, queens, drones, and each other.

Worst case scenario, every bee in a hive has some level of viral infection. After a time there, the bees learn to fly away to healthier homes, or they begin to die younger, and the colony collapses. No mites means no virus.

Then there is *Nosema apis*, an internal parasite. It is ingested by adult bees as a spore, makes itself at home, and grows to produce more spores while continuing to spread. When combined with viruses and pesticides inside our bees, it's even worse, eating a bee from the inside out. The only symptom is that the bee quits eating and dies. The good news is that with probiotics, essential oils, efforts to reduce mites, and enough good food, bees are much more resistant to the parasite.

Which brings us to pasture. Among the acres of crops treated with herbicides, asphalt parking lots, and weed-free lawns, pollinator food does not grow here.

A beehive needs acres of all types of flowers, plants, even weeds, to live. Enough blooming acres all season long will provide enough good food all of the time for every bee in the bunch. But they cannot be treated with pesticides or herbicides. Save a bee, plant a flower.

All these things are going on nearly everywhere, interacting, multiplying, adding up, and piling on, and bees may see better days ahead because of the awareness.

Russians to the Rescue

America's beleaguered honeybees are getting some help from a distant relative.

By William H. Funk

America's honeybees are in serious trouble. We've known this for a while, anxiously watching as populations decline across the continent due to a noxious host of plagues, the greatest of which is a multifaceted disaster called colony collapse disorder (CCD), composed of a number of factors, from neonicotinoid pesticides to the obliteration of natural habitat to *Nosema ceranae*, a unicellular parasitic fungus of Asian origin that weakens bees' resistance to the roiling pesticides they must labor through in their role as pollinators employed by industrial agriculturalists across the country.

Modern large-scale pollination procedures are hard on the honeybee. Hauled by the hundreds of thousands in tractor-trailer rigs to pollinate a range of crops—including cucumbers, pumpkins, and melons; sunflowers; and apples and almonds—honeybees must endure the inherent stresses of this wholly abnormal lifestyle while being increasingly subjected to chemical and biological threats, the latter mostly of foreign origin.

A deadly parasite, the varroa mite attaches itself between the wings of a honeybee.

SOURCES FOR RUSSIAN HONEYBEES

Russians are highly resourceful, and so they don't build a lot of brood early in the springtime until there is plenty of food available and the weather is settled. By the time the bees hit full-stride, approximately ⅓ of the crops needing pollination have come and gone. Hence there are a limited number of breeders for Russian queens because lack of demand in the commercial pollination world.

When you introduce a pure-mated Russian queen into any hive of bees, eventually all the bees in the hive will be Russian. If your hive requeens itself, the new queen will mate with any and all drones in the area, and the offspring will be Russian hybrid bees, which are not nearly as resistant to varroa mites and usually have an unpredictable temperament. Instead, when it's time to requeen, buy another pure Russian queen, so your hive maintains varroa resistance and gentle behavior.

You can find a Russian queen breeder at Russian Honeybee Breeders Association (www.russianbreeder.org).

—Caleb Regan and Kim Flottum, editor-in-chief at *Bee Culture* magazine (www.beeculture.com)

Our honeybees (*Apis mellifera*) aren't native to the Western Hemisphere either; they originated in southern Europe and were brought over by the early colonists. Some conservationists have even expressed concern about their varying impacts on our some 4,000 native bee species.

But the fact is, modernized agricultural practices almost completely dominate the U.S. farming industry, and these bees—whose ancestors were as foreign to America as most of their human keepers'—are absolutely critical to maintaining our current rates of crop production.

ONE CULPRIT

Amid the vicious brew of harms that causes CCD, a tiny mite plays a central role in our bees' accelerating disaster. The aptly named *Varroa destructor* (commonly the varroa mite) is an external parasitic mite that, like a tiny tick, attaches itself to the bee's exterior and sucks its blood (bees' yellowish blood, or hemolymph, doesn't carry oxygen, a job performed by the tracheal system, and so doesn't contain the red pigment hemoglobin). This can be enough to kill the affected bees over time, but worse yet is the infection that varroa mites spread through the entire hive. The bite of this mite, which targets only Apis species, inflicts a disease called "varroosis," resulting in depleted weight gain, underdeveloped body size, deformities of the wings and abdomen, decreased lifespan, and, in the male drones, infertility.

A significant mite infestation will lead to the death of an entire honeybee colony, usually during the hungry months of late autumn through early spring.

The varroa mite is currently believed to be the single most destructive parasite of our honeybees, producing the greatest detrimental economic impact on the beekeeping industry, and thus on some of the industrially raised crops mentioned above.

Controlling this exotic menace is fraught with difficulties: the inherent dangers of pesticide application, the time-consumptive methods of removing drone pupae from the hive, and the regular replacement of honeycombs to deter absolute infestation.

An even more desperate measure is described in a 2015 report by the Centre for Agricultural and Biosciences International: "This involves moving the parent colony approximately 4 meters from the original colony site. A second hive containing newly drawn combs and the queen is placed on the original site, causing foragers to return to this hive, creating an artificial swarm. Further management procedures are undertaken after nine days and three weeks."

It looks like a lot of physical work for the average backyard beekeeper to do over and over, but what if other critters might help in taking on these deadly mites for us? Certain species of pseudoscorpion have been known to prey on varroa mites and have been considered for introduction into the U.S., as have microbial agents such as fungal pathogens.

The problem with using non-native organisms to combat a non-native threat to your non-native bees is, obviously, the accelerating influx of exotics whose long-term effects on their new ecosystems, despite careful preliminary lab research, are often hypothetical at best.

Perhaps one of the simplest and least ancillary damaging methods might be the application of essential herbal oils. Thyme and spearmint have proven effective against varroa, while lemongrass contains antifungal and antiviral properties. How effective this tactic would be at the scale needed for mass pollination isn't clear.

POTENTIAL NEW SOLUTION

Given the economics of what's at stake, researchers are reaching even further afield. Enter the Russian honeybee, of the same species as the "Italian" bee we depend on in the U.S., but a hybrid native to extreme southwestern Russia, in a chilly region called Pimorsky Krai, bordering China and North Korea.

There, this particular *Apis mellifera*, brought east by Ukrainian settlers in the dying days of Czarism during the 1890s, has coexisted with the varroa mite for more than 100 years.

Hoping they might understand this acquired resistance, researchers from the USDA Honey Bee Research Lab in Baton Rouge took a trip to find out for themselves in the 1990s.

They discovered that the Russians were indeed twice as resistant to varroa, as well as being highly resistant to yet another diminutive bug, tracheal mites, which are likewise harmful to Italian bees. In a remarkable example of the speed with which evolution can adapt some species to new environments, during this short window of time, the hearty Russian bees developed a 50-percent rate of resistance to varroa.

Even in those relatively sunny days before the deathly cloud of CCD eclipsed the American beekeeping industry, varroa mites, first detected in 1987 in an apiary in Wisconsin, were already taking a heavy toll.

In 1997, an increasingly desperate USDA Agricultural Research Service (ARS) sent agents to Russia's Far East to collect 100 queen bees from 16 dispersed beekeepers for transport to the agency's holding pen at the ARS Honeybee Quarantine Station on Grand Terre Island in the Gulf of Mexico south of New Orleans.

Lilia De Guzman is a research entomologist with the lab. She says, "In Russian honeybees, there is a suite of resistance mechanisms (brood and mite removal to name two) that acts as one to substantially suppress mite infestation."

I asked her about the remarkable speed with which the Russian bees developed resistance to varroa mites. De Guzman noted that "development of resistance can be observed in a comparatively short period of time because both bees and mites have short generation times; both are exerting selective pressures on each other."

Total freedom from varroa, even for the adaptive Russian bee, is, according to De Guzman, a doubtful expectation: "No, I don't think full immunity is achievable. It would be nice to think so, though, just not likely. I don't think 'immunity' is the right

An adult female varroa mite (top) feeds on a developing honeybee. Varroas can wipe out entire colonies.

A family of varroa mites (above) found at the bottom of a honeybee brood cell.

Honeybee larvae infected with American Foulbrood become a putrid mess.

word when you are talking about varroa mites; I prefer using resistance or tolerance."

So long as the Russian strain can keep varroa infestation to a manageable level, in other words, it's the best we can hope for ... and a far cry from the devastation varroa has heaped on the American beekeeping industry thus far.

The testing was thorough. Russian queens were introduced into Italian colonies that had been treated to reduce mite populations below detectable levels. Varroa mites were simultaneously being reared in strictly segregated colonies to provide a source of inoculum mites for the test, and purely Italian colonies were maintained as watchdogs for any potential threats the Russians might be bringing to North American bees.

The results were clear: non-resistant (purely Italian) colonies had 65 to 75 percent brood infestation, while the mixed Russian/Italian colonies had an average of 48.1 percent. Based on this study, 40 sturdy Russian queen bees were selected as breeders to lead the charge against varroa for America's struggling Italian bees.

FROM EAST TO WEST

Charles Walter runs Walter's Wholesome Goods out of Morgantown, West Virginia. He relates his experience with Russian bees, and the effect they've had on his honey business. A friend urged him to try Russians, and, while initially dubious, he gave them a go. The results were immediately gratifying, he says, with an "explosive growth" of his colonies and an upward spike in their overall health that clearly "outperformed the

OTHER DISEASES AFFECTING HONEYBEES

Thirty or so years ago, beekeepers could be relied upon to inspect their hives for problems, make a diagnosis, and take action. Today, it's a little more complicated with so many new diseases and problems. Many of these conditions exist due to improper management of the hive by the beekeeper, so do your epidemiology homework and build your understanding of common bee diseases and treatments.

American Foulbrood. One of the most significant diseases, caused by a spore-forming bacterium, AFB attacks older larvae and pupae (see photo above). Signs include perforated brood cappings and pupal cells that "rope out" and adhere to a stick when poked. Treatment involves burning infected hives and using antibiotics.

European Foulbrood. Caused by a different bacterium than AFB, this disease usually occurs due to stressful conditions in the hive: queenlessness, attacks by pests, and bad management by the beekeeper. Diagnosis can be performed only under a microscope, but perforated cappings are not present. Treatment includes requeening and antibiotics.

Chalkbrood. Caused by a fungus and related to stress, chalkbrood occurs in spring, but is sporadic and usually found in low levels in colonies. Symptoms include larvae appearing as pieces of chalk—white to green "mummies" found near the entrance. While there is no known treatment for chalkbrood, proper hive ventilation to avoid moisture is a preventive measure; requeening and comb replacement also help.

Tracheal Mites. The *Ascarapis woodi* takes up residence in the honeybee's breathing apparatus. The mites are not visible to the naked eye, and therefore diagnosis can be made only upon dissection. Symptoms include K-wings (wings that protrude out from the body, unable to fold correctly), bees unable to fly, and bees crawling around the hive entrance. Treatment includes menthol and grease patties in late summer and early fall.

Nosema. Caused by a spore-forming microsporidian parasite of the adult's digestive system, nosema results in the affected bee being unable to absorb nutrients. The parasite also may activate viruses. Symptoms are not readily apparent but include K-wings and dysentery. Treatment includes the antibiotic fumagillin, though this has risks and may be hard on the bees.

Varroa Mites. Varroa are permanent residents of the hive and are responsible for large-scale colony loss since 1987. Understanding the varroa problem is not an easy one, and much can be learned from books and websites. However, the most important thing to note is that the levels of varroa must be monitored closely and treated if numbers pass acceptable thresholds. Luckily, varroa can be seen with the naked eye, so there are several methods of monitoring their numbers. Treatments include hard pesticides, essential oils, and formic and oxalic acids.

— Karen K. Will

An abundance of pollen helps bees maintain the health of the hive.

Italians" he'd raised for years. He was pleased with the acceptance of the Russian queens by the Italian workers and drones; together they're now producing "gobs of honey."

Sometimes more traditional apiarists stubbornly stick to their traditional bees, Walter said, and this can cause problems such as "swarming," in which more than half of a colony, led by their imperious queen who has left behind eggs containing her royal successors, succumb to a building dissatisfaction with their surroundings and float away as one in a gyrating, humming cloud.

Once out of the hive, the secessionists gather thickly on a tree trunk, surrounding their leader, while the colony's ace foragers scout out a new home, swiftly scanning the surrounding area for a more suitable area rich in resources and distant from competitors. When a likely new locale is found, a scout will return to perform variations on the famous "waggle dance," one of the most complex forms of nonhuman communication, to persuade other scouts to follow her back to a potential hive site — the more excited the scout's dance, the better the locale's conditions.

Domesticated queens need abundant drawn combs in which to lay their eggs and ample space to expand the brood nest, or they'll go elsewhere. Aside from assiduous upkeep, the real solution to swarming, Walter says, is for people to accept the superiority of Russian bees and make them the dominant domestic bee in the U.S. They are especially excellent for the backyard beekeeper interested in honey production and working gentle bees.

The importation and dissemination of Russian bees, and their increasing acceptance among apiarists, offers a promising means of combating at least one major factor of CCD, and thus helping to ensure the continued cornucopia of farmland whose global importance will only grow along with the world's booming human population.

"More and more people are giving Russians a try," Walter says. "They were suspicious at first, but once they see the results, they're not going back. Russian bees are the best thing since sliced bread."

Slathered, of course, in delectable, homegrown Russian honey.

> (Modernized) agriculture practices almost completely dominate the U.S. farming industry, and these bees ... are absolutely critical to maintaining our current rates of crop production.

Healthy Bees 157

Saving the Honeybees

Businesses educate future beekeepers.

By Andrew Moore

Available pollen supplies are essential to a healthy thriving hive.

Most people would flee from a dark cloud of honeybees buzzing around them. Scott Derrick relishes the frenetic buzz—at least when he's dressed in a full-body protective suit.

The Blythewood, South Carolina, man is a beekeeper and a businessman. Derrick spent 18 years creating flavors for Lance foods and fragrances for Yankee Candle and Bath & Body Works before trading his corporate job for more time at home with his family and his new hobby of beekeeping.

"My grandfathers kept honeybees when I was younger, and it always intrigued me. But I never got to do much with them because I was so young. And that memory always sat in the back of my mind. So I just started one day," Derrick says.

In 2004, Derrick started a honeybee removal service called Blythewood Bee Co. Since then, he's climbed into attics, up trees, and into other uncomfortable spaces to remove buzzing hives plaguing residents.

Around this time, Derrick also translated his olfactory abilities into products for beekeepers.

After three years of trial-and-error experiments, he had a eureka moment. Using a honeybee pheromone called nasonov, Derrick created a spray called Swarm Commander to attract honeybees to a designated area. It is now sold across the U.S. and internationally in Australia, New Zealand, and Sweden.

Derrick also began selling protective suits, smokers, hive frames, and his pheromone liquids through an online store. But as orders piled up, so did the complaints from his family that the house smelled like Swarm Commander. He had to expand.

Derrick opened a successful brick-and-mortar shop in Blythewood, making it the third beekeeping supply store to open in the Midlands. It has become the meeting place for the Blythewood Beekeepers Association, a group he started two years ago for the area's beekeepers.

Tom Dukes, a Lexington resident and novice beekeeper, says the shop offers a better alternative to mail-order products because "you need products fast when you need to attract a swarm or need to get rid of bees in the attic."

Derrick loves that he is able to help his clients. But it is his love for the honeybee that drives his work. "Honeybees are so important to the human race. Our diets would be so different without them because they pollinate our fruits and vegetables," he says.

SAVING THE HONEYBEE

About three-fourths of the world's food crops depend on pollination, according to a report released by the United Nations Intergovernmental Science-Policy Platform on Biodiversity and Ecosystem Services. And more than 40 percent of invertebrate pollinators—bees and butterflies—are "facing extinction."

Honeybees are not native to the Americas and were first brought to North America by English settlers in 1622. Although not native to the American landscape, wild colonies of bees spread quickly as white settlers moved out across the continent.

Since the 1940s, the number of managed honeybee colonies in the United States has declined from 5 million to 2.5 million because of various threats—invasive species, diseases, pesticides, and habitat destruction, according to the U.S. Department of Agriculture.

"Varroa mites are the biggest threat for honeybees," says Dr. Keith Delaplane, director of the University of Georgia's Honey Bee Program. "And we have environmental degradation occurring. Not just through coal mining, but also through urbanization and crop sterilization. We just seem to be reaching a tipping point."

The declining health of honeybee colonies was heightened by the arrival of new diseases and pests in the 1980s, according to the USDA. And in the 1990s, the varroa mite, which was introduced from eastern Asia, created more concern among the industry as it began to kill colonies.

In 2006, a more mysterious and alarming threat appeared as beekeepers across the United States reported colony losses of 30 to 90 percent. It was due to colony collapse disorder (CCD), a disease defined as a colony that has randomly died except for the queen and immature bees. Researchers have not yet found a specific cause.

South Carolina's managed honeybee colonies have a history of devastation and reform. In 2011, an average colony loss of 22.9 percent was reported, according to the Bee Informed Partnership's National Management Survey, which is part of a USDA-sponsored research program.

In 2012, an average colony loss of 41.4 percent was reported, making South Carolina 13th out of 50 states with the worst colony loss. And in 2013, the last year data was made available, an average colony loss of 29.5 percent was reported.

Pesticide use, varroa mites, and colony collapse disorder are major threats to South Carolina's honeybee colonies, says Tom Ballou, president of the Mid-State Beekeepers

> Danny Cannon, owner of Bee Trail Farm, Lexington, South Carolina, says the new store has made bee season "less stressful" for him because he can get supplies more quickly if he forgets something.

Scientists point to different factors when discussing the decline of the honeybee.

Association. He adds that pesticide use is the "biggest problem in South Carolina" and that it's "causing honeybees to starve."

Derrick blames the use of neonicotinoids, an insecticide used to control various pests. "Seeds are coated with these products and they're destroying our honeybees. Until the government stops being reactionary, change will be tough," Derrick says. "We need to ban neonicotinoids like Europe did."

In 2013, the European Union banned the use of three types of neonicotinoids after several studies linked the insecticide to honeybee colony collapse. Today, two-thirds of the world's crops are exposed to neonicotinoids, including 90 percent of corn and 60 percent of soybean acres.

A study conducted by the Environmental Protection Agency (EPA), and published in January 2017, found neonicotinoids didn't harm honeybees or their hives when used on corn, berries, and tobacco, but did cause harm when used on cotton plants and citrus trees.

Gus Lorenz, associate head of entomology at the University of Arkansas, says he and other researchers were disappointed by the EPA study. He says his research conducted in the mid-South shows that "neonicotinoids pose no threat to honeybees" because there is "very little" pesticide present when plants begin to bloom.

Jay Evans, research leader for the USDA's Bee Research Lab, says "diseases have had a bigger impact on honeybees just because there are so many (diseases) in different parts of the country. It doesn't mean that the pesticides don't have an impact ... I believe honeybees are sensitive to them (neonicotinoids) for sure. Now, I think the key work has to do with exposure rates and ingestion and whether or not they have relevant levels of insecticides."

Janet Knodel, extension entomologist at North Dakota State University, says neonicotinoids applied during bloom could be "deadly to honeybees" but that she is "on-the-fence" until she sees more data. She says "withdrawing insecticides right away without an alternative is not the right solution" because it leaves growers without protection against pests.

NEW REGULATIONS

There is one threat that South Carolina beekeepers didn't see coming: governmental regulation. West Columbia considered an ordinance last year that would require the city's beekeepers to hold a permit. It also sought to implement lot size regulations—7,500 square feet for one hive and 5,000 square feet for an additional hive. The city abandoned the ordinance after the Mid-State Beekeepers Association formed a grassroots response as a means of educating the city's planning committee.

Solutions have been organized on a statewide and national scale to solve the honeybee conundrum. Then-President Barack Obama established the first-ever federal pollinator strategy in June 2015. Because of this, the Agricultural Department announced $8 million in incentives to farmers in five states who designate parts of their land for honeybees. The Agricultural Department also provided $3 million to reseed Midwest pastures with alfalfa and clover, providing food for honeybees.

In South Carolina, Clemson University and the South Carolina Agriculture Department established an online program in 2014 that allows the state's beekeepers and farmers to compare notes on the locations of hives and areas designated for pesticide to avoid poisoning. The South Carolina Beekeepers Association holds yearly conferences that include input from a variety of researchers. Also, many of the state's local associations hold beekeeping courses.

EDUCATING THE PEOPLE

South Carolina businesses are addressing the issue through education.

Derrick started teaching beginner courses earlier this year to residents interested in beekeeping. "Honeybees are social insects and beekeepers are social people. So they're kind of a perfect match," he says. "And the number of interested residents who have come through the doors has been astounding. So I think businesses like mine can help bring back the honeybee."

There are several benefits that beekeeping can provide to humans and the environment, according to Utah State University's backyard beekeeping guide.

Beekeepers can collect up to $200 worth of honey from each hive. Those who eat the honey are provided health benefits such as anti-inflammatory, antiviral, and antioxidant effects. Also, keeping bees is good for the environment because it aids in the pollination of nearby fruits, vegetables, and plants.

Despite being an enthusiast, Derrick teaches his students to have less interaction with their honeybees—a more natural approach to beekeeping.

"They need to adapt to the threats. If we continue to treat them with chemicals and give them a crutch, they won't adapt. We're enabling them to die," Derrick says. "Some colonies will clean the mites off of each other. Why? Because we got out of the way."

ONE BEEHIVE AT A TIME

As flowers bloom across the Palmetto state and bees begin to buzz, Derrick is preparing to hold more classes and handle more shipments of supplies as he also worries about the store.

The company has already outgrown the 1,800-square-foot store with its expanding inventory, which includes honey, smokers, pheromone sprays, hive frames, hives, protective clothing, pest control, and live honeybee queens.

He's already begun to formulate his five-year plan.

"I want a 5,000-square-foot building added behind the shop where we can make our own woodenwares. And I want to purchase the property behind the shop to raise about 20 hives so that I can provide more bees to residents and get more honey," he says.

Derrick may also expand his focus to wild bees such as the orchard mason bee, a species that spends most of its time alone in its mud compacted nest.

"I know honeybees will survive because they've suffered through more than man," he says. "And more people are starting to understand why they should be helping them."

An observant and caring beekeeper is key to the survival of the bee.

A Primer for Rearing Queen Honeybees

The art of queen breeding is a valuable skill in any apiarist's arsenal.

By Jim Cameron and Jeanne Malmgren

The queen bee truly lives up to her royal reputation: An efficient, untiring yet graceful monarch that can ensure either the survival or the demise of her subjects, she is the key to a honeybee colony's operation.

Filling up to 1,500 cells a day (at the peak of the season) with fertilized ova that will hatch into worker bees, she's attended by a fanatically loyal following of nurses that fan her, clean her, and generally see to Her Highness' comfort as she goes about her sole and constant chore of laying eggs. The mystery and reverence surrounding this winged ruler have long played major roles in the lore of beekeeping—and rightly so.

Queens are, however, exceedingly delicate creatures and are subject to any number of mishaps. A ruler might have an accident on her initial mating flights, for instance, or she could be replaced by a new, younger queen (in a process called supersedure), or she might—for reasons often unknown—suddenly begin to lay useless drone brood.

A hive can't get along without a queen bee, though, and since one can be lost all too easily, it behooves a serious apiculturist to learn and practice queen-rearing methods before necessity drives him or her to replace a royal layer.

When these basic techniques are mastered, a beekeeper-turned-queen-breeder can also use that new knowledge to create totally new colonies, divide old hives, revive sickly ones, or even raise queens on a large scale for sale to other apiarists. The possibilities are abundant, so if you're already a practicing beekeeper (with any number of hives), you can use the methods described in this article to widen your range of abilities, delve deeper into the mysteries of queen production, and maybe even begin a side business to augment your income from honey sales.

DO IT YOURSELF, SIMPLY

All queen-rearing methods are centered on one basic fact of bee biology: Nurse bees in a hive can turn 1-day-old female (worker) larvae into queens by enlarging the young grubs' cells and feeding them a steady diet of hormone-rich royal jelly. Hence, every technique is based upon introducing tiny, still uncurled eggs (which stand up in their cells and look a bit like slivers) or hatched 1-day-old larvae (which recline and may be beginning to curl) to a group of queenless—and thus highly motivated—nurse bees.

The easiest way to raise queens, and the one most often used by hobbyist and backyard beekeepers, is the Sommerford system, named after the Texas apiarist who developed it at the beginning of the 20th century. This simple and natural technique allows the bees themselves to choose the brood cells in which they'll nourish and rear a new queen, ensuring production of a strong, healthy ruler that's especially adapted to a particular hive in a particular location—unlike a packaged queen, which may be unsuited to her new environment.

To raise one or several queens the Sommerford way, first select your best and busiest hive, then remove two frames of brood comb (sealed cells filled with eggs) and another frame that contains honey, the queen, and a number of adhering bees.

Next, install them all in an empty hive or a nucleus (a small, temporary hive, usually called a nuc—pronounced "nuke"—that's used just for this purpose), tucking the brood frames snugly in the middle racks. It's much better to do this during a good honey flow—that is, when many nectar-producing flowers are in bloom. If that isn't possible, provide the deprived parent hive with a feeder of sugar-and-water syrup or thinned honey. Then leave the hive alone for nine to 10 days. The deserted bees will soon become aware that their queen is gone and will start building queen cells in the remaining brood frames.

Later, when you open the hive to inspect the new peanut-shaped structures that contain the royal-jelly-fed pupae, destroy any cells that are uncapped, small, or appear to be defective (these will be dark and smooth-sided). Carefully extract the healthy cells, along with a bit of surrounding comb. Handle these pupal cocoons with great care, as excessive shaking or jarring can damage a developing queen.

These perfect cells can then be pressed together with bee-covered frames of worker brood and some empty drawn comb into empty hives or nucs to start new colonies; or the waxy "queen bundle" can be affixed somewhere along the top of a frame in an established hive. As each cell hatches (usually 16 days after the egg was laid), its young virgin queen will emerge, investigate her surroundings, and establish her

Queens can lay up to 2,000 eggs each day during the spring.

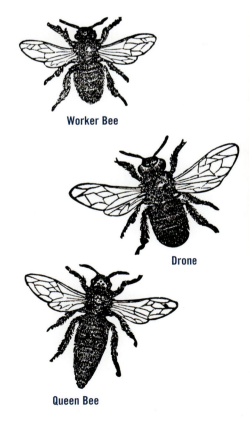

Worker Bee

Drone

Queen Bee

Healthy Bees **163**

sovereignty in the hive. Afterward, she'll take off on the first of several nuptial flights, during which she'll mate with a number of drones that will fertilize her for a two- to three-year life of egg production.

Honeybees feeding a queen larva in an uncapped queen cell.

VARIATIONS ON A THEME

An offshoot of the Sommerford system is the Miller method (named for Dr. C.C. Miller, a contemporary of Sommerford who was a physician before he took up beekeeping).

With this method, the breeder actively "encourages" her bees to produce viable queen cells in the following way: The beekeeper puts a frame of empty drawn comb in the middle of a nuc, along with a queen, lots of bees, and other frames of brood and honey (as previously described).

After a week—when the originally empty frame is full of eggs, larvae, and capped brood—the breeder uses a sharp knife to cut carefully along the bottom edge of the wax comb, directly beneath clusters of hatched larvae that are still in the cells. These larvae should be 18 to 24 hours old. (The distinction between egg age and larva age sometimes gets confused in beekeeping literature. An egg normally takes about three days to hatch. Most queen-rearing discussions refer to the larva's age. Hence, a 1-day-old grub was actually laid about four days earlier.)

If the larvae have curled all the way into the shape of the letter C, they're already too old. After

THE MAKING OF A QUEEN

I used to depend on two beehives to provide me with about 100 pounds of fresh honey each year, but upon inspecting my tiny apiary after an unusually severe Ohio winter, I discovered that the cold weather had entirely wiped out one of my colonies! I knew once spring came I could restock my empty hive with a mail-ordered bees-and-queen package, but I decided, instead, to use the remaining hive community to establish a new colony—complete with its own queen!

My procedure wasn't terribly complicated either. It should be well within the abilities of any backyard beekeeper, and the "queen making" skill can be an important one for any apiarist to master.

Before I could use the "trick," however, I wanted to make sure my remaining colony was at its peak strength. So I waited until May, when the bee population had "blossomed" along with the spring flowers. I then opened the hive, examined the insects' brood box and located the queen. I let her crawl between my thumb and forefinger, then gently grasped her thorax, or midsection—being careful not to clasp the abdomen, or tail section, where she makes her eggs—and clipped off a piece of one of her wings using cuticle scissors. (I knew I didn't need to worry about stings during this operation, because queen bees almost never attack.)

I then gently transferred the "grounded" insect to my empty hive, along with two frames containing ready-to-hatch brood cells, one frame laden with honey, and another containing pollen. The four racks provided food stores and, most importantly, a source of soon-to-emerge young workers (known as nurse bees) that would tend to all the queen's needs.

Once the colony-starting elements were in place, I closed up my "reborn" hive and blocked off most of its entryway so the temporarily shorthanded residents could defend their supplies from any invading "robber" bees. (I removed the entrance reducer two weeks later.)

So far, so good. But how, you may wonder, did the strong hive find itself a new queen? The answer is simple: The bees made themselves one.

the beekeeper places the trimmed frame in a queenless hive, the resident bees will automatically draw out beautiful queen cells along the bottom edge, and the infants within will be nursed into queen pupae that can be removed after 10 days in order to start new colonies or to requeen struggling ones.

Another simple variation on the queen-rearing theme is the double-brood-chamber method, which is particularly well-suited to the small-scale beekeeper who's short on equipment or space but wants to create a new queen and thereby increase her winged flocks. In this method, a normal brood nest (with queen, attendant bees, brood frames, and honey stores) is left intact on the bottom story of a hive. Over this are placed, in succession, the regular queen excluder, a honey super or two, another excluder, and the second queenless brood box.

If frames of honey and young unsealed brood are positioned in the top section, in due time the workers will raise several queen cells that can then be collected for requeening colonies or for storing in nucs.

Queen cells have an appearance similar to a peanut.

QUEENS FOR SALE

Compared with the amateur "backyard" methods we've described, rearing queens for the market requires considerably more skill, greater precision in timing, and to-the-minute record keeping. And because the biggest demand for queens usually comes in the spring, most commercial rearers live in warm climes, where they can get a jump on the season.

Techniques vary slightly from one apiarist to another, but breeding marketable queens—a process that can start as early as February and continue through November in some regions—always involves grafting (or transferring) specially selected larvae into manufactured wax cups that are kept in special "nursery" hives.

The basic system was first laid out in G.M. Doolittle's 1888 book, *Scientific Queen-Rearing*, in which the author recommended using a

---

Worker bees and queen bees come from the same type of eggs. A worker is a sexually undeveloped female, while the prolific queen—an insect that can lay up to 2,000 eggs a day during the height of the summer season—is a fully matured reproducer.

The "secret ingredient" that makes one female egg develop into a lowly laborer and another into the hive's highness is a bee-made food called royal jelly.

Scientists don't understand how this magic substance works, or even exactly what all it contains—oh, the unsolved marvels of apiculture—but they do know that queen bees are raised entirely on royal jelly, while workers-to-be are fed the mysterious food for only the first three days of their lives.

I had already spotted the tiny white, uncurled "specks" of 1- to 3-day-old larvae in the original hive, so I knew the colony contained some royal-jelly-fed youngsters that had the potential to become queens.

To provide a further stimulus, I created an artificial honey flow by filling three quart jars with a ¼-to-¾ sugar-and-water mix, poking small holes in the containers' lids, and inverting these feeders in the space left by the hive's four missing frames. I then reassembled the hive.

Within 10 days, the bees had created eight queen cells. I took out a frame containing one of the peanut-shaped holders, and another with two queen cells, and used these—along with some brood—to start two more small colonies.

That left me with five queen cells in the original hive. The first insect to hatch would destroy her unborn sisters. If more than one emerged simultaneously, the throne seekers would fight until only the strongest bee survived to become the new queen.

The addition of a frame containing 1- to 3-day-old larvae can help renew a hive that for any reason has lost its queen. In my case, using this technique to increase my apiary meant that I once again had two strong colonies, in addition to a pair of up-and-coming new hives. Best of all, that summer I was able to, once more, harvest a 100-pound honey crop!

— Merrill Schulz

Contracting for pollination with local farmers will take several hives, yet yield a nice profit.

A hive has room for only one queen.

whittled-down toothpick as the grafting tool.

A modern process used at the Blanchet Apiary in Riverview, Florida, illustrates the modernized, four-step process for raising good, market-quality Italian queens.

The breeders first choose a proven laying queen, one with a good record for the past year or two. Once the "mother" has been singled out from her sisters, her back is marked with a spot of bright enamel paint for easy identification (colored nail polish also can be used), and she's normally kept for only one year thereafter. The process of large-scale queen breeding then begins in the single-story "mother hive," a brood chamber containing considerable quantities of young bees, honey, and pollen. Confined to one brood frame by a screen excluder on either side, the queen stays in that narrow home the rest of her days, continuing to lay eggs on the only frame available to her.

Every day, Noel Blanchet removes a frame full of 1-day-old eggs and places it outside the excluder before transferring the queen to a new, empty frame. The racks are rotated in this way for two more days, until one of them contains new larvae ready for grafting.

The best environment for grafting is one that is close to the bee yard, and is well-lit and warm (bee larvae become chilled at temperatures below 75 degrees Fahrenheit). Small outbuildings, or even the back seats of closed cars, have served as grafting spaces for many queen breeders. Blanchet starts the process in January or February of each year by making the special cell cups that will be used to house the embryonic queens. (You can buy these tiny cups, but the Blanchets prefer to save expense by fabricating the cups themselves.)

Dipping a quarter-inch wooden dowel with a tapered end alternately into hot beeswax and cold water, Blanchet makes a series of miniature wax cones. He then affixes them approximately three-quarters of an inch apart, in a row of 12 or so, along a wooden bar made to fit inside a standard hive frame. When the bar is "primed" by brushing its surface with hot water, the cell cups stick to it readily.

The tiny manmade nests resemble the comb cells in which the eggs were first laid, and, if all goes well, the larvae grow into splendid, strong queens in them.

The actual grafting process is a precise function that should be learned from an expert. First, a drop of nourishing royal jelly — stolen from uncapped queen cells in another hive — is transferred, using a tiny spoon, into the bottom of each cup. Then the grafting needle is carefully slid under each almost-microscopic white embryo to lift the specimen from its compartment in the

Bees on the move protect their queen by enclosing her in a climate-controlled swarm.

comb frame to the new cell cup, where it's "floated" onto a royal-jelly bath. For this exacting operation, Blanchet uses a special tool with a curved end (such instruments are offered by most beekeeping supply catalogs).

When three bars full of cell cups have been grafted, they're slipped into slots inside a heavy frame, and the whole unit is placed in a one-story "starter hive" containing eager young nurse bees and plenty of pollen and honey stores, but no queen. After spending just one day in this hive, the cups are transformed by the workers into the characteristically peanut-shaped queen cells, which are then ready to be transferred to a finishing hive.

This final box features two brood chambers, with a laying queen in the bottom (among the usual frames of pollen, honey, and brood) and an empty nest on the top, separated by an excluder.

Once the queen cells—hanging neatly from their bars—are placed in this hive, the nurse bees instinctively nourish and tend them until they're completely capped—usually by the fourth day. Then the time must be watched closely, since it's essential to remove the mature pupae from their communal incubator before they hatch. Otherwise, the first queen to leave her cocoon will methodically rip open the other cells and kill her unborn sisters. Or, if two insects emerge at the same moment, they'll engage in combat until one pretender to the throne triumphs by stinging her adversary to death.

On the 10th day, then, the cell frame is removed and the unhatched cocoons are carefully detached so that each can be placed in an upright position in a nuc, where the virgin queen can be born in peace.

Each nuc, which has a tiny entrance to discourage robbing, contains three small frames of brood, one feeder offering a supply of sugar syrup to the fledgling colony, and plenty of healthy bees.

The queen cell is affixed somewhere along the top of the frames and opens soon after. New, mated queens can be left in their nucs until ready for shipping or direct sale,

Workers attend to a queen bee's every need and look after her brood.

A queen bee lays her eggs while in the care of a bevy of worker bees.

and should be watched closely to determine whether their laying patterns are satisfactory. When a nuc's queen is removed, the minihive must remain queenless for a day before the next pupal cell is introduced, and then the whole cycle begins again.

PLUGGING ... A GOOD CAUSE

For the large-scale breeder of queens, grafting is the method of choice: It's not too expensive, it's time-tested, and, when done correctly, it boasts a success rate of 80 percent to 85 percent. But it's not particularly appropriate for a small-scale beekeeper who'd like to raise a couple of new queens each season for replacement or expansion purposes. For such a breeder, a variation of grafting — called plugging — may be the best idea. This innovation — the brainchild of Vern Davis, a Florida beekeeper — is an almost foolproof way to raise good queens in one's own backyard. It calls for a minimum of equipment and virtually no advanced skills.

The beauty of Davis' easy-to-practice method is that the breeder need not invest in nucs, own specialized tools, or make cell cups; nor does a "plugger" have to master the exacting skill of grafting.

This process begins with the selection of a mother queen from those available in the breeder's apiary. Davis advises choosing a bee that's not only a good layer but one whose hive has never swarmed, whose subjects are uniformly marked and gentle, and whose drones are not solid black (a characteristic that tends to indicate a wild heritage).

For this last requirement, it's wise to examine the young, still fuzzy-haired drones that have not yet begun to fly, since older black drones may have flown in from other hives.

While the breeder queen goes about her normal business of laying eggs, Davis puts a stock of eager young bees in the homemade hive that will incubate the queen cells. This special five-frame hive, which Davis designed and built (he assembles all his own bee houses), has a removable quarter-inch hardware-screen bottom that permits maximum ventilation and two holes that accommodate inverted feeder jars in the lid. The cover also contains two slots that can accept the frames filled with plugged queen cells.

The remaining three compartments contain frames of honey and pollen to keep the young colony well fed. To populate the hive, Davis either shakes bees into it through a large funnel fitted into one of the feeder holes, or sets the box temporarily over a well-stocked brood chamber before smoking the bees and hammering lightly on the side of the nursery box, which quickly convinces the young "nursemaids" to move up into the queen hatchery.

For the actual plugging procedure, Davis first heats up a pot of beeswax on the portable electric unit in his workhouse and uses that warm adhesive to "prime" his cell bars. The wax must, of course, be completely melted, but it can't be too hot or it will asphyxiate the larvae when they're attached to the bar. With the cell bars standing ready, Davis puts a pot of water on to boil and goes out to fetch a frame of uncapped brood (less than 72 hours old) from the original breeder hive.

Davis' plugging tool is nothing more than a length of half-inch copper tubing that's about 5 or 6 inches long and has an end that's been tapered, filed, and sanded with wet-dry sandpaper so that it cuts wax comb easily.

After heating that sharpened tip a minute or two in the boiling water, he places the tube over the opening of a comb cell containing a young larva and, with a swift twisting and lifting motion, pulls the cell and supporting comb—along with its rich royal jelly and royal occupant—into the end of the tube. Then he blows sharply through the tube to dislodge the bundle into his hand so he can deposit it carefully on the cell bar, where it will adhere to the warm wax. (Davis also suggests that if you're plugging several bars of cells, you ought to keep a moist towel draped over the brood frame to prevent dehydration of the delicate young larvae.)

And that's all there is to it: Without bothering with special lights, needles, or tiny wax cups, he has the future queen safely in place with her necessary ration of royal jelly and a foundation of comb that the bees can use to build a queen cell around the larvae.

After filling three cell bars with larvae, Davis fits them into a frame and returns it to the nursery hive, where the bees cap and tend the royal cells for 24 to 30 hours. Late the next day, he transfers the cell frame into a special finisher hive he designed to ease strain on his back. This split-level arrangement features a bottom story of two brood boxes separated by a queen excluder.

While the queen is confined to the rear portion, which has half-inch ventilation ports/drone escapes on two sides, the front half serves as an area for honey storage and an entranceway for the bees.

On top of the front section are stacked two or three honey supers. In the uppermost story of this "honeybee high-rise," the frame of newly plugged queen cells is sandwiched between other frames of brood and honey, and a large gallon-jar feeder covered by an empty tin can tops off the entire structure.

On the 10th day, the cells must be separated very carefully before each is placed in a queenless colony or nuc, where the virgin will soon hatch. Since Davis' operation is larger than that of the average plugger, he often, at this point, has to "bank" his queens in a special frame containing row upon row of cages where the young monarchs will be confined until their eventual mating and sale.

A small-scale beekeeper, however, can simply transfer each homemade queen cell to a queenless, well-fed hive, and then let nature take its course.

Whatever system you choose for rearing queens, the royal results—and your increased appreciation for the miracle that is a queen bee—will be well worth the effort!

A hive smoker, used to calm bees, is a handy piece of equipment for a busy beekeeper.

A "good-laying" queen is a valuable commodity, as any apiarist will confirm.

Healthy Bees 169

Winterizing Your Bee Hives Naturally

There may be snow on the ground and ice on the trees, but your bees are a balmy 96 degrees inside their hive.

By James A. Zitting

Believe it or not, bees do not hibernate or sleep all winter. How can that be, you wonder? Their survival depends on the heat they generate as they cluster together in a ball inside the hive. The bees maintain a temperature of 81 degrees Fahrenheit, on average, in the middle of the cluster all winter long.

The process of warm air emanating from the cluster making contact with the cold, flat surface above them results in a build-up of moisture (or condensation), much like the water that forms on a cold glass and runs down to make a ring on your mother-in-law's antique end table. Standing water is never a good scenario, whether it's in a beehive or on an antique end table.

Our local bee clubs usually teach us to give the bees ventilation on top of the hive as well as the bottom entrance; this is to prevent humidity from building up on the ceiling of the hive only to drip into the cluster, freezing them. However, this extra ventilation is problematic because the air draft requires more energy from the clustered bees to maintain an optimal 95 degrees and 50-percent humidity. They'll have to eat more of their stored food (honey) than necessary.

In the wild, bees prefer to maintain a single opening at the bottom of the hive. A single opening allows them to fan fresh air or ventilate the hive as needed. Fanning also encourages excess moisture to be absorbed into the wood, for use in drier times. If there's a serious excess of moisture in the hive, the bees can direct it out through the opening.

LET NATURE TAKE ITS COURSE

So, realizing that the droplets of moisture building up on the cold, flat ceiling of the hive is a manmade problem, I avoid the situation by mimicking nature. My Homestead Hive (a top-bar-type hive) is made with thick wood to emulate a hollow log, and I let the bees seal up all the cracks as they like to do anyway.

BABY, IT'S COLD OUTSIDE

You'll often read about wrapping the hive in tar paper or straw for winter in extremely cold climates. This is a highly debated practice because the hive should never be entirely closed. The bees' cluster produces warmth and humidity, and that air must be allowed to escape; if it can't, the moist air will condense and drip onto the bees, harming them.

What you can do is set bales of hay or sheets of plywood around the hive in late fall to protect it from strong winds. Install ⅓-inch hardware cloth over the hive entrance to serve as a "mouse guard."

Use the winter downtime to repair your equipment and get your extraction area in good order for the busy season.

— Karen K. Will

Snow is a good insulator; don't worry about accumulations on the hives.

I try not to open the hives in the cool of fall. If I must, I'll press the hive parts back together to allow the propolis to reseal the hive.

Propolis. Propolis is a resin that the bees harvest from trees and plants in order to seal the cracks in the hive. It's nature's version of weather-stripping, and yes, it can be annoying. It's sticky and messy, requiring hives to be pried apart. In commercial bee breeding, they have done their best to eliminate the pesky propolis through selective breeding.

In nature, you'll find that the propolis is extremely important to the well-being of the bees. It has medicinal value to the bees as an antibacterial. So if we look to nature as a guide, we should be breeding bees that still have the inclination to make copious amounts of sticky, messy propolis. We need to let our bees breed with the local survivor genetics so that if they want to make messy propolis, they can. Joel Salatin says, "We need to let pigs be pigs." Pigs need to wallow in the mud. We need to let bees be bees and let them make sticky, messy propolis.

Feeding. For winter feeding of bees, we're taught by commercial beekeepers to feed our bees high fructose corn syrup or sugar. The economics are simple: It's cheaper to feed the bees subsidized substitutes. Winterizing the natural way, on the other hand, includes making sure they have enough honey to last the winter. If you're not sure how much to leave, then wait until spring to harvest. It's painful to wait, I know. The benefit is healthier bees.

Protection. In nature, the bees are usually up in a tree where mice and other

Healthy Bees **171**

Even in the snow, honeybees visit early-blooming daffodils to collect pollen and nectar.

varmints can't reach, so to compensate, we need to reduce the entrance of the hive to prevent mice from spending the winter inside the hive with the bees. Use a piece of wood to reduce the entrance of the hive to ⅜-inch high by about 3 or 4 inches long. (Entrance reducers are available to purchase, but anything that blocks the opening will work.) The mice cannot squeeze through the ⅜-inch slot. What this does is make it easier for the bees to defend the opening. In the early spring, before nectar flows, large colonies will rob the weaker ones if they cannot defend the entrances.

Warming. I know you'll watch them from the window of your warm house all winter and wonder how they're doing. "Should I warm up the hive for them?" "Maybe I should wrap them in a blanket?" It's OK to watch, but after they've been sealed into a woody cavity, we need to let them experience the winter as they have done for 10 million years. When we warm a hive, it makes the bees think spring is here, and they'll begin brood production. This will result in your bees eating through the winter stores much faster, and this often leads to starvation.

Snow. You'll wonder if you should clear the snow off the hive. Snow is actually a good insulator, so leave it be. If you get edgy and need something to do, I advocate taking some great winter photographs of the pristine snow on and around your hive.

Feeding Honeybees

Many commercial beekeepers feed sugar syrup to their charges. Two beekeepers offer reasons to discontinue the practice.

By Betty Taylor

Many beekeepers supplement a beehive's honey stores with sugar syrup as a way of helping the insects during lean nectar flows or if too much honey has been harvested. Two experienced beekeepers weigh in on the debate surrounding feeding refined sugar to honeybees.

DO NOT FEED THE BEES

Feeding established hives sugar water or high fructose corn syrup is almost never necessary — nor is feeding necessary when creating nucleus hives (nucs). I hope to convince you that feeding your bees is not only bad for the health of the bees and bad for honey production, but is bad for your bottom line! By learning about nectar flows, forage plants, and how the beekeeping season progresses in your area, you can increase your honey yields, your hive numbers, and the health of your bees.

Over the years, I've discovered that my bees know how to feed themselves and are healthier and more productive when I don't interfere with their nutrition by feeding them "candy" or processed pollen paddies. When fed sugar water and corn syrup, the bees get lazy and do not forage for more nutritious fare. They use the artificial feed to make and store honey, thus greatly decreasing the quality, taste, and nutritional composition of the honey. The bees build up quickly when artificially fed, but then are addicted to feeding. When the beekeeper quits feeding them and the bees must forage on their own, the momentum and any jump on the season are lost.

Some beekeepers think taking away all of the honey and then feeding back sugar syrup is more economical because the profit from the honey outweighs the cost of the syrup. I believe feeding ends up costing the beekeeper more in the health of the bees and in overall honey production. A healthy, strong, well-fed hive produces far more honey, and the honey is of better quality and taste.

Currently, normal yields for my area are 40 to 50 pounds of honey per hive. Each established hive in my apiaries consists of two deep brood boxes and one (what I call "eternal") shallow super. It's always there. The nectar flow has finished here, and after pulling honey for the last time a couple of weeks ago, I left these shallow supers filled with mostly uncapped honey. With this honey and what's in the deeps, the bees will make it through the dearth of summer until the fall bloom. By that time, these top supers will be mostly empty and the bees can refill them in the fall with the bloom from asters, goldenrod, and other fall flowers for their winter stores.

In addition to not feeding the hives, I took 11 three-frame nucs from the strongest hives this spring during the nectar flow. So how did all this "hurt" my honey harvest? I averaged 73 pounds per hive! Yes, I could have squeezed out that last super of honey and increased my yields even more, but I would have paid for such folly in next year's yields. In addition to my honey crop, the bees produced the new nuc hives.

Bees use pollen to create "bee bread" as another nutritious food.

Healthy Bees 173

NOT FEEDING NUCS

Of the 11 nucs created this spring, nine went on to make queens and are now thriving. The bees have mostly filled all the bottom deep hive bodies and, in most hives, are working to fill a second deep hive body.

I started the first six nucs just as the nectar flow was beginning and fed each nuc a partial frame of comb honey (frozen from last year) and then did not feed them again. Five of six were successful. I made the last five nucs a few weeks later at the height of the nectar flow and did not feed them at all. They had only the honey and pollen that were stored in the three frames taken from the original hives. I never fed these nucs. Four of five were successful.

FEEDING REFINED SUGAR TO HONEYBEES

In the beekeeping world, it is common to harvest honey in the fall. In natural beekeeping, we try to leave enough honey to sustain the bees to last until spring. However, many beekeepers feed sugar or high fructose corn syrup to bees.

The main reason beekeepers do this supplemental feeding is a matter of simple economics. The commercial beekeepers have a business to run, and when they do the math, it simply does not work from a financial standpoint to let the bees eat honey. They can make more money selling the honey and buying an artificial substitute. We need to let the bees eat their own honey.

For eons, honeybees have been gathering nectar, mixing it with their own special enzymes, and placing it in the wax cells. The bees create a draft through the hive by flapping their wings in unison to evaporate the moisture from the nectar until it thickens to approximately 18-percent moisture. During this process, the enzymes continue to work, and when the bees decide the honey is ripe, they cap it. Capping is simply when the bees cover the cell with wax to seal off their special winter food. Honey is an amazing food that will last indefinitely.

Another process takes place in the bee hive that few people know about. When the bees bring in pollen, they also add enzymes that pickle or ferment the pollen. This pickled pollen is called "bee bread." This bee bread is even more nutritious for the bees because they can assimilate it more easily. Research shows that more than 8,000 different microorganisms have been recorded living in the bee bread. It is a finely tuned and balanced world of little bugs that I liken to the microorganisms and flora living in our intestines. We simply could not live without them, and neither can the bees.

People will argue that sugar is sugar and it is the same thing

When I checked on these hives, I could not tell which hives I had fed with comb honey and which hives I had not fed until I looked back at my notes. They had all built up well.

I urge you to learn about the seasons in your area, learn when your nectar flows begin and end, learn what your bees forage on, and then adjust your timing for making nucs and for harvesting honey accordingly. You'll be benefiting yourself and your bees.

Honey and pollen are hive byproducts.

to the bees as honey. However, refined sugar and high fructose corn syrup (HFCS) are not honey. They have a different pH and they lack the needed enzymes.

When you change the pH in a bee hive, it affects the finely balanced world of the little bugs, and weakens the colony. When they track pesticides and fungicides into the hive with their little feet, the nutrition within the bee bread is affected.

Another thing that most people don't realize about honey is that when you feed bees HFCS, they stash it in the same cells that nectar is stored in, and, in fact, it gets mixed up with the honey. So when you buy honey from many suppliers, you are getting HFCS and a honey mixture—even if the label says "pure honey," the odds are it isn't.

HFCS is claimed to be toxic to honeybees. We are also learning it isn't good for humans either.

The bottom line is that the bees will continue to be fed artificial sugars as long it makes economic sense to do so. Due to the corn lobby convincing our lawmakers to subsidize corn crops, HFCS is cheap. Since I don't think the government will stop this practice any time soon, we the people must bite the bullet and pay the higher price for natural honey to natural beekeepers. Let's reward the beekeepers who do the right thing by buying their products, and the big players will catch on and change their ways.

Simply put, get to know your local beekeepers. Ask if they feed substitutes and if they place chemicals in their hives. In doing so, you are protecting the bees, the environment, and your own personal health.

—James A Zitting

6

COOKING WITH HONEY

"Sugar still isn't so easy to banish from our diets. Similar to other addictive substances, it's easier to wean ourselves gradually (start by cutting half the sugar in all recipes) rather than quitting cold turkey. Also, for bakers, sugar is second nature. What about when you want to whip up a batch of cupcakes, cookies, or a birthday cake? This is where honey comes into play. Honey is not only more healthful, it imparts a unique, earthy flavor to baked goods that can be altered based on the variety of honey you choose. It can replace sugar in almost any recipe if you follow a few rules."

— Karen K. Will, "Beehive Baking," Page 186

How to Make Mead

Create this delicious and refreshing wine with yeast, water, and honey.

By Amy Grisak

I keep bees at my home here in Montana, and each year we use some of the honey from our hives to make mead. Not many drinks can boast the long and illustrious history of mead—most likely the first known fermented beverage. When honey combines with water and yeast, a delightful reaction occurs.

For the home-brewer, mead is one of the easiest wines to make. Traditional mead is a little on the sweet side, although it mellows with age.

Making mead requires the same equipment as winemaking. Before beginning, make sure everything is scrupulously clean to ensure proper fermentation. Yeast is sensitive, and sanitizer remnants from a previous batch could inhibit growth or taint the flavor of your finished mead.

LET THE BREWING BEGIN

For a basic batch that will produce about 25 bottles of mead, you'll need 16 to 18 pounds of honey, 5 gallons of unchlorinated water, 5 grams of wine yeast, and 2½ teaspoons of yeast nutrient (optional) to aid the process. You'll also need some winemaking supplies. Check out Midwest Homebrew and Winemaking Supplies (www.midwestsupplies.com), or a local home-brewing store.

To begin, bring 2 gallons of water to a boil in a large, non-aluminum pot (stainless steel or enamel is the best to avoid affecting the taste). Reduce the heat and add the honey. Stir until it's completely dissolved, and simmer for 30 minutes. Skim off any scum that forms on top. This helps reduce the cloudiness in the finished mead.

Pour the honey and water mixture into the fermentation bucket, then add the rest of the water. This mixture of honey and water is called the "must."

Meanwhile, if you're using a packet of dry yeast, activate it in ½ cup of warm water for at least 10 minutes before adding it to the must. Allow the must to cool to below 80°F before adding the yeast and the yeast nutrient. Stir the must for at least 5 minutes to aerate the mixture.

Put a lid on the bucket and attach the airlock (a device that allows gases to escape without allowing air to enter the container). During fermentation, the sugar in the honey turns to alcohol and carbon dioxide. Without an airlock to release the pressure, you'll be surprised by a small explosion and a big mess.

Place the bucket in a spot where the temperature is between 55 and 70 degrees. Leave it undisturbed during this primary fermentation. You'll most likely notice it bubbling after two to three days. The primary fermentation will take two to four weeks. Reduced fermentation is evident by a quiet airlock; after it's still, transfer the mead into the carboy (a large glass or plastic container that can be sealed using an airlock).

When you pour the mead from the fermenting bucket into the carboy, be careful not to tip up or disturb the bucket in order to minimize pouring any particulates into the carboy. You'll probably have a little mead left in the bottom of the bucket, but it's best to toss it along with the sediment.

In the carboy, add enough unchlorinated water to bring the mead level up to the base of the neck to reduce the amount of oxygen in this second step.

BOTTLING THE MEAD

You can bottle your mead after it's been in the carboy two to four weeks. Siphon the mead into bottles, and cap them. Again, be careful to leave the sediment at the bottom to have a more refined drink.

You can use wine bottles with a cork. Seal them with wax and store them on their sides. Beer bottles are another option, particularly if you'd like to give samples away to uninitiated mead drinkers. Cap them and store them in a cool, dark area, such as a basement.

Mead develops its true flavor during its time in the bottles, so be patient. Open a bottle after six months to taste how it's progressing, but don't be disappointed. Mellowing a batch of mead for a year is typically the minimum, and as with many good wines, it gets better with age. 🐝

Pour the must (the honey-water mixture) into the fermentation bucket; to produce 25 bottles of mead, you'd need 16 to 18 pounds of honey. The basic ingredient is pure honey; the process begins by boiling water and honey, letting the honey dissolve, and skimming off any scum.

Attach the airlock to the fermentation bucket; this allows gases to escape.

A Homemade Wine Recipe

Use fruits or honey to create a wine from home without fancy equipment.

By Gary Miller

You can make wine out of almost any fruit. In fact, you can make it from just about anything that grows. I have used grapes, pears, peaches, plums, blackberries, strawberries, cherries, and — my favorite — honey.

Back in 1970, a reader asked if it's possible to make wine without expensive equipment. The short answer? Yes.

I started making wine with stuff I could scrounge while living in a one-room apartment. My simple directions follow. They're guaranteed to drive dedicated winemakers up a wall, but they do produce results.

You can make wine out of almost any fruit. In fact, you can make it from just about anything that grows.

HOMEMADE WINE

Get a gallon jug, preferably glass, but plastic will do. Clean it out good. Smell it. Wash the jug with soap (*not* detergent), rinse with baking soda in water, and finally rinse with clear water.

Put 1½ to 2 pints honey in the jug (the more honey, the stronger the wine), fill with warm water, and shake.

Add a pack or cake of yeast (the same stuff you use for bread) and leave the jug uncapped and sitting in a sink overnight. It will foam at the mouth and the whole thing gets pretty sticky at this point.

After the mess quiets down a bit, you're ready to put a top on it. *Not*, I say *not*, a solid top. What you have to do is come up with a device that will allow gas to escape without letting air in. Air is what turns wine mixtures into vinegar.

One way to do the job is to run a plastic or rubber hose from the otherwise sealed mouth of the jug, thread the free end through a hole in a cork, and let the hose hang in a glass or bowl of water. Or make a loop in the hose, pour in a little water, and trap the water in the loop to act as a seal.

Now put your jug of brew away for about two weeks. It's ready to bottle when the bubbles stop coming to the top.

Old wine bottles are best. Use corks (not too tight!) to seal the wine as they will allow small amounts of gas to escape. The wine is ready to drink just about any time.

Use the same process with fruits, except you'll have to extract the juice and, maybe, add some sugar. You'll also find that most natural fruit will start to ferment without the yeast and will be better that way.

Add Honey to Recipes

A variety of dishes lend themselves to substituting healthful honey for other sweeteners.

You've learned all about honeybees and queens, the dangers facing the bees and what to feed them, making beehives, and harvesting honey. Now take a moment to learn about the wonders of cooking with honey. A variety of recipes make use of the sweet treat; it's not just for toast or biscuits, though that is a great way to discover the deliciousness of local honey. Spread your wings in the kitchen, take flight, and turn these recipes into honeyed versions of old favorites.

Gleaned from our extensive archives, these recipes come to you from staff members and readers, from offices to farms, and from one cook's kitchen to your own. Enjoy them all!

HONEY-CURRIED CHICKEN

INGREDIENTS
- ¼ cup honey
- ¼ cup pineapple juice
- 2 tablespoons stone-ground mustard
- 2 tablespoons extra-virgin olive oil
- 2 tablespoons butter or margarine, melted
- 1 teaspoon curry powder
- 3 pounds chicken, cut into serving pieces
- Salt and pepper, to taste

Any light-colored honey works wonderfully well with this sauce, or try a full-bodied honey like buckwheat. Fruit honeys — such as blackberry or blueberry — are especially tasty. Make extra sauce and drizzle baked red potatoes and green beans. Yields 4 to 6 servings

1 Preheat oven to 350°F. Make sauce by combining honey, pineapple juice, mustard, olive oil, butter, and curry powder in small bowl. Set aside.

2 Place chicken in a 13-by-9-inch ovenproof pan. Season with salt and pepper. Pour sauce over chicken and bake, uncovered, for 1 hour and 15 minutes, or until meat is no longer pink. Baste occasionally with sauce as chicken bakes.

3 Remove chicken pieces from pan and arrange on serving dish. Pour remaining sauce from pan over chicken. Serve immediately.

— Kris Wetherbee

HONEY ROASTED PEANUTS

INGREDIENTS
- ¼ cup honey
- 2 tablespoons butter
- 1 teaspoon pure vanilla extract (optional)
- 1½ teaspoons kosher salt, divided
- 1 pound shelled raw peanuts, with or without skins
- 2 to 4 tablespoons granulated sugar

Learn how to make your own honey roasted peanuts with this easy recipe. If you've ever passed a street vendor hawking honey roasted peanuts, you know how good they smell — and now that smell can permeate every room of your house! Serve 'em hot! Yields 1 pound.

1 Grease baking dish and preheat oven to 350°F.

2 In medium saucepan, heat honey, butter, vanilla, and 1 teaspoon salt over medium-low heat, until melted. Stir in peanuts, and then pour mixture out into a single layer in the baking dish.

3 Roast peanuts for 15 to 25 minutes, or until golden, shaking the pan a few times to stir the nuts.

4 Remove from oven, stir to break up clumps, and let cool slightly. Sprinkle on remaining salt and sugar and toss to coat, then serve warm.

— Tabitha Alterman

SUNFLOWER HONEY OAT BRAN MUFFINS

INGREDIENTS
- 1½ cups oat bran
- ½ cup oat flour
- ½ cup whole wheat flour
- ½ cup unbleached flour
- 1½ teaspoons baking powder
- 1½ teaspoons baking soda
- ¼ teaspoon salt
- 2 large eggs
- 1 cup milk
- 2 tablespoons vegetable oil
- 2 tablespoons apple cider vinegar
- ⅓ cup honey
- 2 tablespoons molasses
- ½ cup rolled oats
- ½ cup sunflower seeds

TOPPING
- 1 tablespoon raw sugar
- 1 tablespoon brown sugar
- 1 tablespoon rolled oats
- 1 tablespoon sunflower seeds

Oats and honey make a perfect match! Try these healthful muffins for a snack or a quick breakfast on the go. Yields 12 muffins.

1 Stir together oat bran, flours, baking powder, baking soda, and salt.

2 In separate bowl, whisk eggs for about a minute. Whisk in milk, oil, and vinegar. Stir in honey and molasses. Add dry ingredients a little at a time.

3 Stir in rolled oats and sunflower seeds. Let batter sit at room temperature for at least 15 minutes.

4 Stir together raw sugar and brown sugar plus a few oats and sunflower seeds, and set aside.

5 Preheat oven to 375°F. Line muffin pan with paper cups, if desired.

6 Fill muffin cups ⅔ full. Sprinkle topping over each muffin. Bake 15 to 20 minutes. (A toothpick inserted in the center should come out clean.) Remove muffins from pan to cool.

— Tabitha Alterman

CORNMEAL PANCAKES WITH CINNAMON-HONEY BUTTER

BUTTER
- 2 sticks butter, at room temperature
- 2 tablespoons honey
- 1 teaspoon ground cinnamon
- Pinch of salt

PANCAKES
- 2 cups water
- 2 cups freshly ground cornmeal
- ½ to 1 cup whole milk
- 1½ teaspoons salt
- Tiny pinch stevia or pinch brown sugar
- ½ cup bacon grease, melted lard or butter, or vegetable oil

For the best pancakes, use the freshest whole-grain cornmeal, or grind your own. Soaking the cornmeal overnight will soften the whole grains. You can also make the cinnamon-honey butter ahead of time. Yields 6 to 8 servings.

1 Using hand mixer or stand mixer with paddle attachment, beat butter, honey, and cinnamon on low speed until fluffy, about 3 minutes. Refrigerate in lidded bowl for 1 hour before use if you intend to make into pancakes.

2 he night before making pancakes, bring water to a boil, then pour over cornmeal. Allow mixture to cool to room temperature, then cover, and refrigerate.

3 The next morning, preheat oven to 200°F, or the "warm" setting.

4 Stir milk, salt, and sweetener into cornmeal mixture, adding more or less milk as needed to make a thick but pourable batter. Stir in half the grease.

5 Heat skillet or griddle over medium-high heat. When pan is hot, coat with some of remaining grease. Pour out individual pancakes, about ¼ cup of batter each. Flip them when you see bubbles on top, after about 3 minutes. Cook until golden brown on both sides, about 5 minutes total.

6 Transfer pancakes to oven to stay warm. Repeat with remaining batter. Serve topped with cinnamon-honey butter.

— Tabitha Alterman

YOGURT-HONEY SORBET WITH MACERATED BLUEBERRIES AND JELLY OF MEAD

INGREDIENTS
- 4½ cups plain whole-milk yogurt, plus a little more for plating
- 1 cup plus 3½ teaspoons honey, divided
- 1½ cups whole milk
- 1 cup blueberries
- 1¼ cups mead
- 2 sheets gelatin

This tasty treat features two of nature's wonder foods: antioxidant-rich blueberries and nutrient-packed honey. Finding local honey and berries in most areas of the United States is a snap (try your local farmers market or check www.localharvest.org). Use antibiotic- and hormone-free milk and yogurt from local dairies, if possible. Yields 8 servings.

To make sorbet:

1 Bring yogurt, 1 cup honey, and milk to a simmer over low heat. Strain and chill mixture for a minimum of 2 hours (overnight is better).

2 Churn in ice-cream maker, freeze.

To make macerated blueberries:

3 Combine berries and 3½ teaspoons honey; reserve in refrigerator for about 30 minutes.

To make jelly of mead:

4 Place mead in small pan and bring to a simmer; carefully light mead to burn off alcohol.

5 Rehydrate gelatin sheets by soaking briefly in water. Add rehydrated gelatin to warm mead, strain, and chill for 3 to 5 hours.

To finish:

6 Chill 8 plates.

7 Take some yogurt and draw a pleasing pattern on the plates. Place 2 scoops of sorbet on each plate, then evenly divide berries and jelly of mead. Finish plates with some of the liquid extracted from berries.

— Jessica Kellner

HONEY SQUARES

INGREDIENTS
- 1 cup honey
- 1 cup peanut butter
- 1 cup carob powder
- 1 cup shelled sunflower seeds
- ½ cup raisins
- ½ cup chopped nuts
- ½ cup coconut
- ½ cup toasted sesame seeds

This recipe is a low-cost and delicious homemade food gift you can make during the holiday season. Wrap in aluminum foil or plastic wrap and tie with brightly colored yarn, or tuck the treats into decorated coffee cans, colorful boxes, or baskets. They're even appreciated when stacked up on festively ornamented paper plates. Use your imagination — the whole family's imagination! — when packaging your "kitchen goodie" presents. Yields about 2 pounds.

1 Butter 8-inch square pan; set aside.

2 Heat honey and peanut butter in saucepan. Stir until smooth and remove from heat, then stir in carob powder. Mix.

3 Add sunflower seeds, raisins, chopped nuts, coconut, and toasted sesame seeds. Press mixture into prepared pan. Chill overnight and cut into squares.

By the MOTHER EARTH NEWS Editors

HONEY GINGER ALE

INGREDIENTS
- 1 gallon water
- 1 cup honey
- 1 cup loosely packed hops flowers (optional)
- 2 lemons, juiced
- 2 pieces of ginger, thumb-sized
- ½ teaspoon ale or champagne yeast

Ginger adds a delicious and spicy kick to this soda, and the honey contributes a sweet taste that is richer than refined sugar. Yields 1 gallon.

1 Combine water, honey, and hops in stockpot. Add juice from lemons and bring to a boil.

2 Grate ginger and add to pot. Simmer for 30 minutes.

3 Allow mixture to cool, then add yeast.

4 Let soda stand at room temperature for 24 hours, then use a funnel and strainer to pour soda into bottles. Leave 1 to 2 inches of empty space at top of each bottle and attach bottle caps. Write the date on the bottles and store in warm, draft-free place, ideally at room temperature, for an additional 24 hours.

5 Then refrigerate. For best results, leave the bottles in the refrigerator an additional day or two before drinking.

— Megan E. Phelps

HONEY AND LEMON BALM TEA BISCUITS

INGREDIENTS
- 1 cup butter
- 1 cup honey
- 3 eggs
- 3 cups flour
- 3 teaspoons baking powder
- 1 tablespoon milk
- 2 teaspoons lemon flavoring or lemon juice
- 3 to 4 sprigs fresh lemon balm, chopped

These plump, moist biscuits are a wonderful complement to herbal tea and are only mildly sweet. They will keep for a long time because of the honey.

1 Thoroughly cream together butter and honey. **2** Add eggs and beat well. **3** Add dry ingredients, then milk, flavoring, and lemon balm. **4** Drop by spoonful on ungreased baking sheet, and bake 8 to 10 minutes at 375°F.

— Rhonda L. Brunea, Forestville, New York

Cooking With Honey

Beehive Baking

Put down the sugar bowl and switch to honey with these wholesome recipes.

By Karen K. Will

For some folks, giving up sugar is like giving up breathing—it's just not possible. As Americans, we begin developing our sweet tooth practically from infancy, from sweetened fruit juices to store-bought cookies. But of all the industrial foods out there—modern oils, white flour, artificial sweeteners, preservatives, etc.—sugar may be the most deleterious to our health.

Refined sugar depletes our bodies' B vitamins, which cannot be stored, so we depend totally on our daily diet to supply them. B vitamins are crucial to neurologic and metabolic function, and they are important for treating depression and protecting the body from cardiovascular diseases.

A diet high in refined sugars promotes bone loss and tooth decay—from the inside out—because it upsets the balance of calcium and phosphorus. Knowing all of that, sugar still isn't so easy to banish from our diets. Similar to other addictive substances, it's easier to wean ourselves gradually (start by cutting half the sugar in all recipes) rather than quitting cold turkey. Also, for bakers, sugar is second nature. What about when you want to whip up a batch of cupcakes, cookies, or a birthday cake? This is where honey comes into play.

Honey is not only more healthful, it imparts a unique, earthy flavor to baked goods that can be altered based on the variety of honey you choose. It can replace sugar in almost any recipe if you follow a few rules: Always reduce the oven temperature by 25 degrees; for every cup of honey used, reduce the amount of liquid in the recipe by ¼ cup; and when modifying or creating your own recipes, remember to add a pinch (up to ½ teaspoon) of baking soda to neutralize the acidity of honey (unless the recipe calls for sour cream or sour milk). On average, honey is 1 to 1½ times sweeter (on a dry-weight basis) than granulated sugar.

Since honey varies greatly in flavor and composition, you will experience differences in consistency, flavor, cooking time, and the amounts of other ingredients needed. When substituting all or most of the sugar in a recipe, use a mild-flavored honey (like clover) so it will not overpower other ingredients (unless of course, that's what you're going for).

When switching to honey in baked goods, you'll notice many differences throughout the process: The batter will be thinner; your baked goods will brown more quickly in the oven (this is normal—just watch carefully and make sure they don't reach the point of no return); and the finished products will be springy and retain freshness for a longer period of time.

SAVORY BACON MUFFINS

INGREDIENTS
- 1⅓ cups all-purpose flour
- ¾ cup buckwheat flour
- 1½ teaspoons baking powder
- ½ teaspoon baking soda
- ¼ teaspoon salt
- ¼ cup honey
- 2 eggs, beaten
- ½ cup buttermilk
- 2 tablespoons butter, melted
- ¾ cup sour cream
- ¼ cup minced onion
- ¼ cup thinly sliced green onions
- ½ cup cooked, crumbled bacon

Buckwheat, buttermilk and bacon make these special. Yields 12 muffins.

1 Preheat oven to 375°F. Grease 12-cup muffin pan; set aside.

2 In medium bowl, whisk together flours, baking powder, baking soda, and salt. Make well in center and set aside.

3 In separate bowl, combine honey, eggs, buttermilk, and butter. Stir in sour cream. Add to flour mixture all at once and stir. Fold in onions and bacon.

4 Divide batter evenly among cups in prepared muffin pan and bake for 20 minutes, or until toothpick inserted in center comes out clean. Cool for 5 minutes. Serve with butter and honey.

LIGHT WHEAT SANDWICH BREAD

INGREDIENTS
- 1 cup warm water (about 110°F)
- 2¼ teaspoons active dry yeast
- ¼ cup honey
- ½ teaspoon salt
- 2 tablespoons butter, melted
- 1 egg
- 2½ cups unbleached all-purpose flour
- 1 cup whole-wheat flour

Yields 1 loaf.

1 In large mixing bowl, combine warm water and yeast. Stir and let stand for about 5 minutes, or until frothy. Add honey, salt, butter, and egg, and stir well.

2 In separate bowl, whisk together flours. Add most of flour mixture to yeast mixture; stir until ball forms.

3 Turn out onto floured surface and knead for 5 minutes, gradually adding remaining flour until it's all incorporated. Place dough in oiled bowl (I use walnut oil), turning over once to coat. Cover with plastic wrap and let rise at room temperature for 2 hours.

4 Turn out dough on floured surface and knead for several minutes. Shape into log and place in greased (or nonstick) 9-by-5-inch loaf pan. Press dough evenly into pan, making sure it touches all sides. Cover with plastic wrap and allow to rise again at room temperature for 1 hour.

5 Preheat oven to 400°F.

6 Once dough has risen and peaks above the pan, bake for 20 minutes. Reduce heat to 350°F and bake for another 17 to 20 minutes, or until internal temperature reaches 195°F. Turn out onto wire rack to cool (at least 1 hour) before slicing. Store in plastic bag.

HONEY-LEMON SCONES

INGREDIENTS
- 2 cups all-purpose flour
- 1½ cups rolled oats
- 2 teaspoons baking powder
- ½ teaspoon baking soda
- ½ teaspoon salt
- ¼ cup butter
- ½ cup chopped pecans
- 3 tablespoons finely chopped fresh lemon verbena leaves
- 1 egg, beaten
- ¼ cup honey
- ½ cup plain nonfat yogurt
- 1 tablespoon fresh lemon juice
- 1 teaspoon vanilla
- Honey for topping scones

Yields 8 scones.

1. Preheat oven to 425°F.
2. In large bowl, combine flour, oats, baking powder, baking soda, and salt.
3. Cut in butter until mixture resembles coarse crumbs. Stir in pecans and lemon verbena leaves.
4. In small bowl, whisk together egg, honey, yogurt, lemon juice, and vanilla.
5. Make well in center of flour mixture.
6. Pour honey mixture in well, and mix to form soft dough.
7. Coat 12-inch cast-iron skillet with nonstick cooking spray or oil. With floured hands, pat dough into skillet.
8. Score top into 8 pie-shaped wedges. Bake for 15 minutes, or until lightly browned. Serve warm with honey drizzled over top.

— Kris Wetherbee

RHUBARB CAKE

INGREDIENTS
- 2 cups all-purpose flour
- 2½ teaspoons baking powder
- ½ teaspoon baking soda
- 1 teaspoon salt
- ⅓ cup honey
- 1 egg, beaten
- 1 cup sour cream
- 1 cup fresh sliced (¼ inch thick) rhubarb

TOPPING
- ¼ cup turbinado sugar
- ½ teaspoon cinnamon
- 2 tablespoons butter, softened

Yields 6 servings.

1. Preheat oven to 350°F. Butter 8-inch baking dish or casserole; set aside.
2. In large bowl, combine flour, baking powder, baking soda, and salt. Add honey, egg, and sour cream, and stir until just combined. Stir in rhubarb.
3. Pour batter into prepared dish.
4. In small bowl, mix together turbinado sugar, cinnamon, and butter. Sprinkle over batter in pan, filling in any bare spots with additional turbinado sugar.
5. Bake for 35 minutes, or until toothpick inserted in center comes out clean. Cool completely and serve with cream or ice cream.

APPLE QUICK BREAD

INGREDIENTS
- 3 cups all-purpose flour
- ½ teaspoon baking soda
- ½ teaspoon baking powder
- 1 teaspoon salt
- 1½ cups milk
- 1 cup honey
- 2 eggs
- 1 tablespoon vanilla
- 2 cups peeled and finely diced Granny Smith apples (or other tart apple)
- 1 cup finely chopped pecans

Yields 2 loaves.

1. Preheat oven to 350°F. Lightly grease two 9-by-5-inch loaf pans; set aside.
2. In medium bowl, combine flour, baking soda, baking powder, and salt. Set aside.
3. In large bowl, whisk together milk, honey, eggs, and vanilla. Fold in dry ingredients until just blended. Stir in apples and pecans.
4. Divide batter between prepared pans and bake for about 45 minutes, or until toothpick inserted in center comes out clean.
5. Cool in pans for 15 minutes, then turn out and cool completely on wire rack. Serve with butter and honey, if desired. Store in plastic bag.

PUMPKIN CUSTARD

INGREDIENTS
- 1 cup milk
- 1 package (8 ounces) light cream cheese, softened
- ½ cup brown sugar
- ¼ cup honey
- 2 eggs
- 1 cup pumpkin purée
- 1 teaspoon vanilla
- 1 teaspoon allspice
- 1 teaspoon cinnamon
- Whipped cream (optional)

Custard makes a tasty dessert. Be mindful that custard requires slow cooking and gentle heat to prevent curdling. Take special care in following the instructions for mixing in the eggs, as well. If the eggs are introduced to the heated mixture too abruptly, they will cook before being completely combined.

1. Preheat oven to 350°F. Grease 6 ramekins or custard cups; set aside.
2. In saucepan, combine first four ingredients. Cook slowly over low heat, stirring constantly, until honey dissolves; do not scald or curdle mixture.
3. In small glass bowl, beat eggs. Whisk a few ladlesful of heated mixture into eggs to temper the eggs before pouring egg mixture into saucepan. Remove saucepan from heat. Stir in pumpkin and spices.
4. Pour mixture into ramekins, filling about ¾ full. Place ramekins in larger baking dish with 1 inch water, and bake for 1 hour and 15 minutes, or until knife inserted in center comes out clean.
5. Serve warm or chilled, topped with sweetened whipped cream, if desired.

— Dawna Edwards and Marci O'Brien

PUMPKIN SPICE POUND CAKE

INGREDIENTS
- 1½ cups pumpkin purée
- ½ cup brown sugar
- ½ cup honey
- ⅔ cup oil
- 2 eggs
- 1 cup all-purpose flour
- ⅓ cup whole-wheat flour
- 1 teaspoon baking soda
- ¼ teaspoon salt
- 1 teaspoon cinnamon
- 1 teaspoon ground nutmeg
- ½ cup oats
- ⅓ cup finely chopped crystallized ginger
- ¼ cup chopped walnuts or pecans (optional)

Serve this spice cake warm with a serving of Pumpkin Custard (Page 189). Yields 12 to 16 servings.

1. Preheat oven to 350°F.
2. In mixing bowl, thoroughly blend together pumpkin, brown sugar, honey, oil, and eggs.
3. In separate bowl, sift together flours, baking soda, salt, cinnamon, and nutmeg. Stir in oats and ginger. Slowly add to pumpkin mixture, stirring until moistened. Fold in nuts.
4. Pour batter into greased loaf or bundt pan and bake for 45 to 55 minutes. Remove from pan. Cool slightly and serve warm, plain or with Pumpkin Custard.

— Dawna Edwards and Marci O'Brien

BODACIOUS BROWNIES

INGREDIENTS
- ⅓ cup butter
- 2 ounces unsweetened chocolate
- ¾ cup whole-wheat flour
- ¾ teaspoon baking powder
- ¼ teaspoon salt
- 2 eggs
- ¾ cup honey
- ½ cup unsweetened, shredded coconut
- ½ cup chopped pecans

Yields 9 brownies.

1. Preheat oven to 325°F. Butter 8-by-8-inch baking dish; set aside.
2. In saucepan, melt butter and chocolate together, or microwave until smooth.
3. In small bowl, whisk together flour, baking powder, and salt. Set aside.
4. In large bowl, beat eggs until frothy. Gradually beat in honey. Beat in small amount of chocolate mixture, then gradually beat in remaining chocolate mixture.
5. Add flour mixture and stir until just combined. Stir in coconut and pecans.
6. Pour batter into prepared dish and bake for 25 to 30 minutes, or until toothpick inserted in center comes out clean. Cool completely before cutting.

BEEHIVE COOKIES

INGREDIENTS

¾ cup sour cream
½ cup honey
2 eggs
1 teaspoon vanilla
1½ cups whole-wheat flour
1 cup finely chopped toasted pecans
¼ teaspoon salt

These cookies call for no oil, sugar, butter or white flour — cookie-recipe staples — so the baked cookie has a unique texture. However, they're delicious and a very respectable "healthy" sweet treat. Yields 3 dozen cookies.

1 Preheat oven to 350°F.

2 In large bowl, combine sour cream, honey, eggs, and vanilla. Mix in remaining ingredients.

3 Drop dough by tablespoonfuls onto parchment-lined baking sheets. Bake for 10 to 12 minutes, or until golden brown. Cool on wire racks.

FRUITY OATMEAL COOKIES

INGREDIENTS

1 cup raisins or dates
¼ cup orange or pineapple juice
1 cup honey
⅓ cup brown sugar
½ cup oil
½ cup peanut butter
2 eggs, beaten
1 teaspoon vanilla or orange flavoring
½ teaspoon salt
2½ cups all-purpose flour
1 teaspoon baking soda
½ teaspoon baking powder
2 cups finely chopped oatmeal

Yields about 60 cookies.

1 Preheat oven to 350°F. Lightly grease baking sheet; set aside.

2 In microwave-safe bowl, combine raisins and juice. Microwave for 30 seconds.

3 Cool, then run through food processor or chop fine.

4 In large bowl, combine honey, brown sugar, oil, peanut butter, eggs, raisin mixture, vanilla, and salt. Mix in flour, baking soda, and baking powder. Then mix in oatmeal. (To chop fine, use food processor.) Dough should be stiff; if it isn't, add a little additional flour.

5 Drop dough by walnut-size balls onto baking sheet lined with parchment paper. Press down slightly with fork. Bake for about 10 to 12 minutes. Remove from oven and flip over with spatula; let stand on hot baking sheet for a few minutes before serving.

— Mildred Hollibaugh

A Guide to Cooking With Honey

Learn tips for substituting honey for sugar, and discover recipes for syrup, jams, jellies, breads, puddings, and muffins.

By Margaret T. Hasse

Cooking with honey has added a lot of adventure to our kitchen experiences, which weren't too tame before. No, I'm not going to hit you with a long "honey is better for you" line (though I'm sure it is). My enthusiasm for this and other all-natural foods is more from the taste standpoint. Natural food deserves natural sweetening, and cooking with honey is fun.

Using fresh local honey will take your cooking up a notch.

I've experimented quite a bit and learned quite a bit since we made the change from sugar. First I read what *The Joy of Cooking* had to say, since *The Joy* is usually a good place to start researching a food preparation problem. Then I asked friends. Then I started trying.

The Honey Trip began when Husband John visited our friendly neighborhood beekeeper to get supplies for my Christmas baking, and came back with a five-pound tin plus a honeycomb (a gift). (Tip No. 1: Whenever possible, buy direct from a nearby source. If you use honey for all or most of your sweetening, you'll need a lot, and this way you'll be able to purchase in bulk and get the best possible price. You'll also be sure that the product meets your standards: unheated, bees fed no sugar or drugs, etc. And quite likely you'll get to know someone — a beekeeper — who can teach you things you didn't know about bees or honey or whatever.)

All the first recipes I prepared with honey tasted so good, and our beekeeper's

> Whenever possible, buy direct from a nearby source. ... You'll also be sure that the product meets your standards.

Cooking With Honey

HONEY SYRUP

This recipe is easy to make and sweetens cold beverages naturally with the taste of honey. Using honey to flavor cold beverages (iced tea, fruit drinks, etc.) caused a minor problem for us: The golden liquid, introduced into a chilled drink, immediately stiffens. We found that we could overcome this difficulty by mixing 1 part water—room temperature or a little warmer—with 3 parts sweetening. Now a bottle of "honey syrup" appears on our table for use with cold foods, or in place of other syrups for pancakes, ice cream, etc. One drawback: Our mixture doesn't keep well and will start to ferment in about a week if unrefrigerated. Which, of course, leads to a homemade Honey Wine Recipe (next page).

prices were so reasonable (only a little more than white sugar per "sweetening unit"), that our use of his wares sort of snowballed—and so did our education.

HONEY IS DIFFERENT TO COOK WITH

First of all, I learned to slow down—because naturally sweetened baked goods brown faster (a difference I like). To keep my modified breads and muffins from over browning before they've cooked through, I bake them a little longer at a lower temperature. When I'm converting a new sugar recipe to honey for the first time, I automatically knock 25 degrees Fahrenheit off the oven setting.

Of course, the same consideration applies to other cooking methods as well as to baking. All dishes made with honey seem to stick a little sooner or burn a little faster. I stir more often than I used to and am forever turning down the flame.

Another point to remember is that honey adds liquid to a recipe: about 3 tablespoons of extra fluid per cup of sweetening or ¼ cup per pound. Even when you allow for that fact, your baked goods will tend to be moister than those made with sugar, and the longer, slower baking that prevents burning also helps keep the texture moist rather than wet.

Finally, honey is slightly acidic so I add a little soda (usually ⅛ to ¼ teaspoonful per cup of sweetening) to most batters and doughs. Not to yeast breads, though, because the leavening thrives in the mildly acidic environment.

SUBSTITUTING HONEY FOR SUGAR

Honey is a natural food, not a standardized, "purified" product. Accordingly, there's some variation in its sugar content and in the proportions of the sugars present. Tupelo honey, for instance, has more levulose and less dextrose than other types and can be identified by chemical examination for those substances. Also, honey's flavor varies depending upon a number of factors such as weather and what flowers the bees have visited.

These "problems" of flavor and lack of standardization make honey less predictable than sugar and probably cause most of the difficulties people experience when they look for the ratio to use in substituting one for the other.

Well, I haven't found the ratio either. There is no one proportion that will always "work," that is always produce exactly the same effect. This lack of an exact, reliable equivalent hasn't bothered me much because I like to consider cooking more as art than science, and the variability of honey is part of what makes each batch an individual achievement.

I have found, however, that light honey is easier to substitute than dark because it's more predictable in flavor and less likely to overwhelm other tastes. (The dark varieties, on the other hand, have a robust quality

that's often a welcome change.) I'm told that the bees' output is "safer" — taste wise — to use if it's aged at least a year, but I can't speak from experience.

At any rate, the sugar in a recipe can generally be replaced with an equal weight of light honey — a rule that works out to about ⅔ of a cup of liquid sweetening to 1 of dry. And, of course, you must remember to deduct about 3 tablespoons of other liquid for each cup of honey you use.

SUGAR-FREE JAMS AND JELLIES

You can make your own spreadable treats from natural honey.

We put up a lot of jams and jellies with honey and one of the first things we learned — the hard way — is that small batches are easier to handle and really do make for better quality. The job goes faster that way, too. Honest.

We made peach-sumac jam with peaches from the fruit market trash bin and sumac extract from roadside staghorn sumac (*Rhus typhina*). Our kitchen also turned out elderberry-sumac jelly from a friend's elderberries and more of the same "sumac extract"; grape jelly from sour wild grapes that grew around the neighborhood, some in town tennis courts; grape jam from other wild pickings — sweet this time — which we gathered on an island in Lake Pymatuning; and spiced grape jam from more of the Pymatuning grapes plus

HONEY WINE

Create your own delicious sweet wine from natural honey.

Honey makes great wine, also known as mead. We recommend using a little less honey than Gary suggests (on Page 180): 1 to 1 ½ pints per gallon jug. Also, we sometimes add about 2 cups fruit juice (we're partial to currant) to the basic mead recipe for a light fruit drink.

When using honey in jams or jellies, work with small batches; rice pudding with honey is a comforting stand-by.

some incredibly sour crab apples foraged in the same area plus spices to taste. For all these concoctions we used essentially the same recipe.

Prepare and measure the fruit or juice. We make batches about the size recommended by the Sure-Jell people (see the direction sheet inside the package) and have had good results with a pound-for-pound substitution of honey for the sugar the instructions call for. Then use the amount of juice specified per lot, less ¼ cup liquid for each pound of honey. With really strong wild fruit, you may want more sweetening, in which case you should use proportionately less fluid. You needn't be exact, though; the process isn't all that scientific: For one thing, you don't know the natural pectin content of the juice.

Mix the honey, fruit, and pectin in a deep pan. (The jelly mixture will bubble up to about double its original volume, so be forewarned.) Bring these ingredients to a full rolling boil and boil them hard until the combination passes the "jelly test," usually 15 minutes or so.

To be honest, that "jelly test" is a sore point with us. We have trouble with the old "sheets off a spoon" version, so we devised our own: Drip a few drops of "jelly to be" onto a cold saucer. If it sets to the proper consistency promptly (in one minute or so away from the steamy heat), the mixture is ready. This indicator works well for us and seems to agree both with the spoon business (at which my mother is proficient) and the verdict of a jelly thermometer.

When the stuff passes whatever test you use, ladle it into hot sterilized jars and seal them. (Be sure those containers are hot. It's heartbreaking, not to mention embarrassing, to have a glass shatter in your hand just when you're pouring it full of your beautiful creation.) If you're fussy about looks, you can skim the liquid before jarring it.

RICE PUDDING WITH HONEY

For a wonderful and comforting dessert, try combining rice and natural honey.

John never liked rice much until we started using the brown kind, and he never liked it at all for dessert until the day inspiration hit him: He'd make good old rice pudding, he thought, but with a few minor substitutions.

To prepare John's version, use brown rice instead of white (he usually starts with about 2 cups cooked grain). Then add about 1½ cups or so of milk, right in the pan in which the rice was simmered.

Substitute about ½ cup dates — more if you have them and want a sweeter, fruitier dish — for the usual raisins.

HONEY WHEAT MUFFINS

SIFT TOGETHER
2 cups whole-wheat flour
2 teaspoons double-acting baking powder
1 teaspoon soda

BEAT
1 egg (large)

ADD
3 to 4 tablespoons honey
1 cup buttermilk
¼ to ⅓ cup oil (I like sesame seed oil)

For this weekend's brunch or your next family gathering, a batch of these muffins will make you the most popular cook in the room.

I've always been told that raised goods baked with honey and whole grains are heavy. Not at all! For proof, here's the recipe for our favorite muffin — yes, I know I said "muffin," but we don't have muffin tins right now, we're trucking around the country in a van and there just isn't room — which I bake in a well-greased 10-inch cast-iron skillet. I've developed this dish since we started living on the road and don't know just how it would turn out in conventional pans.

1 Preheat the oven to about 375°F. Sift the dry ingredients (list at left).

2 Mix the wet ingredients together and add them to the flour combination all at once, stirring just enough to moisten the batter.

3 Pour the dough into a greased skillet and bake it until a toothpick inserted into the center comes out clean — about 30 minutes. Eat the muffins hot with butter or honey or whatever.

My invention is also excellent when you add ½ cup or so raisins and about ½ teaspoon cinnamon to the dry ingredients before mixing, or with some sesame or sunflower seeds thrown in. Other dried fruits and nuts are good additions, too, and I sometimes substitute ¼ to ½ cup wheat germ for an equal amount of the flour.

DATE BREAD WITH HONEY

SIFT TOGETHER

- 3 cups whole-wheat flour (If you get a lot of bran when you sift, add it back to the sifted flour.)
- 1 cup soybean flour (If you don't care for the taste, use less and add more whole-wheat flour and dry milk.)
- ½ cup nonfat dry milk (optional, it's been left out a few times)
- 2 teaspoons soda
- 1 teaspoon salt
- 1 teaspoon baking powder (double acting)
- ⅔ cup wheat germ (or chopped nuts or a combination of both)

For an out-of-this-world honey-sweetened bread, add lots of dates. John, our household date specialist, developed a good bread recipe that uses the fruit. This bread may be eaten hot or cold, and it keeps well when given a chance.

We especially like it sliced and spread with a mixture of cream cheese and honey.

1 In 2 cups water, heat 3 cups pitted and cut-up dates.

2 Add ⅔ cup honey, ⅓ cup oil (John likes sunflower oil, but any good, fairly light-flavored vegetable oil is fine), and 2 eggs. Beat the mixture well—we favor a wooden spoon.

3 Sift the dry ingredients (list at left), then add them to the wet and stir well.

4 Grease two 5-by-9-inch loaf pans, line bottoms with waxed paper and grease the paper. Turn the bread into the containers and bake it at 325°F (300°F in glass) until a toothpick inserted into the loaves comes out clean. Continue the baking another 5 minutes and turn the finished product out onto racks to cool (remove the wax paper right away).

Replace the sugar with honey—about ¼ cup (less if you don't want the dessert very sweet, or if you used a lot of dates; more if the reverse is true). Add a splash of vanilla for good luck and stir well. Cook the mixture over a low flame for about 1 hour and give it more milk if it seems too dry or, as John says, "if it gets thirsty." I sometimes grate in just a little nutmeg, but John never does.

HONEY WHEAT BREAD

Using honey in wheat bread adds a hint of sweetness that makes your morning toast a total treat.

My first successful whole wheat bread was also the first batch I made with honey. Here's how:

For two rather small loaves, take 2 cups warm water (110° to 115°F), add 2 tablespoons honey and a little active dry yeast, or use cooler water and compressed yeast. After the leavening begins to "work," add a pinch or two salt, if desired, and 1 tablespoon oil (I'm partial to sesame seed oil) if you want to. Then add whole wheat-flour to make a dough that is just barely stiff enough to handle; turn it out onto a well-floured board, or what have you, and knead in more flour (just enough so the stuff doesn't stick anymore). Knead the mass for about 10 minutes, or until its texture feels right, or until you're just plain sick of kneading.

Divide the dough in half, make two balls, and place them on a greased cookie sheet or whatever flat pan you can find. Do not use a loaf pan, or you might not get the bread out. Grease the loaves well—I also grease my hands before I shape the rounds.

Put the bread into a cold oven and turn the heat on low (about 200°F) for 20 minutes or so. At the end of this time, pull the loaves out and cut slashes in the tops. Replace the flat sheet or pan in the oven, turn the heat up to about 300°F, and bake the loaves for about 1 hour.

This is a fairly heavy bread, close grained and hearty. We like it hot out of the oven with butter, honey or jam, cold for sandwiches, or toasted. One of the great things about the recipe is the way you can abuse it and still get fine results. I seldom measure anything these days, and often add soybean flour, dry milk powder, nutritional yeast, wheat germ, sunflower or sesame seeds, nuts, dry fruits, etc. More honey makes a sweeter loaf that is especially good toasted. I often eliminate the oil altogether except for what's needed to grease the dough and the pan. The last batch I made was left in the oven at 200°F for over an hour before anyone turned up the heat. It was delicious.

Our favorite spread for our favorite bread is made by mixing equal parts of any real peanut butter (prepared from just peanuts) and light honey. Peanut butter and honey and jelly sandwiches are very popular with us, too. 🐝

Adding a bit more honey to Honey Wheat Bread makes for a delicious piece of toast, any time of day!

> (Honey Wheat Bread) is a fairly heavy bread, close grained and hearty. We like it hot out of the oven with butter, honey or jam, cold for sandwiches, or toasted.

Cooking With Honey

7

HEALTH AND BEE-UTY

"Raw honey has widely been reported to prevent, cure, or alleviate symptoms of a wide variety of health problems affecting the mucous membranes of the body including stomach ulcers, mouth and throat ulcers that result from radiation treatment for cancers of the head and neck, and sinuses and sore throats due to colds or allergies. ... Studies in New Zealand have shown that raw Manuka honey (at left). a honey from the Manuka flower of the Tea Tree, was effective in killing the bacterium *Helicobacter pylori*, which is said to be the cause of most stomach ulcers. This is thought to be due to the antibacterial properties of the honey."
— Lindsay Williams, "Health Benefits of Honey," Page 204

Natural Treatments for Stings

To get fast relief, try one of these treatment options; you likely have what you need in the kitchen cupboard!

By Jami Cooley, R.N.

Bee stings can be deadly if a person is allergic to the venom. If you or a family member is allergic to bee stings and gets stung, remove the stinger and seek emergency medical attention right away. Do not rely on a natural bee sting treatment alone. Use an EpiPen (epinephrine auto-injector) if you have one.

Any person who is stung by a bee needs to be monitored for signs of anaphylaxis (life-threatening reaction). About 3 percent of people stung by bees quickly develop this condition. Signs and symptoms of anaphylaxis include itching/redness; hives/welts; shortness of breath; and feelings of faintness or dizziness.

If there is any concern that a person is developing anaphylaxis, call 9-1-1 right away. You can also take over-the-counter Benadryl, but this will not stop the anaphylaxis; it will only slow it. You must seek emergency medical attention immediately for a bee allergy.

NON-ALLERGIC OPTIONS

For a quick recovery from non-allergic bee stings, you have three things to do to begin the healing process:
- Extract the stinger.
- Clean the wound.
- Get pain relief.

The first and most important treatment for a bee sting is to remove the stinger as quickly as possible and by any means. The bee's hind end contains a sac that holds venom, and it may continue pumping more venom into the skin if not extracted. So, don't be slow about it—get the stinger out. You can use your fingernails, a pair of tweezers, or even a credit card to scrape out the stinger. But, be careful not to break the stinger and leave it buried in the skin.

Second, before using a home remedy, clean the wound with soap and cool water. This will help remove any bacteria that can cause infection.

8 NATURAL REMEDIES

After the stinger has been removed and the wound cleaned, you can use one of these remedies:

1 Ice. Apply ice for 20 minutes. Ice will numb the pain and slow blood flow to the area, which reduces swelling.

2 Honey. A degree of irony resides in this bee sting remedy since honey comes from bees, but honey is excellent for healing wounds. Apply a small dab of honey to the wound and cover with gauze or a small rag for 30 minutes to one hour. (If a person is allergic to bees or honey, do not use this remedy.)

3 Lavender essential oil. Add one or two drops of lavender essential oil to the wound. Lavender oil will help neutralize the venom immediately.

4 Crushed garlic. Crush one or two garlic cloves to release the juices and press it against the wound. Cover with a moist rag or towel and let it sit for 20 to 30 minutes.

5 Plantain. This is not the fruit! Plantain (*Plantago major*, broad leaf, and

Plantago lanceolata, long leaf) is a common weed you'll find around your home. It typically grows in places where the soil has been disturbed. It can also be found growing in the cracks of your sidewalks. Bee stings are never planned, so it may be a good idea to purchase the *Plantago major* plant from a local garden center and keep it at your home. Although it is a weed, it has lovely purple foliage and leaves that look like small green roses. To use plantain as a bee sting treatment, you need to release the juices from the leaves. This can be done by using a food processor or putting the leaves in a plastic bag and crushing them with a spoon. You can even chew it slightly to release the juices. Once you release the juice, press the juicy leaves against the sting and cover with a moist rag or towel for 30 minutes.

6 Baking soda and vinegar. Make a paste using baking soda, a dab of vinegar, and water, and apply it to the wound for 30 minutes. Baking soda and vinegar helps neutralize the acid found in bee stings.

7 Toothpaste. Like baking soda, toothpaste is a base that will help neutralize the acidic bee sting, thereby reducing pain and swelling. Apply the toothpaste to the wound for 20 to 30 minutes.

8 Meat tenderizer. Make a paste using meat tenderizer and water, and apply it to the wound for 20 minutes.

After achieving pain relief with one of these home remedies for bee stings, cleanse the skin by using a wet paper towel or rag and apply a small amount of an over-the-counter antibiotic cream or a natural first-aid remedy to help prevent infection.

A cold gel pack or an ice pack will help with the pain and swelling; use the juice of the plantain weed to help with healing of stings.

A paste of baking soda and vinegar will neutralize the sting's acid; a dab of honey helps that sting (if you're allergic to bee stings, don't use this remedy).

Health and Bee-uty

Health Benefits of Honey

Raw honey isn't just delicious—read on to learn some of the medicinal uses for the golden treat.

By Lindsay Williamson

Honey has many uses as a home remedy.

Before I talk about all of the wonderful benefits of honey, I want to make sure I'm specific about the kind of honey I'm advocating. To experience any real benefit, make sure, first and foremost, it's raw honey. Most of what you buy in a grocery store is heated to remove any "impurities" and to keep it from crystallizing, which is supposedly more attractive to consumers. Heating raw honey destroys enzymes and basically turns it into a simple sugar without many nutritional or medicinal perks.

Honey labeling is barely regulated by the U.S. Food and Drug Administration, and there is essentially no testing to verify what is on the label. When buying honey, seek out local beekeepers and ask them about their beekeeping practices. Ask them if their honey is raw, and how they deal with issues like varroa mites and small hive beetles. Some beekeepers use strong chemicals to fight these pests and traces of those chemicals will remain in the hive. Also, ask them if they ever feed their bees and, if so, do they feed high fructose corn syrup. Feeding bees is sometimes necessary, but should not be used as a substitute for nectar, nor anytime close to harvesting the honey. I would avoid any honey that is produced by bees that have been fed corn syrup of any sort at any time of the year.

Last but definitely not least, honey should never be given to an infant under 12 months old as this could cause rare but very serious infant botulism.

ULCERS AND DIGESTIVE PROBLEMS

Raw honey has widely been reported to prevent, cure, or alleviate symptoms of a wide variety of health problems affecting the mucous membranes of the body including stomach ulcers, mouth and throat ulcers that result from radiation treatment for cancers of the head and neck, and (read on) sinuses and sore throats due to colds or allergies. Bastyr Center for Natural Health reported a study finding that people receiving radiation therapy for cancers of the head and neck were significantly less likely to suffer from ulcers when given 4 teaspoons of honey 15 minutes prior to treatment, 15 minutes after treatment, and then again six hours later. These types of ulcers are the reason many people quit their radiation treatment as it can make eating difficult or impossible.

Studies in New Zealand have shown that raw Manuka honey, from the flower of the tea tree (*Leptospermum scoparium*), was effective in killing the bacterium *Helicobacter pylori*, which is said to be the cause of most stomach ulcers. This is thought to be due to the antibacterial properties of the honey.

WOUND AND BURN DRESSING

The pH of raw honey (between 3.2 and 4.5) along with antibacterial, antiseptic, and other properties make it a superior dressing for wounds and burns. Honey is excellent as a wound dressing as it cleans pus and dead tissue from infections, suppresses inflammation, and stimulates growth of new tissue. It also shortens healing time and minimizes scarring.

Manuka honey has recently enjoyed much praise as a cure for and even prevention of *Methicillin-resistant staphylococcus aureus* (MRSA). This honey by itself and also in combination with antibiotics has undeniably saved lives. That's pretty awesome.

ALLERGIES

People suffering from seasonal allergies may find relief in a daily dose of raw local honey. Because honey is made from the nectar of plants and trees likely causing your symptoms, some say it acts in a way that is similar to an allergy shot. The honey exposes you to miniscule amounts of pollen and propolis that over time may encourage your body to build a tolerance to the very plants and trees causing your symptoms.

For this purpose, make sure the honey is local and also ask the beekeeper about her filtering process. You'll benefit more from a honey that is strained but not super filtered. That way you can get all of the bits of pollen, propolis, and wax that you're after. When it comes to filtering, less is more!

COLDS, SORE THROATS AND BLOCKED SINUSES

Just about everyone knows that honey soothes a sore throat, but did you know that a study from Penn State Medical College in 2007 showed that honey is more effective in treating coughs and sore throats than the leading over-the-counter remedies containing dextromethorphan? Next time you're under the weather, try honey first and see how it treats you.

HANGOVERS

Hangovers are said to be caused by the production of acetaldehyde in the body. Honey replenishes sodium, potassium, and fructose, which aids in recovery. Fructose also acts as a sobering agent by speeding the oxidation of alcohol in the liver. So next time you've had one too many, take a tablespoon of honey.

I'm not writing about anything new here. Throughout ancient history you find that pretty much all cultures and religions documented the importance of honey in healing countless physical, mental, and spiritual ailments. So what better way to start your day than with a spoonful of this divine nectar?

Everyone knows honey is good for a sore throat; it also has myriad other health benefits and uses.

Health and Bee-uty

Bee Byproducts

Honey is but one of the items created by ever-industrious honeybees.

By Karen K. Will

Honey is as sensational as it is sweet, but if you thought that honey-making was the only work occupying bees inside that hive, think again. A mind-boggling array of insect activities is creating amazing stuff right under our noses. And our noses themselves even benefit, since some of these products can be used to treat allergies — as well as other common ailments.

According to the American Apitherapy Society, apitherapy (from the Latin *apis* for bee) is the medicinal use of products made by honeybees. Step into any health-food store, and you'll find a bee-dazzling selection of bee byproducts for sale from Medihoney to pollen to royal jelly. Not only are these products life-sustaining to bees, they can be helpful to humans as well. A word of caution, however: Not all claims are scientifically substantiated.

BEESWAX

Pure beeswax from *Apis mellifera* consists of hundreds (284 to be exact) of different compounds, including saturated and unsaturated monoesters, diesters, saturated and unsaturated hydrocarbons, free acids, and hydroxy polyesters.

Beeswax is made by young bees (2 to 3 weeks old) in the hive, after they feed the young brood with royal jelly and before the young bees leave the hive to forage. Worker bees engorged with honey secrete small, colorless wax platelets (scale-like shapes) from eight wax glands on the underside of their abdomens. These are then scraped off by other worker bees and chewed into pliable, opaque pieces by the action of saliva and enzymes. Once chewed, re-chewed, and attached to the comb, the pieces form the building blocks of the hive — the hexagonal cells of the honeycomb.

Wax, this crucial element of the hive, is used to build comb cells for the young, and, when mixed with propolis, seals cracks in the hive and protects the brood from infections. Beeswax is also used to build storage cells for honey and to cap the ripened cells.

Of all bee byproducts, wax has been, and remains, the most versatile and widely used material. Throughout history, beeswax has been more valuable than honey, and it was even considered legal tender in parts of Europe — people paid their taxes with it! Historically, beeswax was used by artisans to create models; priests used it to embalm bodies; it served as glue to hold together woodwork; it was used to waterproof walls in Roman times; it was a polish and a lubricant; it served as a writing tablet; it strengthened sewing thread; and it was used to preserve food, creating a moisture-proof casing (as in cheese).

Of course, beeswax makes the finest candles, burning clean and long, with little (if any) waxy residue left behind. For centuries, beeswax candles were the only light source used in Catholic churches; they believed beeswax to be a symbol of purity.

Beeswax, left, can be crafted into a variety of items, including holiday candles, below. Royal jelly, opposite page, and propolis, above, are other useful bee byproducts.

Today, beeswax has dozens of uses — from cosmetics, food, and pharmaceuticals to candles, modeling, and polishes. While no longer accepted as legal tender, beeswax is still a valuable product of the hive and an "all-natural," preferred ingredient for many consumers.

PROPOLIS

Bees gather resins from trees, flowers, and artificial sources to make a sticky substance called propolis. The makeup of propolis varies depending on the hive, the season, the area, and the available resin sources, but a "typical" northern temperate propolis is made up of about 50 percent resins and vegetable balsams, 30 percent waxes, 10 percent essential oils, and 5 percent pollen. The chemical composition varies as well, depending on the region's vegetation. Bees use this sticky substance, also known as "bee glue," to patch cracks in the hive and to provide a protective layer against bacteria and fungi. When propolis dries, it becomes hard and impervious.

Historically, beekeepers believed that bees used propolis to coat and seal off the colony from the elements, such as rain and cold wind. However, we now know that bees survive and do better with increased hive ventilation during the winter months.

Twentieth-century research indicates that propolis is used to reinforce the structure of the hive, to reduce vibration, to create a barrier against diseases and

Health and Bee-uty

> Pollen is the primary source of dietary protein for bees, and consuming it enables them to produce beeswax and royal jelly.

parasites entering the hive, to inhibit bacterial growth, or "quarantine" threats inside the hive.

You see, bees like to take out the trash by carrying waste out of and away from the hive. But if a small animal like a mouse makes its way into the hive and dies, it is too large for the bees to carry out. So, they use propolis to seal and mummify the carcass, rendering it harmless to the hive inhabitants.

Propolis has been used for centuries by many cultures for its antiseptic, antimicrobial, and detoxifying properties. In countries where antibiotics are not widely available, propolis is commonly used to heal a wide variety of wounds, including burns, ulcers, and inflammation (hence the nickname "Russian penicillin").

Propolis is said to prevent the growth of bacteria in cuts and burns when used as an antiseptic wash or salve. Similar to honey being used to alleviate allergies, propolis is used as an anti-histamine, and it's commonly taken as a remedy for sore throats.

Just like any other hive product, the properties of propolis vary with the sources used by each individual hive. Therefore, any potential medicinal properties of one propolis may not be present in another.

BEE POLLEN

Pollen, male-gamete-producing material, is formed in the anthers of flowering plants. The major components of pollen are proteins and amino acids, lipids, and sugars. Pollination involves transferring the pollen onto the stigma (the female component) of a flower by wind, water, bird, or insect, with bees being a reliable pollination vehicle for many plants.

Worker bees gather pollen while out foraging, bring it back to the comb, and store it. There they pack it into granules and add honey and nectar (or sugar and enzymes), turning it into "bee bread" through lactic acid fermentation. Pollen is the primary source of dietary protein for bees, and consuming it enables them to produce beeswax and royal jelly (more later).

The effects and benefits of consuming pollen are endless, according to some of the non-scientific literature on the subject. Many people report improvement of chronic problems; others claim bee pollen has cured colds, acne, male sterility, high blood pressure, ulcers, and nervous and endocrine disorders. However, the benefits reported are usually a result of personal experience rather than from scientific studies.

The only long-term, reliable measures on the medicinal effect of pollen are related to prostate problems and allergies. Clinical

Bee pollen has anti-inflammatory properties that may help allergy and hay-fever sufferers.

tests and observations in Western Europe have indicated bee pollen to be effective in treating prostate problems ranging from infections and swelling to cancer (Denis, 1966, and Ask-Upmark, 1967). Bee pollen is used therapeutically, through oral administration, to treat symptoms of hay fever and pollen sensitivity, due to its anti-inflammatory properties.

The major use of bee pollen today is as a food supplement, though its value is frequently overstated without data to back up claims. It's often touted as a "perfect food," though its low content or absence of fat-soluble vitamins make that a debatable claim. Consuming bee pollen is considered beneficial; just don't stake your life on the manufacturer's claims. When considering bee pollen as a food supplement or medicine, it's important to know that pollen from each bee colony is different — pollen from one part of the world is always different from that of another — and no one pollen type can contain all the beneficial attributes of "pollen" in general.

ROYAL JELLY

Royal jelly is a white, fluid, pastelike substance secreted from glands in the heads of worker bees, and fed to all bee larvae in the colony. It's composed of 67 percent

BEESWAX BALM

INGREDIENTS
- ½ ounce beeswax
- 1 teaspoon honey
- 4 ounces olive oil
- Mint extract, to taste (about 20 drops) (optional)

Get some non-medicinal experience handling products from the hive by making this simple, all-natural lip balm. Besides the beeswax, its ingredients are probably in your pantry now.

1 Weigh beeswax and measure remaining ingredients.

2 In small double boiler, add beeswax and melt. Once melted, add honey and oil, and stir for 1 to 2 minutes. Add extract and stir well. (Be aware that the honey will not fully mix with the oil because of the water content, but it's a good healing agent for the skin.)

3 Pour heated mixture into a small glass container or beaker, then distribute into lip balm tins or tubes.

NOTE: Adding more or less beeswax will make the lip balm harder or softer depending on your preference; the harder it is, the longer it stays on your lips. You can also add vitamin E oil or grapefruit seed oil as a preservative. In addition, you can mix oils, such as almond oil, sunflower seed oil, and others, depending on the availability and the product you wish to make. Other oils and butters alter the texture and healing properties of the final product.

—recipe by Andy Olenick

Royal jelly in powder form.

Honey is only one of the many items produced when honeybees gather nectar and pollen.

water, 12½ percent crude protein, 11 percent simple sugars, 5 percent fatty acids, and trace minerals, enzymes, and vitamin C.

Royal jelly is produced by nurse bees when they are 5 to 15 days old; they feed royal jelly to all bee larvae for the first three days of the larvae's existence, but after three days, only the female larvae designated to be queens are fed large quantities of royal jelly, which begins a series of molecular events—an epigenetic modification of DNA—resulting in ovary development.

The queen then matures into a large, fertile, and long-living bee, and she continues to be fed royal jelly exclusively throughout her life.

Royal jelly is harvested from queen cells at 4 days of age. It can only be collected from queen cells because an excess amount is deposited there to feed the queen (she literally "swims" in it), and worker larvae cells consume the royal jelly immediately.

Royal jelly has a pungent odor and a sour taste. It has antimicrobial and antibacterial qualities, similar to other hive products. Research has suggested that royal jelly may stimulate the growth of neuroglial cells, helping treat Parkinson's and Alzheimer's diseases. It's also gotten some traction for lowering cholesterol, suppressing the vascularization of tumors, fighting inflammatory diseases, and treating wounds.

Royal jelly, as intended for humans, is classified as a dietary supplement. The use of royal jelly is mainly linked to its reputation for being a stimulant and its inherent therapeutic value. However, the data required for classifying it as a medicine are not sufficient.

How to Render Beeswax for Use

To make your own candles and more, utilize the wax cappings from your hives' frames.

By Betty Taylor,
Persimmon Ridge
Honey Farm

Many beekeepers discard their wax cappings after honey harvest or simply forget about them until the wax moths have found and destroyed them. You may be one of them, thinking that rendering beeswax is too hard, is too expensive, or takes too much time. I am going to share a simple and inexpensive way to render beautiful, sweet-smelling cakes of beeswax from your cappings that does not require expensive solar or water-jacketed wax melters. You can find most of the necessary equipment in thrift shops or maybe your own garage or storage area.

The setup I've devised uses an old plastic cooler, a light fixture like the type used in a chicken coop with a 100-watt bulb, a foil pan to place in the bottom of the cooler, and some sort of rack to hold the light bulb up off the wax cappings in the foil pan. For the rack, I used the base of an old-fashioned food mill that I bought at a garage sale. Dedicate all your equipment to melting wax because you'll never get it clean again!

1 Put your wax cappings in the foil pan. The pan should be sized to cover most of the bottom of your cooler. Put the pan in the cooler, put the rack over the pan, put the light fixture over the rack, close the lid, and plug it in! If your lid does not close all the way, you can use a sheet of foil to keep the heat in. You will have to watch your melting setup to determine how long it takes your cappings to melt down. With my equipment, it takes 1½ to 2 hours. I have never had my wax catch fire this way, but I keep an eye on it and set a timer to remind me to check it every half hour. Remember beeswax melts at about 140 degrees.

2 After the wax has melted, use oven mitts to carefully lift out the foil pan and pour the melted wax through two or three layers of cheesecloth into a stainless steel container. When it cools, you can remove the cheesecloth along with the slumgum (residue from rendering wax) adhering to the cheesecloth. Save this as it makes an excellent outdoor fire starter. In the bottom of the stainless steel pan, the wax will have separated from any remaining honey, floated to the top, and hardened. Remove this wax cake and rinse off the honey. This honey will be discolored from the heating process and will have lost any nutritional value so it won't be worth saving.

3 Before making candles, you will need to melt and filter your chunk of wax one more time. You can melt it again in your cooler (in a new foil pan that you will save and use only for this cleaner wax), or you can use a non-stick slow cooker at the lowest setting. Once melted, again filter the wax through three layers of cheesecloth into a rubber mold or other container to make large blocks. Your wax is then ready to melt for making candles, or to use in salves or lip balm.

If you don't have a mold, you can filter it into waxed paper drinking cups. Place a wick in the center of the cup, and pour the melted wax around it. After it hardens, you just peel away the cup.

15 Household Uses for Honey

Help your family thrive with honey; the all-natural nectar is a healing powerhouse.

By Allison Martin

Honey is a wonderful tool for healing the body, both inside and out. It is moisturizing, exfoliating, antibacterial, and anti-inflammatory: all boons for our skin. Plus it soothes throats, relieves upset tummies, and even fights off hangovers. But keep in mind that not all honey can be trusted.

1 Wow Wash: For a moisturizing face wash, cleanse your face with honey. It's very simple. Wet your face, scoop out a little bit of honey, and smooth it over your face. It will spread easily. Massage into the skin, then rinse with cold water.

2 Pimple Power: Banish unsightly pimples by dabbing just a bit of honey on the blemish. The natural antibodies in honey should help heal the pimple without harsh acne medicine.

3 Hair Helper: Make a simple moisturizing hair mask with honey. Smooth honey over the ends of wet hair and let it soak for about 10 minutes. Then simply wash your hair as you normally would.

4 Hair Rinse: This highly diluted hair rinse technique can help smooth fly-aways and increase shine. Combine 1 teaspoon honey with 4 cups warm water and pour over hair. Do not rinse out.

5 Bathe in Honey: Add 1 tablespoon honey and 10 drops lavender essential oil to your bath. The honey will help moisturize your skin and the antispasmodic properties of lavender will help ease tense muscles.

6 Burn Balm: Thanks to its anti-inflammatory properties, honey can help heal burns. For a minor burn, apply a cold compress, immerse the burn in cold water, dry the area, apply honey, and cover with gauze, refreshing daily.

7 First Aid: A natural antibiotic, honey can help heal a variety of wounds. Dab honey on a clean wound before applying a bandage.

8 **Sore Throat Soother:** Help ease the pain of a sore throat by swallowing a tablespoon of honey.

9 **Steel Your Stomach:** Honey may help coat and comfort an upset stomach. Soothe a nervous tummy by adding honey to lemon and ginger tea.

10 **Workout Booster:** Supercharge your next workout by taking a spoonful of honey beforehand. The blend of fructose and glucose may give you an energy boost for endurance activities, plus you'll reap the benefits of the antioxidants and vitamins in honey.

11 **Be Fruitful:** For a special fruit bowl, drizzle herb-infused honey on berries and toss. It makes a great breakfast or a sparkling dessert.

12 **Sleep Tight:** If you need a sleep aid, try a teaspoon of honey. Honey may help the body absorb the compound tryptophan, making us sleepy.

13 **Hangover Help:** The readily absorbed simple sugars (fructose and glucose) in honey go straight into the bloodstream and help you bounce back if you were overserved.

14 **Say Cheese:** Fancy up your cheese plate by drizzling honey over goat cheese or blue cheese.

15 **Cough Suppressant:** Studies have shown honey may be more effective than the commonly used cough suppressant dextromethorphan, found in most over-the-counter cough medicines. Take a spoonful to help quell coughing.

NOTE: Do not give honey to babies younger than 2 years old, due to a risk of botulism.

Health and Bee-uty

Bee-Friendly Beauty Tips

Nurture and nourish skin with bee-produced ingredients straight from the hive.

By Gina DeBacker

Visiting more than 2 million flowers to produce a single pound of honey, bees are some of the hardest workers on our planet—and quite possibly nature's best cosmetologists. These wondrous winged creatures pollinate about one-sixth of the world's flowering plant species and about 400 agricultural plants, and from their hard work springs forth a plethora of valuable materials. For centuries, humans have sought the hive to reap these versatile ingredients, many of which are excellent for body care and can be found in countless cosmetic products, from soaps to sunscreens. Relish the fruits of the hive by buying beauty products enriched with bee-produced ingredients or by making some of your own. (Keep in mind that if you're allergic to bee stings or bee products such as honey, you could also have a reaction to other products listed here, such as propolis.)

GIFTS FROM THE HIVE

Hydrating Honey: Used in everything from cooking to body-care products, honey is probably the most coveted treasure from the hive. Rich in enzymes and trace minerals, honey is produced by bees from the wide array of nectar they collect, resulting in more than 300 types, all varying in color and flavor. Eating a spoonful of this natural antibiotic can help soothe sore throats, and applying a dollop onto a wound may help treat the skin. In beauty products, this natural humectant can hydrate skin by attracting and retaining moisture. Apply raw, unpasteurized honey to your face to smooth and tighten skin, then rinse after 20 minutes or so. (Combine with your favorite facial oil such as sweet almond or coconut to make the mixture more spreadable.) Honey can also help exfoliate skin thanks to its gluconic acid, a mild alpha-hydroxy acid. Mix 2 parts honey with 1 part baking soda to make a gentle exfoliant, and apply to your face, letting it sit for 5 to 10 minutes to loosen dead skin cells and refine pores. Because it's antibacterial, honey can also make a great acne treatment. Dab a bit of honey onto a blemish to reduce its size.

Softening Beeswax: The waxy material produced by worker bees to build honeycombs, beeswax is an excellent softening agent. Often used to make candles, furniture polish, and art, beeswax is also highly

BEE MINDFUL

Pesticides, climate change, and colony collapse disorder all hamper bees' ability to thrive. Only buy products from companies that are conscientious about where and how they source their bee-produced ingredients. This way, your purchasing choices encourage the health and growth of sustainable beekeeping operations. Plus, the health benefits of these products are largely dependent on quality. Visit localharvest.org to search for bee products by city or ZIP code.

BASIC BEESWAX LIP BALM

INGREDIENTS
- ¾ ounce beeswax
- 1½ ounces fixed oil such as sweet almond, grapeseed, coconut, or sunflower, in any combination

The skin of our lips is particularly thin and must be protected from the elements. Beeswax's smooth surface protects lips from abrasive cold air and seals in moisture.

1 Put water in the bottom of a double boiler and put it on the stovetop over medium heat. Once it reaches a boil, reduce heat to simmer.

2 Combine oil with beeswax in the top of the double boiler and melt, stirring frequently. Never melt beeswax directly over a flame as it could catch fire.

3 Once melted, allow mixture to cool to 120 degrees, then pour into lip balm tubes, small pots or slider tins. Makes 12 tubes, each holding about ⅛ ounce.

Recipe adapted with permission from *Honey Crafting* by Leeann Coleman and Jayne Barnes.

Use small lidded tins, found at your local health-food store, to store Basic Beeswax Lip Balm.

sought after for its cosmetic uses. Because of its ability to solidify emulsified substances, beeswax is a great emollient in products such as ointments, creams, sunscreens, and lip balms. Rich in vitamin A, it seals in moisture, protects skin, and naturally conditions. Apply a beeswax-enriched salve to soften rough patches of skin.

Healing Propolis: Bees combine beeswax with propolis—a resinous substance bees collect from tree buds—to repair, reinforce, and sterilize hives. Research shows that propolis taken from a beehive may fight off infections caused by bacteria and viruses such

HONEY COCONUT BODY WASH

INGREDIENTS
- ½ cup extra virgin coconut oil
- ½ cup raw honey
- 20 drops sweet orange essential oil
- 10 drops lemon essential oil
- 6 drops chamomile essential oil
- 1 cup unscented liquid castile soap

Moisture from coconut oil, invigorating antibacterial properties from honey, and a tangy touch of citrus make this body wash unique. Experience a home spa day with every shower using this honey-sweet, sunshine-scented moisturizing product.

1 Fill the bottom of a double boiler with water and put it on the stovetop over medium heat. Once it reaches a boil, reduce heat to simmer.

2 Place coconut oil in the top and cover. Simmer until it is melted, stirring occasionally, about 1 minute. To preserve the beneficial botanicals, do not overheat. Remove from heat; take the top pan off the double boiler, and wipe the outside dry with a towel.

3 Put honey into a mixing bowl and add melted coconut oil, using a rubber spatula to get the remainder out of the pan. Whisk ingredients together for a minute, then add essential oils, and whisk to blend.

4 Finally, add castile soap, whisking gently to create a uniform liquid. Do not overwhisk, as this activates the soap bubbles.

5 Carefully funnel mixture into a 16-ounce bottle with a tight-fitting lid. Label with contents and date; use within a year.

6 To use, apply to damp skin in small, upward motions. Rinse well. Makes 16 ounces.

Recipe adapted with permission from *100 Organic Skin Care Recipes* by Jessica Ress, available at motherearthliving.com/store.

BEESWAX VAPOR RUB

INGREDIENTS
- 2 ounces beeswax
- 8 ounces shea butter
- 3 ounces sweet almond oil
- 1 ounce cocoa butter
- ½ ounce coconut oil
- 20 drops eucalyptus essential oil
- 20 drops peppermint essential oil
- Double boiler
- Small pots or jars

The eucalyptus and peppermint in this ointment will soothe a rasping cough. Rub the cream on your chest and feel relief spread all over as you begin to breathe easy.

1 Combine all the ingredients in the top half of a double boiler.

2 Heat the ingredients just until the beeswax melts, then remove from heat.

3 Pour into small pots or jars, while the mixture is still warm.

Recipe adapted with permission from *Honey Crafting* by Leeann Coleman and Jayne Barnes.

---

as cold sores, canker sores, and sore throats. Enjoy body-care products made with this natural antiseptic to eliminate unwanted bacteria. It is especially wonderful in soap, facial cleansers, and shampoo. Thanks to its promising anti-inflammatory and antibacterial properties, propolis may also help repair skin damage such as scars and rashes.

WHAT IS MANUKA HONEY?

Manuka honey, a honey produced in New Zealand by bees that pollinate the native manuka shrub, has become increasingly popular in body-care products. This striking honey can contain a higher concentration of a special enzyme, methylglyoxal, which makes it even more capable of fighting infection.

Using this extra-potent honey may help treat blemishes, reduce redness, and treat similar skin woes. To determine the potency of your manuka honey, check the company website or look for a label that specifies its Unique Manuka Factor (UMF) rating. A rating of 10 UMF or higher is considered therapeutic.

THE PROBLEM WITH ROYAL JELLY

Loaded with amino acids, B vitamins and trace minerals, royal jelly is the milky

Thyme honey is a strong antioxidant and antibacterial.

THYME-HONEY CLEANSER

INGREDIENTS
- ¼ cup pure thyme honey or plain honey
- ¼ cup water
- 1 teaspoon fresh thyme, chopped
- 2 tablespoons liquid castile soap

Greek honey made from thyme flowers is some of the best in the world. It's known for having a mild taste and high nutritional value—thyme has strong antioxidant and antibacterial properties. In fact, ancient Greek soldiers used to bathe in thyme water for extra vigor and strength. Find Greek honey in the honey section of your grocery store.

1 Gently stir all ingredients together. Pour cleanser into a clean container.

2 To use, pour a small amount in the palm of your hand, then massage it gently into your skin. Makes 5 ounces.

Recipe courtesy Janice Cox, co-author of *EcoBeauty: Scrubs, Rubs, Masks, and Bath Bombs for You and Your Friends*, available at motherearthliving.com/store.

Health and Bee-uty **217**

SMOOTH-SKIN TREATMENT

INGREDIENTS
- 1 tablespoon honey
- 1 tablespoon sunflower oil
- ¼ teaspoon fresh lemon juice

After a day spent outdoors in the garden, your hands and feet may need a bit of conditioning.

1. Mix together all ingredients.
2. To use: Massage into hands, elbows, heels, and feet—anywhere skin feels dry. Leave on for 10 minutes, then rinse well with warm water and pat dry.

---

substance that can turn an ordinary bee into a queen bee. It is fed to all larvae for the first three days of their lives, but only a few bees are chosen to continue being fed the jelly. Those queen bees grow 50 percent larger and live about four years longer than the other female bees. Cosmetic companies harvest this exotic substance as some believe it may naturally support skin regeneration and rejuvenation.

Unfortunately, harvesting royal jelly can cause undue stress to a beehive. "The first step to harvesting royal jelly is removing the colony's queen, which stresses them out because they need a queen to survive. As such, bees go into overdrive to produce a new queen," says Dawn Combs, owner of Mockingbird Meadows (mockingbirdmeadows.com). Although few dispute the benefits of royal jelly—both inside and out—we don't advise using products enriched with this product, as the harvesting of royal jelly may weaken bees left behind in a hive, and may even contribute to the death of a colony.

LAVENDER-AVOCADO-HONEY MASK

INGREDIENTS
- ½ fresh avocado, about ⅓ cup
- 1 teaspoon honey
- 1 teaspoon lavender flowers

This mask is perfect for extra-dry skin. Both honey and avocado are naturally moisturizing to dry skin. Lavender soothes all skin types.

1. Mix together all ingredients until smooth and creamy.
2. To use, spread mask on your face and neck and let sit for 20 minutes, then rinse well with warm water. Store any leftover mask in the refrigerator; it may darken a bit, but that will not affect its use. Makes 3 ounces.

ACNE ZAPPER

INGREDIENTS
- ½ cup warm water
- ¼ teaspoon salt
- Pure honey

If you have a minor acne flare-up, this simple treatment will help clear it up.

1. Mix together warm water and salt, and stir well until salt dissolves. Apply a cotton ball soaked in the solution directly to blemish and maintain pressure with cotton ball for several minutes.
2. Use a cotton swab to dab pure honey on blemish. Leave on for 10 minutes; rinse well with warm water.

SOOTHING SKIN SOAK

INGREDIENTS
- 1 cup water
- ½ cup honey
- ½ cup mild liquid soap

This is a wonderful bath for dry, sensitive skin and is gentle enough for children. You can use any variety of honey in this recipe.

1. Mix together all ingredients and pour into a clean bottle with a tight-fitting lid.
2. To use, gently shake to remix and pour ¼ cup into the bath under the running water. Soak for 15 to 20 minutes.

Recipes courtesy Janice Cox, co-author of *EcoBeauty: Scrubs, Rubs, Masks, and Bath Bombs for You and Your Friends*, available at motherearthliving.com/store.

Notes

NOTES

NOTES

Special thanks to all the authors who have shared their beekeeping expertise with our readers over the years. The articles in this book appeared in their original form in MOTHER EARTH NEWS magazine and GRIT magazine, and in our sister magazines published by Ogden Publications, Inc.

ABOUT US

MOTHER EARTH NEWS is America's leading magazine about sustainable and self-reliant living. Founded by John and Jane Shuttleworth in 1970, it is owned today by Ogden Publications of Topeka, Kansas, and boasts a growing circulation of more than half a million. Since the magazine's founding, MOTHER EARTH NEWS has been a pioneer in the promotion of renewable energy, recycling, family farms, sustainable agricultural practices, better eating habits, medical self-care, more meaningful education, and affordable housing. The magazine's mission is extended by six annual MOTHER EARTH NEWS Fairs and a vibrant website.

GRIT celebrates country lifestyles of all kinds while emphasizing the importance of community and stewardship. As North America's premier rural lifestyles title, GRIT publishes articles on a broad range of topics that appeal to those already living in the country and those who aspire to get there. The magazine's readers are well-educated, successful, and share an appreciation for life out where the pavement ends. GRIT offers practical advice, product reviews, livestock guides, gardening, cooking, and other do-it-yourself information, humor, and the inspirational stories of folks who moved to the country and love it.

Publisher: Bill Uhler
Editorial Director: Oscar H. Will III
Merchandise and Event Director: Andrew Perkins
Production Director: Bob Cucciniello
Special Content Editor: Christian Williams
Special Content Managing Editor: Jean Teller
Special Content Assistant Editor: Jean Denney
Book Design and Layout: Matthew Stallbaumer

IMAGE CREDITS

COVER
Adobe Stock/peter_waters

INTRODUCTION
Pages 8-9: Karen K. Will (3); top right, Oscar H. Will III

CHAPTER 1
Page 11: Adobe Stock/Macias. **12-14:** Liz Pepperell. **15:** Fotolia/Robin Arnold. **16:** Amy Grisak. **17-19:** Fotolia (3)/cbckchristine, photografiero, freepeoplea. **20:** iStock/Kevin Russ. **22:** iStock/ProxyMinder. **23:** clockwise from lower left: iStock (5)/Flaming Pumpkin, Zhang Bo, Ovidiu Iordachi, Ludmila Smite, Brandon Laufenberg. **24-25:** iStock (2)/Richard Clark, catnap72. **26:** iStock/Doray Isik, Adobe Stock/kosolovskyy. **27-29:** Michelle Tremaine (2).

CHAPTER 2
Page 30: Getty Images/jmsamese. **32-33:** Getty Images/temmuzcan, Adobe Stock/happyculteur. **34-35:** Getty Images (3)/Paul Loewen, Lex20 (2). **36:** Getty Images (2)/sylv1rob1, Sushaaa. **37:** Adobe Stock/Alexander. **38:** Joseph Berger, bugwood.org. **39:** Arthur Chapman, Wikimedia Commons/Ivar Leidus, Harper's Honey Farm. **40:** David Cappaert, bugwood.org. **41:** Nate Skow. **42:** Fotolia/Ahileos, iStock/Eric Delmar. **44-45:** Getty Images (2)/delpixart, Jeremy Christensen. **46-49:** Lindsay Williamson (6). **50-51:** iStock/Freeartist, Creative Commons/Jordan Schwartz. **52:** Fotolia/popov_ariel. **53:** Fotolia/darezare, Creative Commons/Rainer Stropek. **54-55:** Nate Skow (4). **56:** iStock/Marcin Pawinski. **58-59:** iStock/Michael Meyer, Adobe Stock/zukovic.

CHAPTER 3
Page 60: Getty Images/vgajic. **62-65:** Elayne Sears. **66:** Fotolia/Tesgro. **68:** iStock/Oliver Malms. **69:** iStock (2)/Mark Easey, Glenn Robertson. **70-71:** iStock (2): Basie B., Chris Sadowski. **72:** iStock/bgwalker. **73:** iStock/Pamela Cowart-Rickman. **74-75:** ThinkStock/Marin Poole, iStock/Adrian Assalve. **76:** iStock/Temmuz Can Arsiray. **77:** iStock (2)/akke12, Nathan Fabro. **78:** iStock (2)/Andrea Gingerich, Steven Love. **79:** iStock/Christian Martinez. **80-85:** Rosaline Creasy (9). **86-87:** Fotolia/NRPPhoto, Gordon Cyr, masonbeecentral.com. **88-89:** Gordon Cyr, masonbeecentral.com, Wikimedia Commons/Oregon State University. **90-93:** Lynn Karlin (4). **94:** Adobe Stock: kaciia. **96:** Lynn Karlin, Getty Images/gurineb. **97:** Adobe Stock/Gucio_55. **98:** iStock (5). **99:** iStock, Shutterstock, iStock (5). **100-101:** iStock (2)/Viesinsh, jcimagery. **102:** Steve and Dave Maslowski. **103:** Adobe Stock/losonsky. **104:** Adobe Stock: Vera Kuttelvaserova. **105-109:** Carol J. Alexander (9). **110-111:** iStock (2)/Dieter Hawlan, ProxyMinder. **112-113:** J. Michael Krivyanski (2), Zan Asha. **115:** J. Michael Krivyanski.

CHAPTER 4
Page 116: Adobe Stock/freepeoplea. **118:** Fotolia/gertrudda. **119:** Fotolia (4)/sashagrunge, Africa Studio, Adrian_am13, teptong. **120:** Fotolia (2)/nkarol, andreusK. **121:** Fotolia/Kletr, ThinkStock/Getty Images/Creatas. **122-123:** Fotolia (2)/lovelymama, Brent Hofacker. **124-125:** Adobe Stock (2)/jhk2303, telesh. **126-127:** Getty Images/Ron Bailey, Adobe Stock/Adolfo Rodriguez. **128-129:** Adobe Stock (2)/Franco Nadalin, olgakok. **130-131:** Getty Images/istetiana, Adobe Stock/Tomasz Zajda. **132:** Adobe Stock/yanik88, Getty Images/gmutlu. **133:** Adobe Stock/Belish. **134:** iStock/Mark Ruose. **135:** Nate Skow (2). **136-137:** Scott Bauer/ USDA Agricultural

Research Service, bugwood.org, Nate Skow. **138:** Getty Images/natalie_board. **139:** Getty Images/nonmim, Adobe Stock/Vera Kuttelvaserova. **140:** Getty Images/Groomee. **141:** Adobe Stock (2)/teressa, lightpoet. **142:** Adobe Stock (2)/Andreas, Marina. **143:** Adobe Stock/Davizro Photography. **145:** Adobe Stock/photografiero. **146-147:** Adobe Stock/Silvia Hahnefeld, Getty Images/gurineb.

CHAPTER 5

Page **148:** Adobe Stock/Silvano Rebai. **150-151:** iStock/alexandrumagurean, Kim Flottum. **152:** Kim Flottum (2). **153-154:** Scott Bauer/USDA (2). **155:** Lila De Guzman/USDA, Scott Bauer/USDA. **156:** Virginia Williams/ARS. **157:** Bill Beatty/AKM Images. **158:** iStock/photografiero. **160-161:** iStock/darios44, Adobe Stock/AUFORT Jerome. **162-163:** iStock/ProxyMinder (2). **163:** Nancy Nehring Illustrations (3). **164-165:** iStock (2)/Dana Swisher, Annalisa Troian. **166:** iStock/Hande Guleryuz Yuce, Jessica Lawrence/Eurofins Agroscience Services, bugwood.org. **167:** iStock/Nicola Stratford. **168:** iStock/Dana Swisher, Carl Dennis/Auburn University, bugwood.org. **169:** Jupiter Images. **170-171:** iStock (2)/Andrzej Petelski, Borislav Gnjidic. **172:** iStock/Johan Lundgren. **173:** Getty Images/Kosolovskyy. **174-175:** Adobe Stock/muro, Getty Images/danutelu.

CHAPTER 6

Page **176:** Karen K. Will. **178:** iStock/Trevor Moore. **179:** Amy Grisak (5). **180:** Fotolia/By Man Designs. **181:** Adobe Stock/ivanmateev. **182:** Tim Nauman Photography, Getty Images/OksanaKiian. **183:** Getty Images/Zoryanchik. **184:** Adobe Stock/GreenArt. **185:** Getty Images/bhofack2, Adobe Stock/tongkusa. **186-191:** Karen K. Will (6). **192:** Adobe Stock/Grafvision. **194-195:** Adobe Stock (2)/la_vanda, shaiith. **196:** Adobe Stock (2)/Alp Aksoy, seagames50. **197:** Adobe Stock/olepeshkina. **198-199:** Adobe Stock (2)/manyakotic, matka_Wariatka.

CHAPTER 7

Page **200:** Adobe Stock/David Pimborough. **202:** Adobe Stock/Danie Prudek. **203, top:** Getty Images/no_limit_pictures, Adobe Stock/yanadjan. **203, bottom:** Adobe Stock (2)/eskay-lim, Subbotina-Anna. **204-205:** Adobe Stock (2)/Comugnero Silvana, barmalini. **206:** iStock/Florea Marius Catalin. **207:** iStock/Hans-Joachim Schneider, Glorybee Foods, iStock/Stephan Zaabel. **208-209:** iStock/Plamen Petrov, Andy Olenick. **210:** Glorybee Foods, iStock/Ines Koleva. **211:** Adobe Stock/Catherine Murray. **212-213:** iStock, Adobe Stock/Stephanie Frey. **214-215:** iStock (2)/manfredxy, Public Domain. **261-217:** iStock/Simonyi Zsolt, Fotolia/marysckin.